IMPARTIAL JUDGMENT

IMPARTIAL JUDGMENT

The *"Dean of NFL Referees"*
Calls Pro Football as He Sees It

JIM TUNNEY, Ed.D.
with GLENN DICKEY

FRANKLIN WATTS
New York • Toronto
1988

Library of Congress Cataloging-in-Publication Data

Tunney, Jim.
    Impartial judgment.

    Includes index.
    1. Tunney, Jim.   2. Football—United States—
Referees—Biography.   3. National Football League.
I. Dickey, Glenn.   II. Title.
GV939.T85A3   1988   796.332′092′4   [B]   88-20590
ISBN 0-531-15095-X

Dedicated to the memory of my dad,
who taught me to believe in myself

Contents

Acknowledgments

This book has been incubating in me for a long time, ever since I became aware that the commitment to excellence I witness on the gridiron provides fundamental, direct instruction on how to approach many real-life situations. Writing requires more chair time than I like, which is one reason the book was so long in getting written, but writing also demands concentration and persistence, two skills helpful in all areas of life and therefore good ones to keep honed.

Getting the thoughts down for the first draft is fast and not very complicated. The work, I have found, is in the rewriting and the editing. Having my agent, Basil Kane, and my editor, Kent Oswald, standing by helped me considerably in maintaining the focus. I thank Glenn Dickey, too, for his contribution.

I offered to let my wife, Natalie, read the manuscript in the final draft. She declined, saying she wanted to be one of the first to buy a copy. That's the spirit, hon. Thank you for your faith and good humor.

My biggest thanks goes to my mom, who understands how close a guy could be to his dad. I love her gentle ways and steadfast confidence.

Writing this book caused me to reflect on the forty years I've been officiating. I realize now, more than ever, that working weekend games displaced huge amounts of time that otherwise would have been spent with my family. My four children—Maureen, Michael, Mark and Janet—grew up to become responsible and delightful adults even without a dad on many weekends. They deserve extra credit and I openly thank them for their love and understanding.

To the great coaches and players in the game today, I extend an apology. There are few mentions of their talent and dedication in this book. I could say that since we know the capabilities of past heroes, it is easier to extol their heroics. Or, I could say that because today's coaches and players keep increasing their capacity, future books may overshadow the tributes I give here to past heroes. Both excuses avoid the real reason. The truth is, this book includes little about coaches and players currently in the game because the league told me not to.

Foreword
By John Madden

Jim Tunney taught me that a referee could be human. I never even thought that was possible. I mean, who are these guys?

Ever hear of a kid growing up wanting to be a referee? Or going to college to be one? Then all of a sudden, boom, there they are telling you what to do.

I always felt good when I found out Tunney was going to referee our game. I knew I wasn't going to get any breaks, but I also knew the other side wasn't going to get any either.

He always listened to me, and I got to thinking, "Hey, this guy's all right, for a referee anyway."

I always knew he'd be fair, and I knew he would be in control. Like John Wayne walking into a western saloon and telling everybody to cool down, Tunney had control of everything. The wheels could be falling off, all sorts of crazy things might be going on, but you knew he would step in and sort it all out.

He was the referee for Super Bowl XI (1977), and I was really happy to hear that he would be there. I knew he'd do his part right. All we had to do was to get our part right and we'd be okay, which is the way it turned out—Oakland 32, Minnesota 14. Since I've been in the TV booth, I've felt the same way. When Tunney's on the field, the game will be under control.

The thing that really impressed me as a coach was that Tunney was willing to listen to what I had to say. You know, I made a lot of noise on the sidelines. Some referees would just try to ignore me, so I'd have to yell louder and louder to get their attention. Some officials would argue back. Then we'd really get into yelling. Tunney was never like that. He would listen to what I had to say, and, you know, that was really disarming. That really took the wind out of my sails. He'd listen to me and then what could I do? I mean, I'd made my point. It just didn't make any difference. He still did what he thought was right, but I didn't have anywhere to go.

If a guy argues with you, it kind of gives you some fuel. But if he listens to you, well, that's the worst thing he can do to you. You run out of things to say pretty quick. I kept thinking, "Why am I yelling at this guy? He's not yelling at me." Once I realized that, I had to give up the argument. That happened all the time with Tunney. He worked a lot of our Raiders games and it was always the same. He's such a competent guy, you just know he'll be in control of the game.

It was the same thing with my little pregame routine. You know, coaches aren't supposed to talk to the officials before the game, but I would go into their little dressing room and say I wanted to synchronize my watch. The teams are supposed to be out on the field at, say, 12:58, so that was my excuse. I wanted to be sure my watch was right according to the officials. Actually, what I wanted to do was go in and say hello to everybody. If there had been a call that had gone against us the last time we had this or that crew, I wanted to remind them of it. But it never worked with Tunney. He knew why I was in there, and that meant my little game wouldn't work, so all I got for my effort was a few smiles.

You know, I even argued for him one time. It was after the 1986 season. I was working Super Bowl XX in Los Angeles and I ran into Art McNally, Supervisor of Officials. Amazingly, Tunney hadn't worked any of the postseason games. Now we're talking a lot of games—two wild cards, four divisionals, two championships, and the Super Bowl. Here's a guy who's the best in the business, and he hadn't worked a playoff game.

I told McNally, "There's something wrong with a system that doesn't give the best guy a playoff game. That makes no sense."

McNally gave me the in-house line, a bunch of business about the grading system and all that. I got the impression that behind all that song-and-dance, he agreed with me. He couldn't say it, but I think he agreed.

That really got me to thinking. Here I was standing up for a referee. That was a first. Last year, of course, Tunney worked the AFC championship game between Cleveland and Denver.

Since I retired from coaching, I've gotten to know Jim on a personal basis. He spoke at my retirement dinner in 1979 and again at my fiftieth birthday party, which was also the ten-year reunion of our Super Bowl XI team. I see him at various functions all the time. I have to say that the Jim Tunney you get as a referee is the same Jim Tunney you get in this book or at a charity banquet or at a corporate seminar. I'm sure he was the same when he was in the school business. He's the same guy on the field as he is off—always in control of himself, whatever the situation.

He's a great speaker, with a good sense of humor. He's a real gentleman. You add it all up and he's just one good guy. I'm really happy that he's done this book because he has some special insights. Anyone who needs to understand people and teamwork really ought to read it. Everybody will enjoy it.

I can't believe I'm saying all these nice things about a referee!

March, 1988
Pleasanton, California

Introduction

The summer after Super Bowl XI, I refereed the preseason game between the Oakland Raiders and Seattle Seahawks in the King-dome. I was walking the field before the game when I crossed paths with John Madden. I noticed John was wearing the Super Bowl ring he received for being the winning coach of Super Bowl XI (1977).

With a bit of jest, I said, "I don't understand it, John. You were the coach, and I was the referee. We were on the field for the same amount of time. The Raiders gave you that beautiful ring with all those diamonds, and the league gave me this crummy watch. What's the difference?"

"Because you don't care who wins," he said, dead serious.

I think it just popped into his head, as so many things do with Madden, but he was on the mark.

Coaching is the business of winning and losing. The business of an official is impartial judgment. As an official, I don't care who wins. Officials want only to see the game played fairly. Not necessarily evenly, because some teams are better than others, but fairly, within the rules.

When I was a kid playing on the sandlots, we had to make our own calls. When there was a question about a play, I would tend to give it to the other team. Playing the game was more important to me than haggling over a few inches. I didn't realize then that making the fair call would become central to my adult life.

When officials come into the National Football League (NFL) after having worked college games, they are impressed with seeing the talent of NFL players up close. Being human, they may see one of today's great players and utter, "Wow, there's so-and-so." There are so many great ones.

I understand that because when I came into the league, Jim Brown was playing. I couldn't help but be impressed with his talent.

But you have to get awe out of your head right away. You have to realize that if you've been selected for the NFL, you're there because you belong out there. You have the same standing in your position as every other coach or player on the field— we're all tops out there.

The dividing issue between the officials, coaches and players is how differently we look at competition and fairness. If Jim Brown reached out and gave a guy a forearm shiver—as I saw him do a few times in his career—I had to make the call, whether it was Jim Brown or anyone. The value of fairness, the value of the rules, can't be overwhelmed by individual acts of skill or guts.

In addition to putting awe in our pockets, we have to understand that as officials, we do not make decisions in the usual way. We work in fast-moving, sometimes intense situations. We follow the action. We make quick decisions. However, deciding if an infraction of the NFL rules has taken place isn't the same as making a decision on whether to buy a house, change jobs or sell a stock.

Many young officials and the public at large tend to overlook the distinction that being able to read a play requires little logic, just a lot of technical skill. Officials observe. When an infraction is spotted, the flag falls. Logic is not involved. A good call contains no choices.

What if the defensive tackle jumps into the neutral zone just prior to the ball being snapped, realizes he is too early, and is stepping back, trying to get out of the zone and be onside, but doesn't quite make it and is still partly in the zone as the ball is snapped? The flag falls. "Offside. Defense. Penalty five yards."

Logic would say, "Why penalize someone for putting himself at a disadvantage while trying to do right?" The tackle was not in good position when the ball was snapped. He was backing up, in reverse just when he should have been charging forward.

A "fair-minded" individual might ask, "Wasn't he already penalized by losing his chance to be effective on the play? Where was the disadvantage to the other team?"

That's a fair question, but not one the officials on the play would concern themselves with. You may dispute the logic, but the rules are clear. In that situation, the tackle was offside. Make the call.

Knowing the rules, where to be, what to look for, and calling the play as you see it is being an expert witness. An official relies on what is *observable*. He doesn't evaluate options, determine his feelings about them, project probable outcomes, consider how the variables will influence other situations, and *then* decide. That's the job of the coach, and to a lesser extent the players.

People find it relaxing to watch sports. Humans are clever about inventing spectator sports, from football to chess matches and show jumping. We've invented thousands of them.

For any of them, we could choose to participate instead of only watching, but watching is fun. We have the option of spending Sunday afternoon playing tag football with the kids in the park, but thousands of us go to the stadiums or to our televisions instead. What's the appeal of being a fan?

Part of the answer is that we enjoy watching other people grapple with decisions. After battling our way through endless decisions day after day, it's relaxing to watch someone else put his head behind the ball (or racket or pawn or whatever) and see what he does.

The more you understand the rules and strategies of the game, the more you enjoy watching someone else handle the process of deciding what to do as the situation changes. Knowledge builds appreciation. The relative importance of the uncertainties someone else is facing is interesting to us, even as we grab for the Nachos.

We can admire the intelligence and courage of the decisions. We can feel involved, but free of responsibility for the choices or their results.

The coaches and players, particularly the player with the ball, are the ones having a nervous time of it. Adrenaline flows toward uncertainty.

I believe NFL football is the world's greatest sports spectacle. When you walk onto the field with 70,000 people in the stands and know that you are one of the twenty-nine people in the action, it's a great feeling. You feel you are among the best in a game as competitive as any in the world. It's a thrill. That thrill is part of why I do it.

When I became an official in the NFL, I felt excited and lucky to be part of an event that thousands of fans paid good money to witness. After twenty-eight years, I feel the same way.

I've seen the action, heard the sounds, and met the people involved from the special perspective of an official. Players talk to me. Coaches talk to me—sometimes, too much. I've been with the game from the inside. I'd like to share with you some of what I've seen and some of what I've thought about it.

IMPARTIAL
JUDGMENT

1

The Rookie Year

I thought George Halas would never live beyond the third quarter in any game I worked. The veins in his neck would get as big as pipelines. He was intense.

He always wore a hat. You never saw Halas without his hat, although it wasn't always on his head. When he was angry, especially with officials, he would throw it and stomp on it. His intensity would grow to fever pitch. He was inside every play. He could see the play develop. He knew why a guard didn't make his block, why an official didn't make a call.

With this kind of energy set upon winning, Halas had great difficulty accepting a loss. Losing was a foreign idea to him, even though he didn't win all that many games in the years after I first came into the league.

My memories of Halas are vivid because he was part of the first game I ever worked in the NFL, as a field judge, the 1960 preseason game between the Chicago Bears and the Los Angeles Rams at the Los Angeles Coliseum.

Before the game, Halas came over to me and said, "How ya doin'? What's your name?"

"Tunney," I said.

"Yeah, Tunney. Occidental College," he started, "Athlete of

the Year. Worked the Pacific Coast Conference, SC and UCLA."
Halas had it wired. He knew everything about me, and I was
just a rookie.

Then he said, "Jim, I've been in this game a long time. If
there's anything I can ever do for you, if I can help you with
anything, if there's any play or rule you don't understand, I'll
be glad to help you."

I said, "Thanks, Coach," and walked away.

Wouldn't you know it, a play came up in that first game that
resulted in Halas giving me more "advice" than I could handle.

A Chicago Bears halfback caught a swing pass, turned the
corner, raced down the sideline, slipped trying to avoid a tackler,
and fell. As field judge, I was watching the play.

So was Rams linebacker Les Richter. Richter had a bead on
him. He would have knocked him into the cheap seats, so I blew
the whistle when the runner hit the ground. Richter just stepped
over him; the back got up and ran for a touchdown.

When I saw Halas, he was descending from about twelve feet
off the ground. He really let me have it. He started off with
"You rookie SOB," and went on from there. Halas knew all the
words.

He told me then and reminded me many times over the years,
"You don't blow the whistle until the guy is down by contact."

The very next week, I was up at San Francisco, at Kezar
Stadium, the Bears and the 49ers. Halas came up to me and
said, "Now, you had a tough call last week. You handled yourself
pretty well, but it was a mistake. I told you, if you need any
help, just let me know."

I said, "Thanks, Coach," and walked away.

That was Halas. He'd really work on officials. Whether he was
trying to "help" or intimidate us by yelling, he could be pointed
in his comments. Yet, the thing I admired about him so strongly
was that when the game was over, it was over. If a reporter
came in and said, "That call cost you the game," Halas would
say, "That call didn't cost us the game. We should never have

gotten ourselves into that position." He wouldn't call the league office on an official. His attitude was, the officials are out there trying to do their job.

Halas knew the rules very well, probably because he created a lot of them, and he never felt intimidated by anyone or anything. I've seen a lot of CEOs back off in a pressure situation and say, "I'll get back to you on that." Or coaches say, "I won't know until I see the films." Halas never deferred. He would tell you what he saw right then, this was the play, this was the situation. The films might prove him wrong the next day, but he never squirmed out of it.

Halas was a complex man. He was raw and competitive, and yet he was always conscious of the need for balance in the league. He pushed the idea of a college draft, for instance, at a time when he probably could have built stronger Bears teams without it.

When the league started, coaches and owners could sign players either straight out of college or even while still in college. There were few restrictions. While that was good for the players who were signed and the teams who signed them, it wasn't good for the league, because it created imbalance: The richest teams could pay the biggest price for the best players.

The league kept getting more imbalanced. Fans want their team to win, but more importantly, they want to see a good contest, which requires a fairly even standard of excellence. Halas understood that and fought to get the draft adopted.

Halas was also a very religious man. Sometimes the competitive and religious sides of his personality came into conflict.

If you go back to the early days of the NFL, the 1920s, when Halas's team started as the Decatur Staleys, there wasn't much money in the game. His team became the Chicago Bears, and they moved into Wrigley Field, a bigger stadium than they had in Decatur but still smaller than stadiums in most other league cities. Cleveland's Municipal Stadium, for instance, holds 76,000, which is more than twice the fans that Halas could get into Wrigley. The Bears could make more money on the road than they could at home.

So Halas, a man of direct action, put bleachers on the field. He actually set up folding chairs, three rows of them, on the sidelines. A very devout Catholic, he would have the archbishop, or someone from the diocese, right there on the bench. Always the church.

One day, Halas became irate at an official. He called him every expletive in the language. He suddenly realized the archbishop was sitting on the bench right behind him. He turned around. The archbishop stood up and very peacefully gave Halas the blessing, absolving him of all the sins he had just committed. The archbishop loved the Bears, too.

Under Halas, Chicago's greatest rivalry was the Green Bay Packers. I worked the hundredth game between the Bears and the Packers, played at Wrigley Field in 1975, and I also worked a lot of other games in Green Bay, at Lambeau Field.

I remember one Sunday morning going to mass at St. Willebrord's in Green Bay before the game. Halas was on one side of the aisle with most of his team, and Vince Lombardi was on the other, with most of his players. The priest addressed us. I don't remember all that he said, but he preached on the Gospel of the Good Samaritan and brotherly love and how important it is that we all share the feeling of brotherhood.

I got to thinking about competition, these two teams about to go out and try to kill each other in a few hours. The priest finished his sermon, banged his fist on the lectern, and said "And now, let's go out and beat those Bears!" That's how well accepted that rivalry was.

This story reveals another truth. Football draws from every walk of life. It crosses all socioeconomic, religious, and cultural lines. Some treat it as a religion, which it's not, but it is here to stay. It's durable because the contest is clear. Fans go crazy because there's something understandable to send their energies to. Great sport. Great release. I like it.

* * *

For a time, George Allen was Halas's defensive coordinator. Maybe you remember that Allen was given the game ball when the Bears won the NFL championship in 1963 against the Giants. His defensive strategy was the primary reason the Bears won that day. Or that Halas sued to make Allen honor his contract when Allen was hired away as head coach by the Los Angeles Rams and then let Allen go when he won the case. Halas was fierce when he felt a principle was a stake, pragmatic after he made his point. Then, when it was over, it was over.

George Allen was an entirely different kind of coach; we had everything worked out long before either of us got into the NFL.

Allen and I go back to 1956, when he was coach at Whittier College and I, about age 27, was a high school administrator and a college football official. I worked the Pomona-Whittier championship game that year as head linesman. A top official, Norm Duncan, from UCLA, was the referee.

In the second quarter, Duncan pulled a hamstring, made me the referee, and took over as head linesman so he wouldn't have to run so much.

In the last thirty seconds, Whittier was leading 12–7. Pomona was running out of the single-wing box. The tailback spun around, ran a play starting on Whittier's 8 yard line, heading for the goal line. Just as he got to the goal line, the tailback was tackled, but I saw him go over the goal line, so I gave the signal for touchdown. Pomona won it, 14–12. Back on the 50 yard line, Allen was coming unglued. He didn't think it was a touchdown, but of course he wouldn't.

Monday morning, I got a call from Allen at my high school. "I just want you to know, you cost me the championship. We looked at the films, and he did not score."

I asked, "Where were the films taken from?"

"The press box," he told me.

The press box was on the 50 yard line and well back from the field. The camera had to be 60 or 70 yards away.

I said, "You may be right, but I called it the way I saw it."

"Well," he said, "I just want you to know, you cost me the championship."

We have had a good relationship ever since. No lingering animosity. When Allen was with Chicago, he'd always come by and say, "Hi, Jim, how are you?"

One time when Allen was head coach for the Washington Redskins, they were playing the Dallas Cowboys for the division championship. He came into the locker room before the game and said, "I'm sure glad you guys are here. I'm glad you're the referee, Jim, because I know we'll get a fair game today."

He was just trying to set us up, of course.

I don't know that I was particularly nervous my first year in the NFL, but I was excited. Officials entering now are under more stress. The game and the league have gained such prominence. Being in the NFL was always the greatest, but it wasn't always this big.

My first season I didn't work every week. The league took in eight new officials that season, and I worked only every other week that season. We could work high school and college games if we wanted to, and I did. I would work a Friday night high school game, then leave Saturday to work a pro game on Sunday.

I was 31 years old, and I had never been east of Las Vegas. The travel meant a lot to me. St. Louis one week, Washington, D.C. the next, then New York City, and so it goes. I was excited. A new city each week.

A naive native Californian going to Washington, D.C., I arrived without an overcoat. It was late November. Saturday night was beautiful. In those days, our work was more informal. We didn't have pregame meetings, so my time was my own on Saturday night. I walked around the city feeling great. I went to the Lincoln Memorial, I went to the Washington Monument.

Sunday I woke up and looked out. It was snowing. I had never seen snow coming down live. Oh, I'd been to the San Gabriel

Mountains in California when snow was on the ground, but I had never been there when it was actually snowing.

It had started snowing sometime in the middle of the night. It snowed all morning.

The referee was Bill Downs. I had met him the morning of the game. The American Football League (AFL) was suing the NFL at the time, and because Downs was a veteran NFL referee, they were trying to serve him with papers at the airport. So he came down from Chicago on the train instead, arriving Sunday instead of Saturday.

When I met him at breakfast, he introduced himself and said, "Let's go out to the stadium a little early."

That was fine with me. Downs had been in the league twenty years, so I figured he knew what he was doing. He asked me if I had any plastic rain gear, which I didn't, so we went up and down the streets of Washington, D.C., in a taxi, looking for a store that was open. We finally found an Army-Navy surplus store. I bought a long rain jacket and some cotton gloves, which turned out to be the same as the Redskins would be wearing.

The ground crew had covered the field with a tarp. They tried to push the snow off the field with a bulldozer but couldn't. The owner of the Redskins, George Preston Marshall, was going crazy. He had paid $5,000 for the tarp, which was a lot of money in those days, and the bulldozer was just tearing it up. I remember he kept yelling, "I've got to pay for that tarp!"

We held up the game for about forty-five minutes trying to remove the snow. We finally played the game with half the field cleared of snow and half the field covered with the tarp and the snow on it.

We had four stakes in four corners. That's all that was visible. We had chains, but no goal line except for the two markers at each side. No end zone markers. If a punt was close to the end zone, I called, "Touchback," and brought the ball out to the 20. Nobody complained. Who could tell?

I don't know what the official record is, but we must have

been near it that day with an hour-and-fifty-eight-minute game. Moved it right along, we did. First of all, no one wanted to be out on the field, and there was hardly anyone in the stands. Marshall had sold a lot of tickets. The game was against the New York Giants, big rivals of the Redskins, then and now, but few who didn't have to showed up.

The game? Well, shoot, the lineman would block, make contact, but no one wanted an injury, so it was all light stuff. Both teams used a lot of passes. A lot of hurry-up offense from the first quarter on. It was tough on the receivers. Their hands were frozen in store-bought gloves, long before the days of "stickum."

I learned from this game how you officiate in horrible conditions. You play by the spirit of the rules, but you don't get bogged down by technicalities. If it's close to a first down, it's a first down. You don't measure. You just line up, "First down, let's go."

The players accept this, desire it even, when they know it will be the same on both sides. Fairness is always important. Sometimes technicalities aren't.

The next week, I went to New York, a big thrill for me because it meant being in Yankee Stadium. The sentiment of my childhood dream to get to the mound at Yankee Stadium was still alive twenty years later. I don't think I've ever been in a stadium, before or since, with such a strong history for me as Yankee Stadium had for me that day. The drawing power and simple appeal of sports as drama come through. It was fulfilling. The best tradition of Babe Ruth and Lou Gehrig was still alive. I wasn't on the mound, but I was *there*—at Yankee Stadium.

The New York Giants were enjoying some great years right then. Just a couple of years before, they'd played the now famous overtime game with the Baltimore Colts. The Colts won it 21–17. That game is still generally regarded as one of the classics of all time.

The Giants then had Y. A. Tittle, Frank Gifford, Andy Robustelli, Pat Summerall, Jim Katcavage, Sam Huff—great players. Players like that make pro football what it is.

Coming from Los Angeles, I'd seen the Rams with Bob Waterfield, Elroy Hirsch, Tom Fears, Les Richter. They were great players, too, but the Rams just didn't have the mystique that the Giants did. Maybe the spirit of their being in New York, the Big Apple, made the difference. And Yankee Stadium.

That day, the Giants battled the Pittsburgh Steelers to a 27–24 win, which gave the Giants a winning record for the year. The next three years—1961, 1962, 1963—the Giants would go on to win their division championship.

Being in Yankee Stadium made it real to me that I was in the pros. I had worked some big games at the college level, but the excellence found week in and week out in the NFL meant a new standard. I made some mistakes that first year, but also realized I could "hit the pitching."

2

In the Midst
of Game History

The thrill that comes from witnessing excellence is part of why this work never gets boring. Sometimes you're a part of game history.

The year was 1965. Green Bay Packers against the Baltimore Colts. Don Chandler kicked a field goal to win it for the Packers, 13–10. Before that, he had kicked a field goal to tie it at 10–10. That field goal brought about a rules change.

Chandler kicked the first one a little weakly. The wind caught it as it came down the field, causing it to veer to one side.

The goal posts were then only ten feet above the crossbar. As the field judge I stood underneath. I had to look up and project an extension of the post. Doing that, I judged the kick to be good. Norm Schachter, the referee, was in position back with the kicker. As I signaled good, he threw his hands up, too.

From the 50 yard line, where the coaches are, they couldn't begin to tell whether it was good or not. But Don Shula, then the Baltimore coach, was screaming at Schachter, who said, "Don't look at me. Tunney made the call."

Shula and the Colts stormed the field, protesting, but to no avail. Films later could neither confirm nor deny whether the kick was good.

Schachter never escaped the heat. For months after that, there was a radio announcer in Baltimore who signed off saying, "Good night, Norm Schachter, wherever you are."

Because the game decided the championship, there was debate about that call for the entire off-season. Tom Matte, who had replaced Johnny Unitas as quarterback in that game, used the controversy as a big part of the after-dinner speeches he made to all sorts of groups.

Matte used a cake (I guess it must have been plastic) with goal posts that angled off to the right. He would bring out that cake and make a big deal of awarding it to the officials, who were, of course, *in absentia.* He would open with "I'm here to talk about the championship which was taken away from us."

As a result of that controversy, next season, the goal posts were extended to twenty feet above the crossbar. There must have been other games in that era with disputed calls about field goals, but this was the first disputed call to decide a championship game.

It was the first time I had the sense of "I was there." It also showed me how unflappable you can be when you know you did your job well. As a result of that game, Don Shula and I have had several interesting conversations about goal posts and whether officials can see or not.

The next year, I worked a game at Kezar between the Colts and the 49ers. Before the game, I was leaning against one of the goal posts, waiting for the Colts to finish their pregame warmups so I could talk to the captain. Shula came up behind me and yelled, "Get away from those damned goal posts! The last time you were down there, you kicked the play."

We both smiled.

Just a couple of years ago, we had a game where a field-goal attempt by the other team hit the goal posts and went on through. I signaled good, of course. Shula wasn't upset, but he came over to me and said, "You really get screwed up about those goal posts, don't you?"

Two decades, the memory lives.

In the 1987 season, I was in Joe Robbie Stadium in Miami. The Dolphins were playing the Colts, and Shula, now coaching the Dolphins, was standing under the goal posts. I came up behind him and said, "You'd better get away from those goal posts. They're a jinx for you."

"Oh," he said, "you remember."

"You've never let me forget it," I said.

Other than the way it tests your mettle as an official, the important thing about controversies is that people get it wrong so much of the time. People tend to think that controversy begets vendetta. They assume that anger gets carried over and that it has to be redressed or evened up.

That's not the way it's supposed to be, nor is it the way it is, I'm glad to say. It's true: officials don't care who wins. When coaches understand that, controversy can be a bond between the official and the coach, sometimes the players, too. Honest controversy is always okay between honest individuals.

Earlier, in 1979, in a Dolphins–Redskins game at RFK Stadium, the Dolphins threw a forward pass; there was a collision downfield, and the pass was incomplete. Shula was furious because he thought it was defensive pass interference.

Our rookie field judge, Don Hakes, was covering the play. He said he saw the defender and the pass receiver going after the ball. Equal opportunity, no foul.

Meanwhile, Shula was screaming on the sidelines, yelling at me. From my position behind the quarterback, I'm not going to be making a call 25 yards downfield, but there was no way I was going to let a rookie official go to the sideline to deal with an irate coach. During the next time out, I went over to talk to Shula. I told him the official was in position and saw both players going for the ball, so there was no interference. That didn't satisfy him.

"You've been screwing me for eighteen years," he said.

"It's nineteen, Don," I said.

He laughed. I think my comeback took him by surprise, but once he'd laughed, that was the end of it. He couldn't say anything after that, so he just walked away.

Shula's a funny guy. He'll yell at me every time I'm working a game. Even if it's another official who makes the call, he'll yell at me. I think he gets a big kick out of it.

I've said for years that the best way to know a person is either through a love affair or a confrontation. In a controversy, you find out about the other person, what their basic values are and what kind of self-esteem is working. Shula's all right. Tough and honest, fair-minded.

There's a bond of community that builds up between those who have been in the league a long time, whether as a coach, player, owner, or official. No one stays in the game for decades without really wanting to be there.

After twenty-eight years, I ask myself sometimes, "Why am I still here?" That question comes to mind after every tough game. The answer is simple and always the same: "I love the game of football." There is a real-life significance in getting eleven players together in a huddle and saying, "All right, let's do this together." A shared goal always comes before a shared victory.

When people ask how many controversial calls I've had, I respond, "I think there's a controversial call every game," After the game, without the advantage of video replay, I sometimes wonder if one call or another was right. The biggest difficulty an official faces when a coach or player indicts him by saying "You missed that call!" is not so much whether the call was in fact right but in not giving it any more thought and focusing entirely on the next play.

After the game or season, though, you remember those calls. There was one I made in Super Bowl XII (1978). Denver and Dallas. The Cowboys were ahead, 7–0, in the second quarter.

Dallas quarterback Roger Staubach rolled to his right near the sideline, stopped, threw a pass into the end zone. The pass was intercepted by Denver, which would have been a touchback except that before Staubach released, he stepped on the sideline. I signaled time out, out-of-bounds.

The Broncos thought they were going to get the ball on the 20 because of the interception. I had to be the messenger with the bad news and tell them, "The quarterback was out-of-bounds before the pass. Dallas's ball at the out-of-bounds spot. Fourth down."

Dallas kicked a field goal to make it 10–0.

After the game, the pool reporter came in and said the "Eye in the Sky" showed that Staubach was in-bounds. He asked me about it and I said, "Well, I saw Staubach step on the line."

On Thursday, after the game, Art McNally called me and said, "I thought you'd like to know that our game film showed Staubach did step out-of-bounds."

Well, fine, but that was Thursday. In the meantime, everyone had spent Monday, Tuesday, and Wednesday debating the call.

McNally had waited until Thursday because it was the Super Bowl and there was not a game going on the next week. If it had been during the season, they would have reviewed the film on Monday. Meanwhile, all that time, I was one among many who were wondering, Did I really make the right call?

What you have to do is believe in yourself, you have to know your intention was right, and that your attention was correctly focused. If it had turned out that I had made an error, if the film had shown that Staubach had not stepped on the line, well, I would just have to say that I made the call the way I saw it. Self-knowledge calms a lot of jitters.

One of the worst things an official can do is anticipate. You can't watch a player going up the sideline and say to yourself, "He's going to go out," because then you anticipate and make the call that way even if he doesn't. Then you're in trouble. Man is a teleological being. We move in the direction of our thoughts. If we anticipate one thing, we ready ourselves to see it.

This natural tendency is an advantage in training. All excellent performers learn to use it to improve results. You become better at it through practice, as with all skills, but officials must recognize when *not* to use it. Our whole focus should be on straight observation. No expectations, no anticipation, no preferences.

Still, if all our clear-minded attention results in a furor, no matter. If we make the call and it's unpopular, we just have to live with it.

There was another controversial call in Super Bowl XII, one I didn't make, on a pass by Staubach to Butch Johnson in the end zone for a touchdown. As Johnson hit the ground, he rolled over and the ball came out as he stood up.

At the time, it seemed simple: Johnson had caught the ball and tossed it out as he got up. It wasn't until later we thought, "Did he really catch the ball?" The call was debated a greal deal after the game. Had instant replay been in effect, the play would have been reviewed on the spot.

Because Dallas won 24–10, neither of these calls affected the outcome of the game. The most lasting controversies are the ones about disputed calls which decide a game.

There was one in the Houston–Seattle playoff game in 1987. Seattle linebacker Fredd Young thought that he had an interception and the head linesman ruled it was trapped. Houston went on to win the game.

There was a lot of debate in the Seattle papers the next week about the call. That's always the way it is. Controversy is always a concern of sportswriters; sometimes a concern of fans, coaches, and players—when the call goes against their team. You don't hear much from the coaches, players, and fans of the team which benefited.

Another controversy occurred in the 1981 Oakland–San Diego game, when Raiders quarterback Kenny Stabler fumbled the ball, halfback Pete Banaszak batted it, and tight end Dave Casper kicked it and then recovered it in the end zone for the winning touchdown. That "fumble" prompted a rule change.

Prior to 1985, we didn't have "in the grasp." Stabler was grabbed and spun around, and the ball came out. The referee ruled it was a fumble. Banaszak dived on the ball. When you dive on the ball, it's not likely to stay there. The ball jumped out. Casper reached to pick it up and kicked it. Casper always did get his hands and feet mixed up. He fell on it in the end zone for a touchdown that won the game.

As a result, the referee had ugly phone calls to his home and had to have police protection. It was ridiculous.

For one thing, he wasn't the only one making the call: The whole crew was involved. I've looked at that film dozens of times. I can't see an infraction. Fumbling the ball, legal; Banaszak diving on the ball, legal; Casper accidentally kicking the ball, legal.

The rule since 1979 is that a fumble in the last two minutes can only be advanced by the fumbling player. If that play sequence happened today, no touchdown would be allowed, and the ball would be returned to the spot where Stabler fumbled it.

I'm waiting for the day, and this is going to happen, when there's fourth and goal on the one, a few seconds to play, and the quarterback tries to sneak the ball in. He fumbles before he crosses the goal line, the ball pops up in the air, and his teammate catches it in the end zone. Touchdown?

No, because on fourth down or in the last two minutes, only the fumbling player may advance the ball. Meanwhile, time has run out, and the ball game is over. Talk with me about controversy then?

One time I was asked to help defuse some controversy. When I worked Super Bowl XII (1978) a sportswriter for the *Los Angeles Times* did a very complimentary story about me, and the headline was "NFL Goes to Best Man." McNally approved it because it was important at that time that officials get some good publicity. There had been a couple of controversial calls during the playoffs leading to that Super Bowl.

One of them happened in the AFC championship game that season, between Oakland and Denver. The Broncos' Rob Lytle was headed toward the goal line when he apparently fumbled, with the Raiders recovering on about the 3. The head linesman didn't see the fumble, and he signaled a touchdown. The Broncos won the game by three, 20–17, and went on to Super Bowl XII. That call was critical.

Now there are two things to understand about that call. The first is that the head linesman couldn't see the ball come out. That happens sometimes. He was in his correct position, but the ball came out on the side opposite from him, so his vision was blocked by the player.

That's why officials now "huddle" for conferences in games, to share information and avoid as much of that kind of thing as possible. When I came into the league, even up to that Denver–Oakland game, it was pretty much every man for himself. If you made a call and another official thought it was wrong, he wouldn't say anything about it. But now we'll get together, and if another official had a better view at the play, he'll say what he saw and sometimes the call will be changed. That's when you hear the announcement that "The flag will be picked up. No foul."

There's an old joke in baseball about a runner sliding into third. The third basemen makes the tag but drops the ball. The umpire signals "out" but verbally calls the runner "safe." Both the runner and the baseman are confused. They saw the umpire's arm raised, signaling "out," but heard him say "safe."

The umpire says to both, "You know and I know that he's safe, but 60,000 people in this stadium saw me signal you out, so he's out."

Officials can't let personal embarrassment about a mistake compound the mistake. If we make an error that can be corrected on the spot, we admit it. It's the only way. We want the play to be right.

The second thing to understand about that Oakland-Denver

call is that the one time an official doesn't have to be in a hurry about signaling is with a touchdown. When a touchdown is on its way, everybody in the stadium knows it. Nobody needs the official to throw up his hands.

Officials must wait, watch and confirm that nothing surprising happens in the last half-second, that the runner does cross the plane of the goal line in possession, or that the pass is caught both feet in bounds and not bobbled, or . . . or . . . or. . . . Often a player drops the ball or gets tackled just before his hopes come true. If the official anticipates a touchdown by throwing his hands in the air—well, there's no good place to put your hands when "caught" like that.

There was another call much like that earlier in 1978. Baltimore and New England. Miami coach Don Shula and the rest of the Dolphins were waiting for the outcome. The division title was at stake. If Baltimore won, the Dolphins had a chance to go to the playoffs.

Baltimore quarterback Bert Jones fumbled. The referee thought Jones's forward progress was stopped, so he blew the whistle. New England recovered the fumble but the ball was dead with the whistle and reverted to Baltimore. The Colts scored on the next play and went on to win, knocking Miami out of the playoffs.

Shula got a letter from a parent saying, "How in the world can you stand this injustice? How can I teach my twelve-year-old son that life is fair when this kind of thing happens and keeps you out of the playoffs? You got burned by a bad call. That's unfair."

Shula's reply is legendary. It went something like this: "It's important you teach your son that everything in life isn't fair, that there will be things that go against you sometimes over which you have no control. You just have to accept life as it is. The better you are, the bigger you are, the more you'll accept the bad breaks and get on with life without worrying about what you should have had, what you really 'deserved,' or what was due you. Officials call what they see. A few bad breaks are part of the breaks of the game. I'm sure I've won games and made the playoffs other times because of lucky breaks."

Shula shows a reasonable perspective.

Controversy has another benefit: It helps educate the public. We have excellent analysts on television explaining what to look for. The change to announcing all calls from the field is also an improvement. While most announcements are routine, once in a while the unusual happens and the viewers, sometimes the analysts, too, get a bit of education.

We have an expression in officiating, "untimed down," which covers a rare situation. It occurs when there is a defensive penalty on the last play of a half. If the penalty is accepted, you cannot end the half on that play; you have to have another play. There being no time left on the clock, the extra play is called an untimed down.

A play like that happened in the Minnesota–New Orleans playoff game in January 1988. The last down of the first half, Minnesota ran off-tackle, but New Orleans had twelve men on the field.

The penalty made it a first down and moved it 5 yards closer, so the Vikings went for a "Hail Mary" pass. To explain that the rules permitted Minnesota another down, the referee announced, "There was a defensive foul. Twelve men on the field. We'll have an untimed down."

From the TV booth, Pat Summerall, doing play-by-play for CBS, admitted, "I've never heard that expression." Well, Pat knew the rule, but the words took him by surprise. It is sometimes announced as "one additional down," which leaves out the information that no time is used or needed.

An untimed down is a rarity. It may not have happened during the years Summerall was the punter for the New York Giants. It has happened perhaps only a couple of dozen times in all the games I've worked over the last twenty-eight seasons.

* * *

The media prompted the change to announcing players' numbers on all fouls. We always had informed the coaches which players were involved, because they need to know. Then in the late 1970s, the media requested that we also announce the numbers from the field so that their play-by-play and followup stories could be accurate. We were glad to oblige.

Do the players complain about being singled out? Some do, sometimes. The fans certainly can get more behind the action because they know more about who did what to whom. A better informed fan is a more involved fan.

I credit the networks and their analysts and commentators with educating the viewers more and more. Slow motion, reverse angles, replays, chalkboards, expert discussion, and all the high-tech assistance are better than the old-fashioned locker room blackboard. Go back to that play in the Minnesota–New Orleans game, when there were twelve men on the field. On TV, they were able to come back with the picture and within seconds count off the players right on-screen for all to see.

Because the fans are more sophisticated, they are more inquisitive about the rules. What fans are discovering is that the rules do not always equal out. If the defense jumps offside, for instance, and the offensive guard slugs the defensive nose tackle, the fouls offset *if* there is a change of possession during that play. Offside is a 5-yard penalty. The punch is a 15-yard personal-foul penalty. The fouls offset, but clearly one team "lucked out." Those are the rules.

Fans sometimes think they know more than they really do about fouls. People say to me, "You could call holding on every down." Well, not if you are interpreting the rules according to league philosophy.

The issue in holding is whether the defensive man being held is actually being restricted. If the defensive man tries to roll and get away and he can't, that's holding. He is restricted from where he wants to go. If the defensive man makes the contact, say, he comes straight on and engages the offensive man, that's not holding. The player was not restricted from doing what he intended. You'll see guys all wrapped up, but the contact is considered holding only if the defensive player is being restricted.

Defensive players can be very clever about this. In struggling with an offensive player, the defensive guy will sometimes take the offensive man down, trying to draw a holding foul. The official must be alert and watch the play develop. You can't anticipate. Watch for the restriction. If one player is gaining an illegal advantage, make the call.

It can get pretty frantic in there. The officials watch the snap. Instantly, players are whizzing by. The back might swing out for a screen pass; the linebackers are moving around. It's like trying to work in the middle of a freeway. Nonetheless, you can't be in a hurry. Read the play, see the foul, throw the flag. No more quick decisions; we use a different interpretation in the 1980s than we did in the 1960s and 1970s.

At one time, we didn't allow any movement by the quarterback before the snap. Now we allow him to move his leg, to signal a back to go in motion. He can't bob his head or move his hands or do anything to draw the other team offside. If he does, that's a false start (5 yards).

If there's an overriding philosophy in the league's thinking, it is to "let 'em play." Let the players set the pace. If they set a tempo where there's a minimum amount of fouls, if they're playing the game according to the rules, let 'em play. The minute you see them trying to get an advantage by breaking the rules, the officials have to step right in and be strong with them.

Keeping that balance is one of the toughest aspects of officiating. You are there to enforce all the rules but to let the play move without being "overly officious." One major criticism of an official is that he injected himself too much into the game and made his role bigger than the game itself.

One final point about controversy: I can tell, watching other games, when an official makes a call that saves a lot of controversy. This happened in the 1988 divisional playoff game between Minnesota and New Orleans.

Minnesota punted to New Orleans, the ball hit a New Orleans player, and Minnesota recovered. The side judge was going to give the ball to New Orleans. He knew Minnesota had recovered, but he was set up to signal the wrong way. The head linesman came in and took the call right away from him and said, "Minnesota's ball."

That's good officiating. Nobody noticed it, but had the side judge pointed the wrong way, he would have created a lot of unfortunate controversy.

Every coach and player comes to the field hoping to make game history that day. Officials also want every game to be worth a page in the history books. But when we find ourselves in the midst of game history, we want the reason to be only because we are witnessing coaching and playing excellence at yet a higher level. We don't want the game to make history because of something we did or didn't do. The game belongs to the players.

A proper call is only correct. It isn't historical. Good officiating clears the way for the excellence of the players to determine the game. Players make history when they surpass existing standards. Officials make history only when they flub. We don't seek controversy. We strive to make our performance unremarkable, simply correct.

3

It's All Up to Me

I'm an optimist. I make no apology for that. Who was ever helped by a defeatist attitude? I believe every day is a great day. Don't believe that? Try missing one.

As NFL officials, we're graded more on the mistakes we make than on the number of correct decisions. This reflects a tendency that runs counter to my belief that it's better to "accentuate the positive."

I've learned it works—"What the mind can conceive and believe can be achieved." When we teach ourselves to think in a positve way and take action, we proceed and perform toward success.

When football coaches review game films, they watch for players doing something wrong. "Terrible block, lousy pass."

Some coaches go on to say, "Now, this is the way it should be done," but too often coaches—and bosses, teachers, parents, and spouses—forget that teaching requires setting a positive direction for the learner. We get a better idea of how to do it right if we know clearly what needs to be done. In that sense, it's irrelevant to know what we've been doing wrong.

I made the same mistake when I was a driver-training teacher. (I am brave!) I sat in the right seat with a clutch and brake, but no steering wheel. A nervous teenager was at the wheel. Inevitably, beginning drivers are afraid of oncoming traffic. Somehow they feel that parked cars are less threatening than oncoming traffic. They tend to crowd the curb. If they could, they would drive on the sidewalk.

Being in the right seat, I saw that getting to the sidewalk meant going through the parked cars. When the student driver pulled too far right, I'd say, "Don't hit that car! Watch out for the parked cars."

Invariably, the drivers would move closer to the parked cars. I was putting that direction into their heads. They were thinking "parked car," and that's where they headed.

I didn't realize then what "visualization" could do for learning and athletic performance. In looking at why student drivers kept doing the wrong thing, I eventually saw that part of the problem was in how I was giving them instruction.

When you put the correct picture in your mind, you will tend to move in that direction. When you say, "Don't do that," your mind is distracted from the right thing, having been told to think about the wrong thing.

Ken Venturi, former U.S. Open golf champ and now a golf analyst for CBS, and I discussed this concept in terms of golf. Ken teaches that once you identify the trouble spots on a hole, whether a sandtrap, water, a tight shot through trees or what-ever, you should block that out and focus solely on where you want the ball to go. You think about, visualize, the exact spot where you want the ball to land. It works.

Whether it's learning to drive a car, hitting a golf ball, playing football, or any other skill activity, putting "don'ts" in your mind crowds out the "dos." "Don'ts" slow down getting it right. "Don'ts" are irrelevant if the quest for excellence is alive.

I try to remember that when working with younger officials. As a referee, I'm responsible for the in-season training of our crew. I find I get faster improvement by pointing out what a rookie official is doing right and clearly defining the overall goal. If he's motivated, he'll prepare himself for doing it right the next time.

If you want to get fancy, you can say that man is a teleological being. The mind moves toward the picture it's given—in athletics, chess, cooking, anything. It happens in the mind before it happens in the muscles.

My dad had been a professional baseball player for the Oakland Oaks, a Triple-A team. That made it easier for him to understand my dream—I wanted to pitch for the New York Yankees. Dad always encouraged me even though I hadn't shown much talent. He'd catch me, and say, "Good pitch. Now, remember how you threw that."

He didn't know the term visualization, but his instinct was exactly right.

I wasn't being disloyal in yearning for the Yankees. I lived in California. We didn't have the Dodgers, Angels, Giants, or Athletics yet. The Yankees were my team, with Babe Ruth, Lou Gehrig, Joe DiMaggio, Red Ruffing. I wanted to stand on the mound in the "House That Ruth Built." Trouble was, I couldn't break a pane of glass across a small room.

I kept at it. I played baseball all four years at Alhambra High. Well, I didn't play a lot. The coach didn't know what to do with my level of talent.

But I was there every day. Never missed a practice or a game. First one on the field. Last one to leave. I loved baseball.

Finally, as a senior, I made the starting lineup as second baseman. Coach Bill Hess put me where I could do the least damage. Most high school batters are right-handed and hit between third and short. I understood this, but I was happy to play.

Then the big game came. El Monte and Alhambra were tied for first place in the Moore League. Whichever team won this game would stand alone in first. Boy, we wanted to be number one.

El Monte had a great coach in Terry Bartron. He had developed a powerhouse team around pitcher Tom Morgan, who went on to a long career in the majors.

We were at El Monte. Bottom of the ninth. Two outs. El

Monte had bases loaded. We were ahead, 3–2. I was the second baseman. As our pitcher, Lefty Ray Rubacaba, wound up, I got into the crouch position infielders take and whispered quietly to myself, "Don't hit the ball to me!"

I thought, Oh geez. What if they hit the ball to me? What if it goes through my legs? Two runs will score. Who'll the guys blame? Tunney. Right?

The voice of a loser. Where was my dad when I needed him? Finally a chance to make a difference to the team and I was scared I'd choke.

I didn't get the chance. They hit the ball to our third baseman. He stepped on the bag, forcing the runner for the third out. We win, 3–2. Alhambra is number one. Oh, boy.

That experience festered in me. All those years of practice and I was scared I'd choke.

I went on to play first base for Occidental College. The voice of the winner started to come out in me. I was batting .450. The team was 23–2. Every play, every time, every pitch, I would say to myself, "Hit the ball to me!"

I didn't care about being a star or hero, but I knew I could make the play. Before every pitch, I could see myself fielding the ball and making the play. I saw it in my mind fresh each time. I practiced it every day. When game time came, I was ready.

Although there have been difficult times since then, the voice of the winner has held firm. "Hit the ball to me. I can make the play."

I didn't win all the difficult battles, but none of them defeated me, either. I knew I wouldn't choke. I never backed away.

Visualization is now standard in athletics. Once an athlete learns to visualize his performance, improvement and consistency follow.

I've heard it said a thousand times, "Practice makes perfect." Not so. Practice DOESN'T make perfect. PERFECT PRACTICE makes perfect.

Just going out and whacking at a golf ball a thousand times doesn't lower a handicap. Nothing helps more than concentration and practice. To develop excellence, you have to know what you're doing and intend it the right way every time.

Self-esteem comes in here, too. When Vince Lombardi was coaching the Green Bay Packers, the cameras might catch him on the sideline bawling out a player. What the camera didn't catch was Lombardi going over to the player a few minutes later, putting his arm around the player's shoulders, and building him back up. Lombardi knew the value of criticism, self-confidence, and strong self-esteem to consistent performance.

It was 1971. New York was playing Dallas at Shea Stadium. If I remember the score correctly, it was tied in the third quarter. Jets quarterback Joe Namath went back to pass. His wide receiver, Don Maynard, had put a move on the Dallas cornerback and was all alone in the end zone. Namath laid the ball right in Maynard's hands. Somehow it didn't stay.

Maynard had already set all kinds of receiving records for the Jets, but this time he dropped the pass. The fans in New York can be unforgiving. They were throwing apples, oranges, snowballs, anything they could get their hands on. Maynard had committed the unforgivable sin in football—not holding on to the ball. This time it really counted.

I was standing next to Namath when Maynard came back to the huddle. Joe just leaned over and said, "You'll catch the next one, Don."

I was there in the American Football Conference (AFC) championship game on January 17, 1988, when another hero turned into the goat. It was Denver 38, Cleveland 31, with 1:05 left in the fourth.

On second down from Denver's 8 yard line, Cleveland ran its 13-trap play designed to go inside. Quarterback Bernie Kosar handed off to running back Earnest Byner. Byner found that lane shut down, so he popped outside and swung free.

At the 1, only a stride from the end zone and a chance to tie the game, Broncos defensive back Jeremiah Castille stripped the ball out of Byner's hands and recovered. That ended Cleveland's second-half comeback glory.

Byner had earlier scored two touchdowns and was largely responsible for the fighting chance Cleveland had with 1:05 left, but all the honor that was due him suddenly seemed to evaporate. Byner trudged off the field and sat on his helmet on the sidelines as the defensive squad futilely went out for the last series for Denver.

Kosar bent down and put his arm around Byner. Every player, every coach, every Cleveland Browns fan, knew that the team wouldn't have made the playoffs if it hadn't been for the efforts of Earnest Byner. His "mistake," although costly, needed to be kept in perspective, and it was.

In these two situations, there are plenty of quarterbacks who would have taken their disappointment out in anger. What good would that have done? Nobody wanted to catch the ball more than Maynard or keep the ball and score that touchdown more than Byner.

When something doesn't go our way and we project our anger onto others, as we so often do with our children, spouses, employees, friends, and partners, we accomplish little except our own loss of dignity. It's a defense for our bruised ego to point out another's mistake when obviously they intended the right action.

Namath had enough sense to know what Maynard was going through and planted in his mind that he would do it right the next time. Kosar knew what Byner was feeling. Positive thinking builds strength, and that comes out as grace under pressure. In my book, that's a good deal.

Like every official, I'm in the NFL because I love the game of football. Officials see the game in a way nobody else does. Fans hear the noise and see the plays, but only the players and the officials are in the thick of it, where the sweat flies, where the crunch and the finesse of the action are.

We see the drama as players battle in an arena. We hear the humor, some of it raw, as coaches and players express themselves. There is always a clear-cut outcome—one side wins, one side loses.

Players respect officials because we're in the action with them. The officials are under pressure to make every decision the right one. We respect the players, too. The closer you are to the courage, the more durable your respect. Unless you are on the field with them, you can't fully appreciate the endurance and commitment the players have. It's just incredible some of the moves these guys make, and always under pressure. When they explode occasionally, we understand.

A common trait among NFL players is that every one of them wants to be better than he was yesterday. Any player who doesn't want to be better—he's gone. Instant history. That's why businessmen look to athletics for role models.

Nick Buoniconti, Hall of Fame linebacker of the Miami Dolphins, tells a story about when the Dolphins won the AFC the first time and played Dallas in Super Bowl VI (1972). I worked the game.

Dallas beat Miami, 24–3. In an interview after the game, Buoniconti was asked, "You had a great season. Tell us about it."

Buoniconti summed it up, "We set our goal in July to get to the Super Bowl."

"You mean," the interviewer asked, "you didn't set your goal to win the Super Bowl?"

"That's where we went wrong. We only aimed at getting to the Super Bowl. We should have set our goal to win it."

The next year, Miami set its goal higher. They won Super Bowl VII—and everything else. The 1972 season was the year they went 17–0, which no NFL team has done before or since.

It's a privilege to work with the coaches and players of the

NFL. Men like Vince Lombardi, whose motivational ability would have made him a success in any business. It's no coincidence that several of Lombardi's players from his great years at Green Bay, men like Willie Davis, Bob Skoronski, Fuzzy Thurston, Bob Dowler, Max McGee, and others went on to become successful businessmen by applying the lessons Lombardi taught.

Don't get me wrong: Football is entertainment, not an MBA program. It is a chance to witness peak performance and to see how preparation and discipline help you to stay near your peak for long stretches. Those are skills that can be converted to success in any endeavor.

But peak performance requires a winning attitude and the discipline of optimism. The voice of the loser must be silenced. The voice of the winner must hold steady. You have to go into the situation saying, "I can make the play. Hit the ball to me."

4

You're Only as Good as Your Next Call

Kids grow up dreaming of becoming superstars, not NFL officials. Even though my dad was a referee, which gave me a perfect role model, my dream was to pitch for the Yankees.

From the time I was 4, I went to games with my dad. I'd carry the bag with his uniform. We'd go through the gates, and he'd say, "This is my assistant."

We went to every little rinky-dink high school and junior college field in Southern California as well as the Rose Bowl and the Los Angeles Coliseum. Being a kid, I used to run up and down the bleachers. I remember my dad telling me time after time, "Sit down on the bench and watch these guys. You can learn something."

I remember sitting on the bench with Jackie Robinson when he was playing for Pasadena Junior College. It didn't mean anything to me at the time because who knew what Jackie Robinson was going to mean to sports? He was just another star football player.

My dad coached at Lincoln High School for about eight years. While there, he groomed Kenny Washington, who he said was the finest football player he had ever coached. We both followed his career when he went on to UCLA.

Dad didn't buy into the idea of "stars." He appreciated excellence and commitment and thought there was always more potential to be realized. He avoided laying on the praise and glory stuff. Kenny was a great player, but when he did something wrong, my dad chewed him out, the same way he would any other player who messed up.

Even with all these opportunities to watch my dad being a coach and an official, it never crossed my mind that I'd become an official. In fact, I got into officiating by accident during my freshman year in college when I was recruited to fill in during the summer recreational basketball league.

My dad watched me officiate only once a year or so. It was the same when I was playing. I think I could probably count on two hands the number of times he watched me play. That was fine with me. I didn't want him there. When he watched me, he'd have a checklist of ways to improve when I came home. I mean, he nailed me! But he was always on my side.

When my ambition to get to the mound at Yankee Stadium faded, I decided I wanted to coach. From the time I was in seventh grade, I had studied every coach I had. I learned from the great ones, but I also learned from those who didn't care as much. Watching what coaches were doing that was ineffective taught me how to seek a better way. I was constantly trying to find ways to teach or coach better. All experience is education, if you know what you're after.

Following graduation from Occidental College, I started my first coaching assignment at Lincoln High School in East Los Angeles. I coached football, basketball, and baseball for four years. All those years of preparation and I coached only four years! When an opportunity to get into high school administration came up, it was too good to pass up.

Meanwhile, I was continuing to officiate basketball and football. It was a regular part of my life. A pace that I liked, and the extra income wasn't all that bad, either. It seemed part of me, very natural, but I never had a well-formed ambition to get into the pros. I liked high school and college officiating and wasn't aware of any desire to move to the NFL.

In 1956, I was selected to work football in the Pacific Coast Conference (PCC; now, Pac Ten). A lot of officials were alumni of USC or UCLA, so they couldn't work games involving those schools. Having gone to Oxy, I could.

Meanwhile, I continued to work basketball games at the high school, junior-college, and small-college level. After a city championship high-school basketball game, as I was getting dressed, there was a knock at the door. The man at the door said, "My name is John Wooden. I wonder if you'd be interested in working major college games?"

I said, "Absolutely."

And he said, "I'll put your name in."

Jess Hill, athletic director at USC, also recommended me. Hill knew my work from football in the PCC.

Working basketball in the 1960s was great. Johnny Wooden was having his great years. The whole sport was in an upsurge.

I always admired Wooden's philosophy. He didn't believe a lot in scouting opponents. His thinking was "If I can prepare my five guys to play the best they can, I'm not worried about what the other team can do."

As a kid, I played more basketball than football. I preferred its more continuous movement. When I started officiating, the same appeal drew me. This was the era of the fast break. I loved running up and down the floor all night.

I also loved the speed of the decision making. In basketball, you can easily make 200 decisions a game, compared with 10–20 for the average NFL game. Yet, officiating football is more mentally draining because of the intricacies of the rules.

The rules are much more complicated in football than most people realize. I always knew that if I had to choose between football and basketball, I'd choose football. The plays and the players are more varied. Eleven people, each with a different task, working together for the same purpose makes the game more complex.

In 1959, I worked two nationally televised football games that gave me some early visibility. After the season was over, about

February 1960, Bob Austin, who had left the NFL to become head of officiating for the newly forming AFL, called me and said, "We're going to need officials, and we'd like you to referee in the AFL."

I had never really considered working pro games. My ambition at the time was to work up to the biggest college games. But his offer certainly gave me cause to think. Austin told me he was going to be in Los Angeles the next week, so we arranged to talk about it.

Two nights later, Mike Wilson, NFL supervisor of officials, called. He said Norm Schachter, Dutch Heintz, and Bud Brubaker, three NFL officials from the Los Angeles area, had told him about me. They thought I might be interested in working in the NFL.

"We understand you've been offered a contract by the AFL," Wilson said. "Don't sign it until we have a chance to talk to you."

It was exciting to have such great options. Having done nothing aggressively, I was being courted by two leagues. So I met with both.

The AFL offered me the position of referee and $2,000 for the season. The NFL offered $1,800, but as a field judge.

I wanted to be a referee, because that's what I'd been doing in college officiating. I liked being in charge, but I decided to go with the NFL, choosing security over position. The NFL had been around for forty years. I remembered when my dad was working in the All-American Conference (in the late 1940s), it folded. I wasn't sure the AFL would last.

Joining the NFL as a field judge meant I wasn't thrown right into the thick of things. Then, as now, officials come into the NFL in a position other than referee. It helped me tremendously to find several mentors among the other officials. To be able to work with great officials like Bud Brubaker, Norm Schachter, Art McNally, Stan Javie, Ron Gibbs, Bill Downs, George Rennix, Dutch Heintz, Dan Tehan, and others who helped me in those early years was a blessing.

With all the officiating I'd done, it surprised me to suddenly realize I had never been to a pro football game. I'd seen a few on television, but the first pro game I attended was the first pro game I officiated. It was a preseason game between the Bears and the Rams in the Los Angeles Coliseum. At least the surroundings were familiar.

During my first season in the NFL, I met Sid Borgia, head of NBA officials. I ran into Sid as I arrived at the St. Louis airport on Saturday. He invited me to the Hawks game that night, during which he said, "I've heard of your work in college. How would you like to work in the NBA?"

I said, "I'm flattered. I'd like to think about it."

Officiating pro basketball is a full-time job. I was then in my second year as assistant principal at Lincoln High School. I was concerned that if I took a leave from my career in education, I would be at the whim of the NBA. I turned it down. Family, security, all that.

My ambition was to work up through the ranks and become a high school principal. Officiating was a great change of pace for the weekends, but that's all I figured it was—a change of pace, not a livelihood in itself. I would come home from school on Friday and pack for the game, glad for a switch from the continual, mundane decision making of school administration. The drone of "I don't have enough chalk for my classroom" type of problem was relieved by jumping into the midst of a hot game.

Then boom. I changed my career route. While principal at Fairfax High School in Los Angeles in 1966, I met one of the Fairfax alums, Herb Alpert. I asked if he and the Tijuana Brass would perform for the kids at school. He said, "I'd love to. Nobody ever asked."

In 1968, Alpert asked permission to use the school as background for a television special called "The Beat of the Brass." He and the Brass spent three days filming on campus.

He surprised me one afternoon by asking, "Why don't you come to work for me."

I said, "All I play is the whistle. What can I do for you?"

Not many people know the philanthropic side of Herb Alpert. He established an educational foundation to create a school in which the students would participate in designing the curricula and all school policies. He had a daring vision, one that is consistent with the level of trust he has in people, teenagers included.

He asked me to create that school. His concept was well matched to my views on nurturing and how to develop an environment in which learning was the central activity.

The dream of every educator is to have his own school. This was an opportunity to try some of my favorite ideas about leadership and motivation, which I found were difficult to institute in a public school system.

Alpert and his foundation seemed to be the open door. I went to work to design the opening plan.

In the second year, Alpert's financial picture changed, and he had to abandon the project. We remain close friends, and he continues to give his energies and money in many ways for the good of others.

Having taken a leave of absence (safety planning, again), I returned to the Los Angeles city schools, first as a principal of Franklin High School in Highland Park, then as principal at Hollywood High.

Yes, THE Hollywood High School. This was as much an educational experience for me as I intended school to be for the students. I probably learned more about how to cope in a high-tech, sophisticated environment than the students learned about European history and algebra.

One thing became very clear: the perceived glamour of rubbing elbows with football heroes gave me an immediate advantage on campus. I am fully persuaded that it was easier to lead students and faculty toward common goals because of how they viewed my work in the NFL. It was a self-fulfilling prophecy of the best kind.

National recognition helped as I moved on to the assistant

superintendency of the Bellflower (California) Unified School District. In fact, when I was later appointed superintendent, I am sure that the demonstrated ability to make hard decisions in a fair way on Sunday afternoons played an important part in my appointment.

All this time I'd been doing public speaking. I realized that the same concepts and practices I was using with young people to develop leadership, teamwork, and mental management would work, reslanted, with the nation's executives. I joined the National Speakers Association in 1975.

What motivated me to leave the school business was the possibility of reaching so many more people. The desire to extend these principles to more and more people has been a driving force throughout my life.

The constant in these career steps was my "change of pace"—officiating. An important change came there, too.

As a field judge, I was responsible for only my own actions. When the league made me a referee in 1967, I became responsible for the training of our crew. I was a teacher again, and it felt good. As a teacher and coach, if the students didn't do well, I felt responsible. In the same way, I felt responsible for the success or failure of each member of our crew. A large part of that responsibility involves positive reinforcement and maintaining my own morale and energy.

Leadership begins with setting a strong example. It's my job to be "on" for every game—alert, precise, prepared. Organizational behavior is reflective. If I expect the crew to be ready, I must be.

One technique is to use mental management before, during, and after the game, especially during. Stay focused on the play in progress. That's the only play which deserves attention.

This is as true in a blowout as it is in a score-for-score battle in which the next play could be the winning touchdown. The heart of officiating is to treat every play as equally important, giving it your full attention.

Wayne Gretsky, the all-time scoring leader in the NHL, has

won every honor possible in his sport. At the tender age of 23, he had won a number of them more than once. After winning one more, he was asked, "With all the awards you've already won, what is there to look forward to?"

Gretsky replied, "Tonight's game."

Able to stay in the moment and ready, Gretsky understands focus and what it brings you.

Some may call it anticipation or psyching yourself up. It's no different for officials than it is for players. The essential requirement is to prepare mentally for each game.

Experience teaches that you can't float on your résumé. Great records and awards don't help with real-time performance. Distraction is the enemy.

This attention to real-time performance is similar to an entertainer who must appear in the same role or with the same repertoire nightly before a new audience. Every repeat performance is supposed to be as good as the best ever. That's the challenge for officials. When you stop to think about it, that's the challenge for anyone with excellence as his goal.

When officiating high school and college games, I didn't look at the rule book in the locker room before a game. My feeling was "If you don't know the rules by now, Tunney, you'll never know them." I learned better.

I review rules all through the year, with a daily focus during the season. I go over the basics again and again. Every week. Even if I think I know every one of them cold, I take the time. I direct my attention. I push them through the memory bank. It has to be fresh knowledge to be fast knowledge. I can never be too prepared.

There was a new rule on the kickoff in 1987. If a kickoff goes out of bounds, the ball is placed on the 35 yard line, not rekicked as it had been. While it happened only two or three times all last season in the games our crew worked, when it did, we were prepared.

We put the ball on the 35 yard line. I turned on my microphone and explained it to the crowd. No hesitation. A simple thing, because we were prepared.

If you are not prepared, if you have to think about the rule, you give the coaches, players, and fans the impression that you're not in control. More than that, you know yourself you weren't ready.

Crew preparation on rules and mechanics is specific and extensive, but on the field, performance depends on each official being totally focused. Mental management is always tougher than being in shape and solid on the rules, because no one can help you with it. No one is in your mind with you. You are its only driver. If you don't maintain your focus, the moment will slip by. The maxim for all officials is true: You're only as good as your next call.

5

No Time for a Cheeseburger

September 14, 1987. The game seemed to deserve the anticipation that had built up. Might be the biggest game of the year. New York Giants, champions of Super Bowl XXI (1987), against the Chicago Bears, champions of Super Bowl XX (1986), at Soldier Field. First ABC Monday night game of the year. Plenty of hype. A packed stadium of 67,704 fans and nearly 40 million around televisions.

This was also the first regular-season game for the crew assigned to me that season. We had worked only two preseason games together. We had a second-year man and a fourth-year man. As NFL tenures go, that's not a lot of experience for a game that might develop Super Bowl intensity.

Third quarter. Chicago 24, New York 7. Third down and 2 on New York's 28 yard line. New York quarterback Phil Simms drops back to pass and gets a big rush from the Chicago defensive line. I'm right there behind Simms. We're looking at more Bears and bigger bears than the San Diego Zoo ever had.

Simms scrambled. I did, too. Just as he started to throw, he was hit, and the ball hit the ground. I ruled "incomplete pass."

When the ball hit the ground, it bounced straight into the hands of Bears defensive lineman Steve McMichael, who had run it into the end zone. When he turned to look my way, he saw me waving my arms back and forth, signaling incomplete forward pass, not the upright signal for a touchdown.

This was the second year of instant replay. Up in the replay booth was the instant replay official. We call him—"God." That evening, God wasn't just anyone; it was Art McNally, supervisor of NFL officials, my boss. He was reviewing the tapes, trying to determine whether it was an incomplete pass or a fumble.

If Simms's arm was going forward when the ball was released, it is an incomplete pass when the ball hits the ground. If the ball was knocked out of his hand while he was not in a throwing motion, it is a fumble.

After looking at all the angles to determine pass or fumble, McNally tried to relay the information by wireless Telex to the umpire on the field, Hendi Ancich, but the transmission didn't come through.

I had to go to the instant replay telephone, located behind the home-team bench, to talk with McNally. I picked up the telephone and said, "I'll have a cheeseburger, a diet Coke, hold the fries."

McNally said, "What?"

I said, "Never mind. What do you have up there?"

He said, "We're ruling that play a fumble."

I said, "Well, fine, but I called it as an incomplete pass and blew my whistle."

When the whistle blows, the play is dead. It didn't matter whether my call was right or wrong. The play was dead as soon as I blew the whistle, and you can't go on as if it were a recovered ball and continue the down.

McNally agreed that the play had to be ruled dead. "But," he said, "it really was a fumble. Place the ball on the New York 19 where the ball hit. It'll be fourth down, New York's ball. Now, go out there and announce it."

I walked to the middle of Soldier Field, in front of 67,704 Bears fans who saw me as the villain who had stolen their touchdown. I turned on my microphone and said, "Although instant replay rules it a fumble, I called it as an incomplete pass and blew the whistle. It is New York's ball, fourth down.

I wanted to go home.

But I couldn't. I had to concentrate on the next play. Fourth down—Sean Landetta back to punt. I had to focus on my responsibilities. Watch the snap of the ball, watch the kicker's foot contact the ball, watch for roughing the kicker, watch for holding. While I watched, New York punted, and Chicago's Dennis McKinnon returned the ball 13 yards.

What was I thinking as I ran downfield? Did I blow that play? No. That play is dead. History. Gone. I can never change it. But if I let my mind dwell on the last play or if I worry about self-image, I'm not going to be effective for the next call. What I had to do was some fast mental reorganization. In psychobabble terms we call it "self-talk." I had to tell myself that I had a split-second decision to make, and I made it, on the spot. I couldn't think now about whether it was right or wrong.

I can't control game sequence. I can't decide whether it's going to be a pass or a run. I can't anticipate players' strengths or mistakes or see everything from all angles with one pair of eyes. What I can do is concentrate and do the best I can on every play.

Unless you have the discipline to stay right there, in the moment, and take the heat once in a while, you won't last as an NFL official. You must be able to stand out there and take abuse from coaches, players, and fans; but NEVER give it to yourself.

Most officials have learned this by the time they get to the NFL. Every NFL official has worked in high school and college football before being selected. Not surprisingly, every official played football at some level. I played college ball. Many NFL officials, such as Lou Palazzi, George McAfee, Jack Nix, George Murphy, Frank Sinkovitz, Joe Muha, Gary Lane, Pete Liske, and Dean Look, were NFL players who continued their love for the game through officiating.

Officials have to be clear, and clearheaded. We're not out there to make a touchdown or a great tackle. We're out there to do a good job. If there's one thing you want to hear when you walk off the field, it's a coach saying, "The officials gave us a hundred percent and were fair."

Unfortunately, that doesn't happen often enough. Usually, we're treated like offensive linemen—we get noticed only when we make a mistake. We get criticized more than praised. For some officials, that's psychologically the toughest part of the job. Being graded by our supervisors every week, every game, every play is a constant reminder that we are expected to be perfect— and a little more.

The supervisors grade us by reviewing videotapes of our games. They give little attention to the overall content of the game. Their emphasis is on individual calls made or not made. They run the tape back and forth to see what really happened. It is the ultimate in Monday morning refereeing. On the field, we don't have the luxury of reverse angle or slo mo. . . .

Some fundamentals aren't included in the grading. Control of the game, for instance. If the officials lose control of the game, it will get out of hand, with a lot of pushing and shoving, even fighting; then the fans get rowdy and start booing. Fans come to see a football game and don't like it when the game degenerates into a hockey game.

For the good of the game as well as the protection of the players, officials must stay in control. Even in hot games between rivals, if the officials are in control, problems don't occur. The fans instinctively grade an official on his poise and command, but the league's rating system doesn't.

Most officials have a sense of being decisive. They see a play and make the call. That's the way they run their lives, whether as businessmen, doctors, or teachers. We read plays as quarterbacks read defenses. We see a foul, we throw the flag. But we don't anticipate. It's not a foul until it happens. There are no "maybes"; at least there aren't supposed to be. Wait, watch, if it happens, make the call.

I don't see a lot of ego gratification coming out of it. It's not like saying, "Hey, look at me, I'm a referee. I've worked twenty-eight years and three Super Bowls." If that happens, you're dead. You're out of the moment and therefore out of focus. That's murder for an official.

You also can't start thinking you're more important than any player or the ball. The players determine the game. Officials must never forget that.

Another must: Officials are like Caesar's wife. Our integrity must be above suspicion.

The league is concerned about the amount of money that's bet on pro football. Because gambling is sometimes tied to the criminal element of our society, if there is any indication that gamblers are near the game, the league steps in.

That's why Paul Hornung and Alex Karras were suspended in 1963. It wasn't so much that they were cheating. They were betting on their own teams. But simply to avoid a possible association with the fringe element, Commissioner Rozelle acted quickly and directly. "Out. Both of you, out."

The league is also cautious about the image of its officials. It doesn't want anyone thinking that someone could get to an official to fix a game.

I probably had an advantage in understanding this because my dad was a steward in thoroughbred racing. He was the official in charge of seeing that the race is run fairly. Horse racing, then as now, is legitimate. My dad was a highly ethical man. He was aware that the gamblers watch the stewards.

When I was in college, I would go down to the racetrack and drop by the paddock area to say hello. He'd say, "How are you?" and that was about all.

I asked him once why he wouldn't talk to me more. He told me, "Others don't know you're my son. If they see me talking to you, they might become suspicious. Gamblers assume the races are fixed. I don't talk to anyone other than owners, trainers, and jockeys between races."

Remembering that, if one coach comes up to talk during the pregame warmup, I make it a point to go over to talk to the other coach. It evens out the impression. I don't want anyone in the stands or on the field thinking I might be partial or that there might be an unfair advantage. My job is detached observation and impartial judgment.

It's not enough for an official to do the right thing. You have to look as if you're doing the right thing. I want the gamblers to know "There's no use even approaching that guy." In twenty-eight years in the NFL, I've never had a gambler approach me in any way.

I stay out of bars (mostly because I don't drink), and I don't go places where there's a lot of betting. When I'm traveling, if somebody wants to talk about the NFL, that's fine, but it's always in general terms. I never talk about coaches. I never talk about players. My usual response is "I only know what I read in the newspapers." The most casual comment might be interpreted as "That guy has some inside information."

Before the start of the season, either Warren Welsh, the head of NFL security, or his assistant, Charlie Jackson, will come to the officials' clinics to talk about the outside influences that affect the game. Their agenda always includes gambling, the money that's being spent, the kind of information gamblers are looking for, and drugs.

Once players get hooked on drugs or gambling, the gamblers can get to them. Once they're hooked, the gamblers are right there, knocking on the door. That's why the league is so concerned about drugs, not just because of the damage drugs do to the players directly but because the high cost of addiction often leads to gambling and threatens the game's integrity.

The league has a strict rule about officials drinking. From the time an official leaves home the day before the game until after the game, he's not allowed to have alcohol. The league's policy is to avoid the airport bars. The league says wait until you get home.

It's a common-sense recognition of human nature. Too many people jump to conclusions. The league doesn't want even one disgruntled fan to see an official having an after-game drink and say, "Ah, those guys drink all the time."

People take a strong position about officials, usually negative. It's important to the league and to the integrity of the game that we maintain a higher standard than that of the general public.

The "Caesar's wife" syndrome goes with the job. It is just one of the restrictions all officials accept. The restrictions don't bother us, because we're generally the type of people who would live our lives thoughtful of public scrutiny.

Since I've been in the league, there's never been a scandal involving officials. The league gets the credit for this because it has a consistent standard of excellence in its selection process. It follows up with reminders of its policies constantly and effectively.

The officials deserve the most credit for staying mindful of the policies and the spirit behind them. Our job includes the obligation to preserve the integrity of the game by being a watchdog of our own actions, both personal and professional. It is only through each individual holding himself accountable for both the appearance and the substance of his actions that the integrity of the game is ensured.

That established, the focus is forward. The path to growth is premised on the recognition that your next call is more important than the last one. When you blow one, the best thing to do is put your embarrassment in fast-forward. Get past it fast. The next play, your next opportunity, is only thirty seconds away, and that's not enough time for a cheeseburger.

6

An Official's Training—
Rules, Interpretation,
and Fitness

NFL officials move up through the system similar to the way NFL players do. We start officiating with high school games. College-conference supervisors select the best to move on to the collegiate level. The NFL supervisors recruit only from the major college conferences.

Except for a few distinctions in the rules and the strength and skill of the players, football is basically the same game whether it's being played in the Pop Warner League or the Super Bowl. At all levels, it's a game that requires concentration and preparation in players and officials alike. Only officials who work the junior levels with precision and effectiveness move on through the ranks.

The criteria for officials are the same at all levels, but the NFL has by far the most intensified training program. Shorty Ray, as technical adviser on rules and officiating from 1938 to 1956, is credited with giving the program its more formal structure. The standards he set earned him the distinction of being the only official so far to be voted into the Hall of Fame.

Through the years, the program has been strengthened by Ray's successors—Mike Wilson, Joe Kuharich, Mark Duncan, Mel Hein, and the present supervisor of officials, Art McNally.

The training program is administered by the league's Department of Officiating in New York. Under McNally since 1968, the program becomes increasingly professional and demanding as the impact and presence of the league grow.

As supervisor, McNally is responsible for the entire program—the recruiting, the training, the assignments, the observing, and the final evaluation of each official. Assisting him is a staff of five assistant supervisors—Jack Reader, Nick Skorich, Joe Gardi, Tony Veteri, and Bob Rice. The assistant supervisors are responsible for observing and grading the performance of each official in every game. They are assisted by a staff of approximately twenty instant-replay officials and game observers.

In the press box at every game is one instant-replay official and one observer. The instant-replay official plays "God" on reviewed plays. The observer gives an on-site evaluation of officials' performance and the overall conduct of the game. He charts the play-by-play and records any unusual events or incidents.

On the field is a crew of seven game officials. The referee is crew chief and responsible for general oversight and control of the game. During play, he takes a position in the backfield 10–12 yards behind the line of scrimmage and favors the side of the quarterback's throwing hand.

The umpire has primary responsibility to rule on players' equipment as well as their conduct and action on the scrimmage line. His position is approximately 5–8 yards downfield in the vicinity of the linebackers.

The head linesman is responsible for ruling offside, encroachment, false start, actions pertaining to the scrimmage line, and for the chain crew that handles the down box and yard markers. He is located at the side of the field and sights down the line of scrimmage at the beginning of each play.

The line judge straddles the line of scrimmage on the side of the field opposite the head linesman. He keeps the time of the game as a backup for the stadium-clock operator. In addition, he has responsibilities similar to those of the head linesman.

The back judge operates on the same side of the field as the line judge, approximately 17 yards downfield. He has primary responsibilities for his sideline and rules on forward pass completions or interceptions.

The side judge operates from the same side of the field as the head linesman, 17 yards downfield. His responsibilities on his side of the field are the same as those of the back judge on his side.

The field judge takes a position approximately 25 yards downfield, times the interval between plays on the 30-second clock, and makes decisions involving catching, recovery, or illegal touching of a loose ball beyond the line of scrimmage. Together with the back judge and side judge, the field judge rules on pass interference and actions involving kicks.

The home team staffs the chain crew, stadium-clock operator, and the 30-second-clock operator.

The time and effort spent in coordinating the intricate working relationships among officials, the chain crew, and the clock operators have a direct relationship to how efficiently the game proceeds. The goal is for the intricacy to be invisible and the game to proceed smoothly and effectively.

The training of the game officials involves both physical and mental components. The league is stringent in its requirements for expert knowledge of the rules. The *Official Rules of the NFL* runs to 127 pages and is filled with complicated, intricate, interrelated, and sometimes confusing playing rules.

Clipping, as an example, is a simple foul that all can see. The rules say that clipping is not allowed from behind below the waist, except in close line play. However, even in close line play, an offensive lineman may not clip a defender who at the snap is aligned on the line of scrimmage opposite another offensive lineman who is more than one position away when that defender is responding to the flow of the ball away from the blocker. Got it?

Other rules appear contradictory unless you understand the intent and spirit that underlie the league's philosophy on player safety and game integrity. While the game of football is easily understood in the overall, the art of rules interpretation depends on years of study and application. I find it takes a good official coming from a major college conference three to five years to understand the NFL's thinking and direction well enough to make consistently correct distinctions.

One of the most complicated areas to understand is where you enforce the penalty. The spots of enforcement in the NFL are considerably different than college and high school rules, and there are exceptions within the exceptions.

During a punt, for example, if the receiving team commits a foul after the ball has been kicked, the spot of enforcement for that penalty is from one of three spots: the spot where the receiver fouled, the spot where the receiver caught the kicked ball, or the spot where the ball became dead. The penalty is enforced from the spot that is the most disadvantageous to the team committing the foul. The exceptions to this are illegal touching of the ball by the kicking team or the failure of the receiving team to keep the kicked ball. Got it?

In addition, many of the rules are complicated in the first reading. For instance, a defensive player may not block an eligible receiver at the line of scrimmage except when that receiver is lined up within 2 yards of the tackle OR when the quarterback leaves the pocket area OR hands off the ball to a back. Got it?

These distinctions are derived from years of experimentation to adjust to the continuous improvement in coaching and playing techniques and to make the game more exciting. In the blocking rule above, if the defender can block the receiver at any time, the passing game is severely limited. The rule is designed to create flexibility in the passing offense.

To master these distinctions, the league requires all game officials to pass a 200-question rules examination in the spring of every year. Currently, the test is compiled by Norm Schachter, a former referee and now one of the instant-replay officials. Dr. Schachter is also the coeditor, along with Art McNally, of the *Official Rules*.

The test presents play situations, real or imagined, in generic language. A sample:

A's ball, 1st and 10, on A's 28-yard line. A1, QB, back to pass. B1, cornerback, blocks A3, wide receiver, below the waist at LOS. A1 completes a pass to A3, who runs to the A 40, fumbles and B2 recovers the ball at the 50. Ruling:

    (a) A's ball, 1st and 10 at A 45
    (b) B's ball, 1st and 10 at the 50
    (c) A's ball, 1st and 10 at A 33
    (d) A's ball, 1st and 10 at A 40
    (e) _____

The answer is C. Team B may not block a receiver who is lined-up more than 2 yards from a tackle at the line of scrimmage. Although Team B ended up with the ball, they committed a foul before its recovery. The ball reverts to the offended team, and the penalty (5 yards) is enforced from the line of scrimmage. It's first down for Team A.

Had A3 been a tight end positioned next to the tackle, the block by B1 would have been legal, and Team B would have taken possession of the ball at the 50.

The rules test is mailed to each official in April. Officials in various geographic areas get together for informal and voluntary study sessions. The purpose of conferring is not so much to be sure you know whether the penalty is a 5-, 10-, or 15-yard infraction but to understand the reasoning behind the intent of the rule.

The test is due at the league office in early June and is graded by the supervisors and returned to each official at the officials' clinics, held in mid-July. Officials from the eastern half of the

United States meet in Pittsburgh one week, and those from the western half meet in Denver the next. These workshops run from Thursday through Sunday, and each session follows a similar agenda.

Topics covered include league procedures and policies, review of old and new rules, field mechanics, videotape study of special play situations involving fouls, team formation, and officials' positions. Officials in each position attend special sessions to discuss specific areas of responsibilities.

First-year officials start the workshop one day ahead to cover the "basics" in greater detail. Particular emphasis is given to the differences between college and NFL rules, and they receive instruction in a myriad of operating procedures unique to the league.

The chief thing to understand is that officials don't learn the rules once and forever more. The clinic is the starting point for the in-season training of officials. It continues on the field, game by game. There the essence of the game and the rules is learned.

A lot of people believe the game starts at one o'clock on Sunday. That's not so for the officials. We assemble on Saturday afternoon for video study and rules review.

As a referee, I am responsible for the training of the six other men on our crew. Each official brings to this meeting the weekly rules test the league requires of every official during the season. This is a three-page variation of the 200-question preseason exam.

During the rules portion of our pregame meeting, we review the answers to each question and make sure that each official understands and agrees with the interpretation. It is critical that we go on the field with like minds.

Next, we review a video of the game we worked the week before. The supervisor assigned to our crew has already critiqued the game video and recorded his comments on the play-by-play sheet. If one of us made a mistake, he's seen it, and we'll read about it here. He often questions us as to what we saw and why we called a particular foul.

His question might be "You called pass interference on this play, but on the tape I can see no contact. What did you see?" That's what we call a "direct question." The official who made the call must provide the supervisor a "direct answer," such as, "The left arm of the defender pushed the receiver in the back while the ball was in the air." There's no place to hide with such close scrutiny.

The assistant supervisor assigned to our crew stays with us half of the year so that he can chart progress and/or need for improvement by any individual official or the coordination of the crew. Every third week he is with us at the game, but he reviews our game video for every game we work.

The responsibilities of the assistant supervisor and mine as the crew chief are similar in that I am also looking for ways to improve crew performance. One of the things the supervisor counts on is that I have done my job.

During the pregame video review, I am looking for teamwork communication and coordination and discuss these mechanics with our crew. Along with the video of our last game, we review "McNally's Weekly Highlights," compiled from all games played the previous week. This video, sent to every crew, targets our attention to current league philosophy and helps ensure uniform interpretation of the rules.

Officials give no consideration to teams or players, only to play situations. It is not important, for example, for us to study the plays or formations of the teams for whom we will be officiating the next day. No matter what a team does on any given play, we are trained to be ready for it. We are trained to expect the unexpected, and this includes snowballs, power failures, fan discourtesies, and spectacular plays.

The toughest plays to cover are the kicking plays—kickoffs, punt returns, and field goals. The players are widely spread, and it requires immediate adjustment by all seven game officials to cover the action. We call it "keeping the play boxed in."

Pass interference, grasp-and-control, quarterback pass, or fumble and sideline catches are among the more difficult plays to cover. The key to making the right call is to be in the proper position. These plays are more difficult to cover because the play happens so quickly.

From the time we assemble on Saturday afternoon until we are back at the airport Sunday evening, our crew is together the whole time. The Saturday video review session usually lasts 3–5 hours, concluding mid-evening. Often, Saturday evening dinner is by room service as we continue our video study.

Sunday morning is church time. Catholics go to mass, and on our crew, as with many others, non-Catholics attend also in the spirit of family and togetherness. This may seem inconsequential, but actually it is subtle and strong. Officials are independent and strong personalities. This is as much a job qualification as rules knowledge. However, a crew works well together only if it merges and becomes a cohesive unit.

Then comes breakfast, followed by an important meeting— rules review. Yes, again.

Two hours before game time we meet the league security man assigned to our crew at the designated area at the stadium. Usually an ex-FBI agent, the security man is responsible for the safety of the officials from then until we depart for the airport after the game.

Each official has designated pregame duties. One of my responsibilities as referee is to coordinate television communication. I work with the producer and director of the network crew and with the local field manager.

The field manager positions himself at about the 25 yard line and relays to me by hand signals the director's request for commercial time-outs. Television depends on split-second timing. The league has contractual commitments with the networks that specify commercial time. It is imperative that I be alert to their requests. While final authority on the operation of the game is mine, cooperation with the networks is good for the game.

My next responsibility is to inspect the game balls. The rules require that the home team supply twenty-four league-approved Wilson footballs at the stipulated pressure—11–13 psi. Then I inspect my radio mike and thirty minutes before game time conduct an audio check on the field.

While the umpire's primary pregame responsibility is player equipment, an added component since the introduction of instant replay is the inspection and operation of his communication equipment. He wears a headset that receives and transmits information between the instant-replay official and himself.

The head linesman meets with the chain crew and works out their positioning on the field. He informs them as to how and when to move the chains for a first down and the proper procedure for measurement.

The line judge meets with the electric-clock operator to discuss communication techniques on starting and stopping the stadium clock. In addition, he discusses special timing situations that require exactness.

The back judge and side judge meet with the ball boys on each side of the field to go over proper methods of relaying fresh balls into the game.

The field judge meets with the 30-second-clock operator to coordinate communication techniques for starting and resetting the 30-second clock and confirms that the clock has been properly tested that day.

By thirty minutes before game time, the entire crew goes onto the field for inspection of players, equipment, and the field. We check the alignment of the goal posts, the positions of the corner markers, the setback markings on the sidelines, and other details.

The fans in the stands see us walking around and probably do not understand that each official is carrying out prescribed duties. It is only through this level of attention to detail that the game is the same every week, stadium to stadium.

Back in our dressing room, I double-check that the checklist has been completed. Our final ritual before leaving the dressing room is for each official to place his hands on the football to signify that we are going to work this game as a unit. For every game that I have been a referee, my final words to our crew are "Concentrate. Every play. And enjoy the game."

Now the fun begins. Let's "play ball."

Once the game is over, each official fills out the "Official's Game Card" indicating the score, elapsed time, and the fouls he called. As the referee, I summarize those fouls on a separate card and send all game cards to the supervisor of officials along with a copy of the play-by-play sheets.

While it may appear that our crew's job is done as we head for the airport and home, I ask that each of us use the travel time to analyze our individual performance and give a written critique of its separate components. This is not a league requirement, but I find that reviewing performance immediately after the game reminds me of what I did well that day and what I want to work on. With this self-evaluation, I begin the mental preparation for next Saturday's video study. The fine points discovered in an immediate review become integrated with my overall knowledge faster and better than in a delayed review.

The ability to be frankly honest with yourself is also important in terms of physical fitness. Professional football players are skilled athletic performers. Officials should be no less. When I walk onto the field to be a part of an athletic contest, I want to feel like an athlete. That means I must be able to keep up with them, and look like one, too.

This doesn't mean I need to a world-class sprinter or have the moves of an O.J., but physical strength and stamina are essential to officials in all positions. The league is aware of this, too. While

SELF-EVALUATION FORM

(Note: This form may be used by each official in our crew to review and evaluate his performance of each game. It is best to complete this form as soon as possible after each assignment.)

GAME NO. ___ _____ VS. _____ DATE: __ / __ / __
        Visitor   Home

RATING:

		RATING:
PREPARATION		( )
PERSONAL APPEARANCE/PHYSICAL CONDITION		( )
JUDGMENT	—Making proper decisions concerning violations of rules.	( )
DECISIVENESS	—The manner in which judgment is exhibited. Did my decision result from the normal flow of the game, or did I inject myself into the game unnecessarily?	( )
POISE	—Reaction to pressure conditions: Self-control.	( )
ALERTNESS	—Awareness of game conditions: down—distance—time.	( )
MECHANICS	—Position coverage during down: movement.	( )
KNOWLEDGE OF SPOTS OF ENFORCEMENT	—Aware of EVERY foul and its proper enforcement.	( )
TEAMWORK	—Working with and assisting others.	( )
GAME SENSE/ "COMMON SENSE"		
CONCENTRATION DURING GAME	—Did I stay "focused"? —Was I really "in" this game from start to finish?	( )
OVERALL PERSONAL RATING FOR THIS GAME		( )

SUMMARY COMMENTS:
A. What I did well today: _____
B. What I want to work on: _____

	RATING SYSTEM:	1-2-3	4-5-6	7-8-9	10
		Fair	Good	Very Good	Excellent

the downfield officials usually have a little more running to do, each position requires agility and a quick sprint.

As with the rules, strategies, and techniques, the requirements for physical examinations have changed over the years. In the early years of my tenure, the 1960s and the 1970s, the league required only a cursory examination by a friendly family physician. The league issued scant criteria. The standard was solely the doctor's. Not what you would call comprehensive, it was the "Turn your head to the side and cough" and "Can you see the eye chart on the wall?" type of exam. If you could see the wall, you were fine.

Today the league has more stringent requirements and is openly more concerned with the level of fitness for officials. The emphasis is on cardiovascular health. Since 1986, with the encouragement of Kenneth Cooper, M.D., the Dallas cardiologist who created the well-known aerobics-fitness program, the league has required a treadmill stress test, along with clearer criteria for measuring fitness.

In addition to the annual exam, which takes place in June, all officials are weighed at the preseason clinic in July and again about the middle of the season. The clinic weigh-in is a normative standard only.

While there is no fixed limit for the ratio of height to weight, if it is out of proportion, it will become detrimental. A part of the weekly video review by the supervisors is to observe the appearance and mobility of each official. Is he fast and agile enough to stay with the play? Does his weight or level of fitness prevent him from being in position to make the call?

The increased concern by the league is certainly in concert with my perspective. Since grammer school, physical exercise has been a part of my daily life. "Calisthenics" didn't inspire me. What I liked was strenuous full-court-press basketball and running bases. After lettering in basketball and baseball in high school and college, I played competitive AAU basketball until I was 35.

But the dramatic incentive for adopting a disciplined, daily regimen of exercise was the death of my dad from a massive heart attack. He was only 59.

My dad had been a great college athlete and had officiated high school and college football and basketball for nearly twenty years. With a job change at age 40, when he became a steward at California racetracks, his life-style became more sedentary.

His sudden death awakened me to a sense of the future. I began a program of long-distance running. It wasn't easy. I discovered that sprinting on the basketball court wasn't the same as holding in there mile after mile.

The daily regimen since 1967 has been a daily run and situps. In 1979, I met Dr. Cooper and joined his program. We were both surprised when I broke Roger Staubach's treadmill record.

During that first treadmill stress test, I was running at the twenty-four minute mark, feeling ready to quit, when Dr. Cooper, who was monitoring my heart rate, casually mentioned that Staubach's treadmill record was 27:05. Suddenly I was determined to beat that.

I managed to keep running, stopping at 27:15. I was exhausted. Cooper was ecstatic. He told me that Staubach's record was the best of the Cowboys. Cooper said he wanted to call Staubach and tell him.

Lying on the recovery table, still weak from the effort, I said, "No, that's not important to me."

Cooper was insistent. He went straight to the phone and called Staubach at his real estate office, motioning to me to pick up the other phone.

"Roger, this is Dr. Cooper. I just called to tell you that Jim Tunney, a 51–year-old referee, just broke your treadmill record."

I was glad Cooper had me on the extension. Staubach's response was classic. "Well, Dr. Cooper, that just proves that his heart is better than his eyesight."

Roger is 16 years younger than I. He has since come back to

beat me. We enjoy this informal competition. So does Dr. Cooper.

Having my level of fitness quantified gives me a measuring stick. Each year when I return for the annual physical, I can chart my improvement. Like the performance reviews by our NFL supervisors, reporting to Dr. Cooper takes away any chance to find excuses for not maintaining or improving.

My current exercise program is a run of three or four miles, interspersed with fartleks, alternating every other day with a twenty-eight-minute workout at the level 6 work load on the Schwinn Aire-Dyne exercise bike. These aerobics workouts are combined with daily situps and weight training for muscle tone.

The training concept behind fartleks was developed by Gösta Holmer, chief coach of the Swedish team for the 1948 Olympics. It incorporates the valuable idea that physical training should be enjoyable as well as hard work. It consists of alternating fast timed sprints with normal pace running and walking over varied distances and terrain.

To fulfill the concept, you must specifically include variety in training terrain and distance. It admits, even requires, a sense of enjoyment while maintaining a demanding workout. It recognizes the fact that athletes train harder if monotony is relieved, which includes seeking out situations that are new and challenging. Running down rutted, muddy roads in a rainstorm, vaulting a few fallen logs in a run through a forest, and trudging up sand dunes are all good possibilities.

The spirit of fartleks says that a training routine of straight road running with a few stairs runs thrown in lacks imagination and creative self-involvement and therefore dulls the spirit. A dulled spirit reduces the body's ability to naturally endure. Variety is added but doesn't replace fundamental self-discipline and the initiative that fuel any training effort.

It is preferable that exercise be enjoyable if you require it as part of your daily contributions to good health and longevity. Incorporating fartleks into my training program has added enjoyment to something I feel I must do for myself. I feel great, which is the whole point.

When you look at the league's twin emphasis on rules knowledge and physical fitness, you see that the league's criterion is the same as every serious coach believes in—*Mens sana in corpore sano*. The late Dr. Carl Trieb, my physical educator at Occidental College and a mentor, impressed this ancient maxim into my awareness. I remember him saying that the "key to understanding the formula of 'a sound mind in a sound body' is to notice which leads—the mind leads the body."

7

Game Highlights: "Ice Bowl" to "The Catch"

December 31, 1967. The "Ice Bowl," Dallas at Green Bay. My eighth year in the NFL, my first year as referee. The last thing I expected was to pull a playoff assignment. I'd spent most of the season working the lesser games. That was the first year for the New Orleans Saints, and our crew worked three for them. This was expected. You don't put a crew with a rookie referee into the big national games. Prudence dictates that you keep them on smaller games with regional telecasts.

I was surprised—thrilled, even—to be named as an alternate for the NFL championship game in Green Bay. The problem was that I was also officiating college basketball at that time and had been assigned to work the semifinals and finals of the Far West Basketball Classic in Portland, Oregon, on Friday and Saturday nights. To be at the NFL championship game, I'd have to leave home Friday night to be in Green Bay for our meeting on Saturday. Obviously, I couldn't be in both places.

I called the supervisor of officials for the college tournament and asked if he could switch my assignment so I could work the preliminary games on Thursday. He couldn't do it. He said, "We'll just take you off the games."

I didn't want to lose that assignment, because I was still trying to build a career in officiating college basketball, but, given a forced decision, the choice was easy. The thrill of working the NFL championship game more than compensated for the disappointment.

Norm Schachter and I arrived in Green Bay on Friday night in blizzard conditions and minus five degrees. We'd taken our overcoats and our thermals. I wasn't as unprepared as I'd been in Washington in 1960, but we weren't prepared for what we would face.

The weather turned worse on Saturday—more snow, more ice. We searched for extra gloves and thermals.

On Sunday, my own mother wouldn't have recognized me. I was bulked up with long johns, two thermal shirts and a plastic bag with a hole opened for my head around my chest under my shirt and plastic bags on my feet between two pairs of socks. We used every trick we knew to trap body heat, then added an overcoat and earmuffs.

Pat Harder, the other alternate, was on the Dallas side of the field, and I was assigned the Green Bay side. As alternate, my assignment was to write a running account of the down and distance for each play. Ever try to write with two pairs of gloves on?

Even with all the extra layers, the cold was numbing. There were blowers on the sidelines to blow heat toward the players. Somehow I managed to find a way to stop in front of the blower no matter where the play began or ended.

Don Chandler, the Green Bay kicker, had his right foot in the blower most of the game. Bart Starr, the Packers quarterback, would stick his hands in it every time he came off the field. I had my backside to it as much as I could.

The linemen were tough, though; they wouldn't be caught dead over at the blowers. It was a kind of pride. Coach Vince Lombardi started with his usual short-sleeved shirt on! It wasn't until the second quarter that he relented and put on a jacket.

I felt sorry for Schachter and the other five officials on the field. Line Judge Bill Schleibaum had his whistle freeze to his lips. When he pulled it off, three layers of skin came off with the whistle. Joe Connell, the umpire, got frostbite on his face.

That day, I started the habit of sticking my hands inside my belt to keep my fingers warm. I always felt an official should keep his hands out of his pockets. You don't want to look as if you're taking a stroll in the park. But an official needs fingers that move. The cold was enough to drive this Californian home, except that six colleagues had it worse than I. Even so, my idea of a change in the weather is when the temperature drops from seventy-five during the day to sixty at night.

I didn't feel particularly worried about Harder. He's tough, and a Wisconsinite. Cold wouldn't dare penetrate his Badger discipline.

Most games played in that kind of cold move along quickly and easily because the players want to get it over with, too, but this "Ice Bowl" had an extra dimension of intense rivalry.

Some background: For two decades starting in the mid-1960s, the Cowboys were consistent winners, five times in the Super Bowl in the 1970s. But they didn't start that way. As an expansion team, they were under .500 for their first five years. They had won a conference championship in 1966—but then had lost to the Packers, in Dallas, in the league championship game. That meant that the Packers went to Super Bowl I, and won. It also meant that the Cowboys were eager to avenge that loss in this game.

Even though they weren't acclimated to that kind of weather, the Cowboys played a tremendous football game. The hitting was incredible; everybody played as if it were a warm-weather game.

It wasn't. It snowed and sleeted throughout the game, blowing into our faces the entire time. The temperature at game time was thirteen below zero, the coldest December 31 in Green Bay history. Lambeau Field had an underground heating system to keep the field thawed, but this day was too cold for it. The field was as hard as a rock throughout the game.

When Bart Starr charged the 2 feet needed to get behind Jerry Kramer and score the winning touchdown, it was thirty-one below zero. Several players had frostbite, and Lombardi said later he had gone for the touchdown because he didn't want to subject either side to overtime. A field goal would have only tied it. He was willing to risk losing it just to have it over. Player safety was more important than winning at any cost.

Cold as it was, it was an honor to be there.

The scheduling conflict in that game in effect ended my officiating for the PCC, which wasn't willing to deal with "schedule conflicts" and a silent priority to the NFL. I had worked several full seasons and never missed an assignment, but I recognized the problem was more than this one inconvenience.

The problem stemmed from the old rivalry between colleges and the pros. Colleges often get upset because the pros recruit their officials from the colleges. The pros have no choice—the college conferences are the best source for officials—but that doesn't make it any easier for the colleges to accept.

That I might lose basketball assignments was important to me, but more important was that I was assigned as a rookie referee to an NFL championship game. This started a nice run for me: in the twenty-eight years I've been in the league, I've been awarded twenty-six playoff assignments. I'm proud of that.

Let me make a distinction about postseason games. All playoff games are important, because they count. One team goes on, and one team goes home. That's a contest.

The Pro Bowl, on the other hand, is a postseason assignment, but it's just a party, a celebration, not a contest. It's always fun to work, and I worked it every year for my first five years, but for an unusual reason. In those years, it was held in the Coliseum, and was a charity event. It was managed by Paul Schissler, who didn't want to spend any more money than he had to; he would use only Los Angeles area officials to save airfare expense.

The year before I came into the league, Joe Gonzales was the field judge in the 1960 Pro Bowl. That year, Scooter Scuddero of the Washington Redskins took a kickoff at the 2 yard line, but thought he was in the end zone. He touched it down and then tossed the ball to Gonzales. If Gonzales had let it go, it would have gone into the end zone as a free ball. But Gonzales caught the ball, signaled touchback, and took it out to the 20.

The supervisor of officials, Mike Wilson, came unglued because Gonzales had made such a bad mistake. He was so angry he wouldn't let Gonzales work the Pro Bowl game ever again.

When I came into the league in 1960, Gonzales and I were the only field judges in the Los Angeles area. With Gonzales on the out list, I automatically got the Pro Bowl for the next five years. No honor in that, only lucky geography.

In the 1964 Pro Bowl, Eagles linebacker Maxie Baughan was covering a back on a pass pattern. As the back was going downfield, he pushed Baughan, or so Maxie thought. Maxie came screaming at me, and I told him I thought it was a minor collision, not a foul.

"He pushed me!" Maxie screamed. "I could have had an interception on that play!"

I said, "Max, Max, don't get excited. This is only the Pro Bowl. This is fun."

Maxie glared at me and said, "Fun, my ass. There's a difference of three hundred dollars to the winner."

That helped me put it in perspective. There's no such thing as a "fun game" for a player. Winning, and winning only, is the name of his effort.

The NFL puts in special rules for the Pro Bowl—no blitzing, no zone defense, for instance—to keep the game wide open. The league wants to make it entertainment. They're not interested in who wins.

But it's hard for a player to play with intensity all season, then tell him that a game is just entertainment. Players are programmed to play to win. You can't put them in neutral.

For an official, though, the Pro Bowl is more relaxing. It

doesn't compare with the pressure and excitement of a championship game, where one side goes home for the year.

Every individual who wants to be at the top of his game, whether a coach, player, official, CEO, or anyone, either learns to enjoy the pressure or stops growing toward excellence. Stress can be an invigorating experience if you see the effort as a challenge and within your ability. Championship teams always do.

That stress can be healthy has become so well understood it has been given a name. *Eustress* is good stress, entirely different from *distress*. To the extent possible, plan plenty of eustress in your life: It energizes you. As much as you can, eliminate distress: It saps your strength.

Dr. Hans Selyc, the late expert on stress, often made the point "Stress won't kill you; distress might."

It is the attitude with which you look at stress that makes the difference. Enjoy the moment, as "stressful" as it may be. Again, the greater self-confidence you have and the more attention you give to preparing yourself for the task, the easier the stress is to handle. Give me the championship games anytime. There's plenty of eustress there.

Like the Cleveland-Denver AFC game, January 1988. That was a great game. I didn't want it to end. I'm not a fan, I have no favorites, but if Cleveland had scored in their last dramatic attempt, the game would have kept going.

It was one of those ideal games; everything went well. There was not one mention of the officials having influence on the game. The players decided the game, which is the ultimate goal of any official.

The week before, there had been some controversy in the Denver-Houston playoff game. Denver quarterback John Elway, operating out of the shotgun, was thrusting his hands forward before the snap, and the Houston linemen were pulled offside five times.

The rule says that any player in the shotgun formation who

extends his hands, unless he's a punter or a holder for a field-goal attempt, must immediately receive the ball. (There has to be some flexibility in those situations because at times teams will fake a punt or field goal and snap the ball to another player.) Looking at the game films, Cleveland coach Marty Schotten-heimer insisted that Elway was violating the rule.

In our pregame officials' meetings, we discussed the possibility of what to do if Elway violated the rule. At a press conference, Schottenheimer and Denver coach Dan Reeves also talked about it. Schottenheimer was very calm, saying basically that he would rely on the officials to make whatever call was necessary.

Merlin Olsen and Dick Enberg, of NBC Sports, sent word through their producer, Larry Cirillo, that they wanted to know what I, as the referee, would do if Elway moved his hands early. I sent back the message that if they saw a flag on the field during the game they would know a foul had occurred. I never call a foul before the game.

As it turned out, Elway's actions during that game were not remotely close to being a foul. Maybe the Broncos realized that since Cleveland was aware of it, there would be no advantage. I give credit to the coaches for dispelling the controversy by saying, in effect, let's play football.

The preparation of our crew was excellent. We were ready for anything. It was the first game the umpire, Ben Montgomery, and I had worked together, so we worked out ways to communicate quickly on the field.

Only one problem came up: Our field judge, Dick Dolack, pulled a hamstring on that 80 yard Broncos touchdown pass in the third quarter. NFL mechanics call for a field judge to be at the goal line when the runner crosses. We don't have many field judges who can keep up with NFL wide receivers, and Dolack was moving as fast as he could to keep up with the play when he pulled his hamstring.

As in all playoff games, there was an alternate official assigned to our crew. This time it was Jerry Seeman, a thirteen-year veteran and a referee for the last six or seven years. Ironically, he was the one who made the call on the fumble by Earnest Byner, the play that decided the game.

Another marker of all-star quality in that game was the respect each team had for the other's ability. There were no verbal battles, no bickering, very little of the pushing and shoving that you get in some emotional, physical games. Denver and Cleveland transcended the game of intimidation and played full-out football.

Cleveland quarterback Bernie Kosar is a cool one, even though he's so young, just 24 at the time of this game. Denver had gotten off to a big lead, 28–3 at one point, but the Browns came back strong in the second half. With just about four minutes to go, Denver scored to go ahead, 38–31. Then the Browns started a drive of their own.

It was an exciting time, because you could see that the surge of emotion and momentum was now in the Browns' favor. Early in the drive, there was a time-out, and Kosar went to the sidelines to talk to his coaches. When he came back to the huddle, I told him he had one time-out left.

"Well," he said, "just another day at the office." Kosar is one who knows how to manage stress.

He showed it again at the end of the game when the Browns' fine drive collapsed as Castille stripped the ball from Byner. From where I was, back with Kosar, you could see that Denver had recovered the fumble. But Kosar didn't leave the field. I went down to the pileup. Seeman was yelling, "Orange ball. Orange ball." I signaled that Denver had the ball.

Kosar had come downfield, and said to me, "They really did recover it, didn't they?" trying to resign himself to a new reality.

The hug he gave Byner more than showed Kosar's strength. Another player said, "I love you, Earnest." It was a great family feeling.

For those watching the game, it was over. Denver had won. But there were still some key plays for the officials.

All Denver had to do was get a first down to run out the clock; Cleveland had no time-outs left. On the third down, Elway ran the ball to his left and went into the "quarterback slide."

The rule says that the quarterback is not to be contacted when he slides. The spot where the quarterback starts his slide is where the ball is down. When we measured, Denver was short of a first down.

The Broncos had to give the ball up, but their punter, Mike Horan, was in the end zone. I was thinking, What's going to happen here?

The obvious answer is that the Broncos would take a safety and then try a free kick from the 20. They couldn't afford to take a chance on the kick being blocked, because blocked kicks are sometimes recovered for touchdowns.

The snap was low, which would have cost the Broncos the game if it had been fumbled, but Horan caught it and ran laterally in the end zone to use up time before he ran out of bounds for a safety. As he ran out of bounds, one of the Browns pushed him.

There were some who thought a personal foul should have been called on the Browns. It was a judgment call. The Browns' defensive man had to ensure Horan would go out of bounds. If he had hit him with an elbow, that would have been something else, but he pushed him in the action of the play. It wasn't a late hit, and it didn't carry unnecessary force.

After a safety, the team committing the safety must free kick the ball at their 20 yard line. As the Broncos were setting up to free kick the ball, both coaches wanted to be sure of the procedure.

Eight seconds left to play.

Reeves wanted to know where Cleveland would get the ball if Denver kicked it out-of-bounds. I told him that it would be where it went out-of-bounds, or at the 50 yard line, whichever would be more advantageous for the Browns. Reeves told Horan just to kick it as far as he could.

Schottenheimer called me over to tell me that his kick returner, Gerald McNeil, would fair catch the ball. I told McNeil to make sure that he signaled for a fair catch by waving one hand clearly above his head while the ball was in the air.

One more bit of drama: One second ran off the clock when McNeil touched the ball. The clock doesn't start, in the last 2 minutes, when the ball is free kicked until the ball is touched. But a fair catch precludes the clock starting. The clock, however, now showed 7 seconds, and I had to tell the timer to reset it to 8 seconds. The Browns needed much more than 8 seconds; their final pass attempt fell incomplete, and the game was over.

We got off the field in a hurry. Our assistant supervisor of security, Charlie Jackson, had told us before the game to get off the field as soon as we could after the game because there would be police dogs on the field and the dogs don't know the difference between a good official and a bad one. I hustled.

For another classic confrontation, go to Pittsburgh. Take either year, the 1978 or 1979 AFC championship game. Both featured Houston and Pittsburgh—unusual in itself to have team repeats—and I worked both. A triple coincidence. Working a championship game two years in a row is as unusual as working two straight Super Bowls.

The second game was a hardship game in terms of weather. It wasn't as cold as Green Bay in 1967, but it wasn't a day at the beach, either. Ice and snow everywhere and all of twenty degrees.

One of the wise sayings among NFL officials is "slow whistle." Don't anticipate. Otherwise, what happens is you see a runner like Houston running back Earl Campbell get hit and about to go down, you blow the whistle, and about that time, Campbell either doesn't go down or he fumbles. You're stuck with the sound of the whistle in the air. For that reason, some officials use a finger whistle so they have an extra couple of seconds to slow them down.

During a break in our crew meeting on Saturday, the seven officials and two alternates went out in front of our hotel and stomped out the words "Slow Whistle" in the snow. When we resumed our meeting in Supervisor McNally's room, we took him over to the window to show him we were indeed thinking "slow whistle."

The field at Three Rivers Stadium had been covered by a tarp, but it had no heating element underneath. An hour before the game, the field was frozen. Two dozen men struggled to pull the tarp off as 60,000 fans huddled to stay warm.

The hardy fans were waiting to see the resumption of what was becoming a great rivalry. Houston and Pittsburgh had already played twice during the regular season. Pittsburgh ended as the AFC Central Division champion, and Houston had come through as the wild-card team. The winner of this game would head to the Super Bowl.

Thirty minutes before game time, Houston coach Bum Phillips confronted me as we came onto the field. "Jim," he said, "we're not going to be able to play on this field. Earl can't run on a frozen field. He needs some traction, and this is like an ice rink. We could play hockey on this field."

"You're right, Bum," I said. "We can't play a game on this field. I think you should just call it off and tell all these people to go home."

Bum instantly realized the foolishness of his remark. He laughed and said, "Yeah, I guess you're right. It's going to be the same for both teams."

Earl Campbell did have a down day, and the Steelers won the game. What I remember most about the game was a controversial call in the end zone, late in the game.

Houston wide receiver Mike Renfro had caught a pass in the corner of the end zone. The question was whether he had possession with both feet in bounds. Field judge Bill O'Brien was on the end line, and side judge Don Orr was on the sideline. They were both in position to see if Renfro made the catch.

In the NBC booth, Merlin Olsen was saying that it looked as if Renfro were in when he caught the ball. Meanwhile, on the field we had made no decision.

Houston quarterback Dan Pastorini agreed with Olsen. He said to me, "Mike caught that ball."

I told Pastorini, "I don't know how you could determine that; I couldn't, and I was thirty yards from Renfro, about the same distance that you were." I called a crew conference to see what each official had seen.

Crew conferences are important in officiating. It's no different than a CEO calling his top VPs together to get their information before an important decision is to be made. There are two important "keys" in any crew conference or in a top CEO meeting. One, ask the right questions. Information is of little value unless it is pertinent to the solution. Two, listen to the answers. Far too often the person charged with the decision, whether it is a referee or a CEO, has already formed an opinion as to what the decision should be. Information is irrelevant to a closed mind.

When we have crew conferences, I ask everyone what he saw. I'm looking for something positive. If one official says he saw the receiver with both feet in bounds and another says he thought the receiver was out, I'm going to favor the in-bounds view.

This decision was clear-cut. Feet not in. No catch. No touchdown.

Instant replay was not in effect then. Had it been, this would have been a perfect call to review. The NBC tape was inconclusive. Fans were sure. In Pittsburgh, they saw him out. In Houston, they saw him in.

Back in Houston that night, the Oilers were treated to a rally at the Astrodome. An effigy of me was hanging from the rafters. Bum Phillips told the crowd the officials who made that call should have been spanked with a mesquite branch.

Bum had a unique perspective on the game. He knew each game was important, but he knew that in terms of the arms treaty, or the Persian Gulf, football is way down in the list of priorities for the world. I always felt that if he had his choice, Bum would rather be riding the range than riding herd on a bunch of primo dons.

When Bum would get upset, he let his anger come out. Yet, he had a strong enough sense of humor that he could hold a balanced view. He coined the maxim "There are only two kinds of coaches: those who have been fired and those who will be."

Most people think of being fired as a devastating experience. I know how upset I was when I was "fired" by Herb Alpert; I had never lost a job before. When you get fired, you tend to drop some self-esteem.

Isn't it strange that we often let outside conditions—ones over which we have no control—diminish our self-esteem. Self-esteem is the belief we have in ourselves. It is controlled only by us. It can never be eroded unless we let that happen. It's not something anyone can take from you.

But Bum, who was fired by the Oilers, then later by the Saints, never felt that way. He had a high opinion of himself, and his self-esteem wasn't affected by being fired.

When the Oilers lost the first of those championship games, Bum made a promise to the Houston fans. "We knocked on the door this time," he said. "Next year, we'll kick it down."

Despite that promise, the Oilers were never able to get past that final hurdle and into the Super Bowl.

Probably the best thing about those games was that Pat Harder was our umpire. Pat and I worked together for thirteen years, an NFL record for crew longevity.

Pat Harder is an amazing man. All-American fullback at Wisconsin, number-one draft choice with the Chicago Cardinals, later traded to the Detroit Lions, for whom he played on the 1952 and 1953 championship teams.

As a player, Harder was always overshadowed. He played with Elroy "Crazylegs" Hirsch at Wisconsin. With the Cardinals, he was the leading scorer in the NFL two consecutive years. He played in the same backfield with Charley Trippi, Paul Chrisman, and Elmer Angsman. They were known as the "Million Dollar Backfield." Just imagine what their price would be today!

Harder did everything. He kicked off, kicked extra points, ran the ball. He still holds the record for most points after a touchdown in one game. He did that twice. He holds the record with Paul Hornung for most points scored in one game—nineteen. His records still stand after thirty-five years and a lot of technological improvements. As a running back, he was All-Pro twice and leading scorer 3 straight years. Pat Harder should be in the Hall of Fame.

Harder was tough as nails. When he played for the Detroit Lions against the Cleveland Browns, he broke Len Ford's jaw. Harder didn't try to "juke" defensive players; he liked to run over them. Against the Browns, when Ford came up to make the tackle, Harder just hit him with a forearm that was stronger than Ford's jawbone.

Many years later, when Harder was working on our crew, we had a game in Cincinnati. Bengals coach Paul Brown had been at Cleveland when Harder broke Ford's jaw and hadn't forgotten.

During the game in Cincinnati, Brown kept up his running abuse against Harder, even though Pat was doing his usual good job. At the 2-minute warning in the first half, I told coach Brown, "We have a good umpire out there, and he's doing a great job today. Lay off him."

Brown said to me, "I'm still mad at him. He broke Lenny Ford's jaw."

Brown wasn't mad at Harder for what he was doing that day but for what he did some twenty years before. To this day, Brown hasn't forgotten it. I know for a fact that Brown didn't want Harder working his games. He felt Harder had something against him, which just wasn't true.

When Harder was the umpire, the players knew not to try to

get away with anything. He not only would call a foul; if a player got in his way, he'd knock the player down. I've seen a linebacker trying to push him aside and Harder throwing a forearm to get the linebacker out of there so he could stay with the play.

Harder was a great official. It's a shame that he retired from the league without having the chance to work a Super Bowl.

Harder retired before the 1982 NFC championship game, Dallas at San Francisco, a classic that went down to the wire with tough line play and steady intensity. Harder would have loved it.

Like the Oilers, the 49ers had been frustrated by one team—the Dallas Cowboys. Three times in a row—1970, 1971, 1972—the 49ers won their divisional championship, only to lose to the Cowboys in the playoffs each time.

The 49ers then fell on bad times, not making the playoffs for 9 years, until Bill Walsh resurrected them in 1981. The 49ers won their division and beat the New York Giants in the first round of the playoffs. Who next? Who else? "America's Team," at Candlestick Park in San Francisco.

The game was everything you'd want in a championship game, back and forth for sixty minutes. The Cowboys led, 27–21, with just under a minute remaining, but the 49ers were on the Dallas 6, third and 3, when Joe Montana rolled out, looking for a receiver in the end zone.

My job is to stay with the quarterback, so I followed Montana to the sideline, with Dallas defensive end "Too Tall" Jones and linebacker Mike Hageman after him. They were right on top of Montana when he threw what was almost a jump pass into the end zone. "Too Tall" thought he was throwing the ball away, but 49ers wide receiver Dwight Clark went up in the end zone over Dallas defensive back Everson Walls to make what became known as "The Catch."

I didn't see the catch because my responsibility is to watch the quarterback and the onrushing defensive linemen. Right after the ball was thrown, "Too Tall" decked Montana, and I watched to make sure there was no extracurricular stuff going on. There wasn't; it was a clean hit by "Too Tall."

As I was watching, I heard the roar of the crowd, so I knew the pass must have been caught. I could feel the thrill that comes with being part of an unforgettable moment in sports.

I don't know who came up with the expression "The Catch," but it's history now. With that big a play, you're always concerned about whether the receiver came down in bounds. On this play, there was no question.

The game wasn't over. The Cowboys would try to get into position for a field goal. As the Cowboys were driving, I had a tough call to make.

Danny White went back to pass and fumbled as he was hit, with the 49ers recovering. White argued that he had been hit in the act of throwing, which would have made it an incomplete forward pass. The Cowboys would have still had the ball.

To his credit, when I said, "No, Danny, the ball was a fumble," he recognized it was over and walked away. The films later showed that there was no question; it was a fumble.

The 49ers ran out the clock and walked off the field with their first NFC championship win. I went back to my hotel room so I could watch the news and finally see "The Catch."

8

My Dart Stuck

In 1972, I was selected to referee Super Bowl VI. How the league made the playoff-game assignments was a mystery to all of us. I had the feeling the names of all the officials were on darts, that the supervisors, blindfolded, threw the darts at boards that read "divisional," "championship," and "Super Bowl," and if your dart stuck, you worked that game.

That seemed acceptable to me because the competition to get into the NFL is stiff enough to assure competence in everyone. For playoff assignments, the supervisor of officials selects from among a group that, like the players, includes the best in the world in their position.

I didn't spend a lot of time worrying about the selection process. This was a goal come true. I was excited. It couldn't have happened at a better time.

Let me go back two months to November 1971. In one week's time, my life changed dramatically. I had decided to get a divorce, leaving four children at home, the oldest of whom was 18 and the youngest 7. I left home the day after my son, Mark, had his eleventh birthday.

At that time, I was working as educational director for the Herb Alpert Foundation. This was much less frenetic than being a school principal. No more of those twelve-hour days that had been so common for me. There were fewer problems for which there were no resources to improve, and it was rewarding to work.

A week after my separation, Alpert called me into his office and said he'd been forced by other factors to close the foundation. "You mean, I'm fired?" I said.

"Well, I don't like to put it that way," he said, but that was the upshot.

Boom. I was without a marriage and without a job. I was assigned the Thanksgiving Day game in Detroit. I was glad to be traveling that week.

An offer came along to work as vice-president of marketing for a new athletic clothing manufacturer. I took it. I needed a job, but I sensed from the beginning that I was just marking time. The job lasted only six months before the greater satisfaction of public education drew me back into school administration the next fall.

Then, in January, Art McNally called and said, "Congratulations. You've got the Super Bowl." Talk about highs and lows coming together.

As thrilling football games go, Super Bowl VI wasn't one. Dallas beat Miami, 24–3. It was a mismatch from the opening kickoff. Nothing significant occurred in terms of officiating, either.

It was exciting to have been honored with the assignment, but what I remember most about the game happened before I even arrived at the stadium.

I had picked up a bad cold. The night before the game, I called a member of our regular-season crew, field judge Dick Dolack, who is a pharmacist every day but Sunday in Muskegon, Michigan. I asked what I could do to get me breathing again. He recommended something from the corner drugstore.

Back in the hotel room, I took two capsules and went to bed, but not for long. I broke out in a rash from head to toe, had chills, felt terrible, and the only thought whirling through my head was "My God, tomorrow's the Super Bowl. What am I going to do?"

I called Dolack again, and he suggested a hot bath with Epsom salts, to draw the allergic reaction out of my body, and a prayer. I sat in one bath after another most of the night, slowly feeling a little better than terrible. I managed three hours sleep, at most.

Yet, the next day I felt fine. The chills were gone, and my head felt clear. The excitement of working the Super Bowl blocked all physical ailments from my mind. It was a case of two teams, 100 million fans, one boss, and myself not being disappointed.

I think anybody who has been involved with the Super Bowl as a coach, player, or official gets caught up in the whole scenario. The Super Bowl is pomp and pageantry as well as a championship game. For three hours, nothing else seems to matter. War could be declared and no one in the stadium would notice. It's a form of temporary amnesia.

No other sports event gets so much attention. The Olympics, the World Series, and the World Cup probably come the closest, but as the NFL has grown in presence and team excellence, the impact of the Super Bowl has become dominant. This is not only my ranking. *The Timetables of History* lists the results of the Super Bowl first.

You have to grow up fast through the hype or it will swamp you. The attention is exhilarating. Something to enjoy but also something to respect, like the ocean. There are riptides amid the fun and excitement.

Super Bowl VI was played in New Orleans, in what we think of as the sunny South. That day the wind-chill factor put the temperature into the low thirties. The officials wore turtleneck sweaters to keep warm. The game went well. I had no uneasiness. I worked a good game.

That game was the last Super Bowl to be played in Tulane Stadium, the original home of the Sugar Bowl. The stadium, now razed, was old, and the stands looked as if they might fall at the slightest tremble. None of the 81,023 fans seemed concerned when the stands swayed with their booming and stomping.

I had worked in Tulane Stadium many times already. The New Orleans Saints' franchise began in 1967, my first year as a referee. Since I was the only rookie referee, Supervisor of Officials Mark Duncan assigned our crew to the rookie Saints three times. It is unusual for a crew to be scheduled with any team more than twice a season. We assumed the league was hiding us in case we screwed up.

I had officiated the Saints-Falcons game that year. I believe it was Sunday of Thanksgiving weekend. Everyone in the crew took their wives, and we arrived a couple of days early to tour the sights of New Orleans.

The Saints' record at that juncture was 0–9, and the Falcons were not much better at 1–8. I noticed when we came down to breakfast the morning of the game that the headline writers of the *Times-Picayune* were calling it the "Super Bowl of the South." The city was in ecstasy about their beloved Saints, even if their first year was a test of loyalty.

By kickoff time, 81,022 loyalists were in Tulane Stadium, ready to find something to cheer about. Talk about frenzy.

Al Hirt played the national anthem on his horn. I was standing on the sideline not far from the first row of box seats and noticed an empty seat in the first row. I wondered why that seat was empty with the entire stadium packed. It may have been the only empty seat.

Next to the empty seat was a nicely dressed elderly woman complete with hat, veil, gloves, the works. My curiosity was piqued. I stepped over and inquired, "Ma'am, I noticed that empty seat. With the stadium jam-packed, I wondered why."

She replied, "That seat belonged to my husband, and he died."

She didn't have any awkwardness in her voice. I felt a little shy about it, but I asked, anyway, "Why, I'm surprised one of your friends hasn't joined you."

She answered, "I asked, but they were all going to the funeral today."

Talk about dedication to "dem Saints."

That and other experiences that indicate the loyalty and dedication of fans have taught me never to underestimate the magnetic power of sports. Dedication has an odd strength. Coaches try to inculcate it in their players systematically because it is such strong glue for a team. Players like it in fans because the energy is fed back to them. That fans "wave" with it is pretty easy to understand when your team's winning, but "dem Saints" were 0–9 that day.

Super Bowl VI was a runaway—Dallas 24, Miami 3. The Cowboys rushed for a record 252 yards and their defense limited the Dolphins to only 185 yards. This is the only Super Bowl in which one team didn't score a touchdown. I guess Bob Lilly, Leroy Jordan, Chuck Howley, Mel Renfro, and the rest of the Dallas defense remember that.

My favorite memory is looking over to the area where I had talked to the nice widow lady at the Saints game and seeing her again, this time with an agile-looking octogenarian next to her. When I said hello, she introduced me to her "new boyfriend," who she admitted was a Cowboys fan.

I looked for this delightful pair at the first Saints home game the next season, but the seats were occupied by noisy teenagers who gave unintelligible answers to my questions about her. I felt a sense of loss.

My second Super Bowl was a bigger thrill for me because it was played in the Rose Bowl in Pasadena. I had grown up in San Gabriel, California, just four miles from the Rose Bowl in Pasadena, where I had watched Jackie Robinson play for Pasadena Junior College.

Jackie was already a star. I was about 8 years old. He was about 18. Because my dad was the referee, I got to sit on the bench alongside him. I felt lucky to be there.

Several years later, my dad refereed the Rose Bowl game between Illinois and UCLA. I can picture where I was sitting in Aisle 21. Buddy Young, who later played halfback for the Baltimore Colts, scored three touchdowns that day—Illinois 45, UCLA 14.

I had even coached and played in the Rose Bowl. When I tell people that, their eyes get big, and then I have to tell them it wasn't the New Year's Day game.

I played offensive end for Occidental College. Each year we played Cal Tech in the Rose Bowl. We would have around a thousand faithfuls. Not a crowd to get a team wild. The students at Cal Tech preferred the labs, I guess.

Later, as a coach at Lincoln High and as a principal at Franklin High, we played several games there, again with but a smattering of fans in the stands.

With those memories as background, it was an extra bonus to work in the Rose Bowl in Super Bowl XI, the Minnesota Vikings and the Oakland Raiders. This was the first time a Super Bowl was scheduled in the Rose Bowl. I liked the coincidence.

Actually, I thought Tommy Bell would get the assignment. So did he. Tommy had worked two Super Bowls and had announced before starting the 1976 season that he would be retiring after 15 years in the league. He was the sentimental choice, but I got the call. I guess my dart stuck and Tommy's didn't.

People thought Tommy and I were in competition throughout the latter part of the 1970s. It was always "Bell and Tunney," "Tunney and Bell," when referees were mentioned.

I've never felt competitive with any other official. I'm sure Tommy didn't, either. We were good friends. We shared ideas. There was never any animosity or jealousy if one of us worked a bigger game. Tommy was disappointed on that one, though. I understood. I would have been, too.

The way the league office made assignments for the playoffs

and the Super Bowl game added to the excitement. There was no advance notification as the playoffs started.

Each week as the assignments were made, you hoped you *wouldn't* be chosen. The hope was forward, for a bigger game next week. The risk was that "your dart" didn't stick on any board and the playoffs would pass with no assignment at all.

Now—and since the early 1980s—the league informs the officials after the last regular-season game whether they are assigned to work in the playoffs. You have to work a playoff game to have a shot at the Super Bowl. Back then, the league office wouldn't tell you until the week before a game whether you were working, and if you worked a playoff game, you didn't work the Super Bowl.

As the first assignments were announced and I wasn't selected for the divisional, I anxiously thought Hey, I could work the Super Bowl. I know what the ten finalists for "Miss America" feel like as they hear the names being called. You don't want to be named as "Fourth Runner-up," but more than that, you want your name to be called.

Simple arithmetic is also at work: There are eight postseason games and fifteen crews. We each had our own opinion of our ability and performance that year, but you had no idea how the league rated you. As the weeks went by and I wasn't selected for either of the conference championship games, it was all or nothing for the Super Bowl.

But I just had a feeling. When I got the call from Art McNally, ten or eleven days before the game, I was excited. "All right!"

I knew I'd worked hard to get it, but I also knew that others had worked hard, too. Of the fifteen referees now in the NFL, there are only eight who have worked a Super Bowl. Nearly half of the referees who work week in and week out haven't officiated even one Super Bowl. I think of that often. Still, my goal is to work a fourth.

I can't say exactly why I got the assignment for Super Bowl XI. I thought I'd had a good season, but I don't keep a diary of my good calls or negative grades, so I can't honestly say whether my performance was better that season than others. With the charge of memories I had stored about the Rose Bowl, getting that particular assignment was very special for me. I remember every hour, every moment.

In my speeches, I sometimes tell a joke about that day. Before the game, I was pacing back and forth in my uniform, waiting to walk out in front of over 103,000 people, when a young woman stopped me.

"Excuse me," she inquired. "Are you the referee for today's game?"

I puffed up and replied, "Why yes, I am."

She continued, "Are you nervous?"

I said, "No, I'm never nervous."

She asked, "Then what are you doing in the ladies' room?"

In truth, I wasn't nervous that day. There wasn't anyone on the field who was more relaxed that day than I. I had earned the right to referee that game, and I was—home.

I had worked games that season with both Oakland and Minnesota. Raiders coach John Madden had gone 13–1 that season and beat Pittsburgh for the AFC championship. Vikings coach Bud Grant had gone 11–2–1 and had won the NFC championship by beating Los Angeles. The quarterbacks were ready, too. Ken Stabler for the Raiders. Fran Tarkenton for the Vikings.

Every Super Bowl has a special significance to the teams playing. That one was especially important to Oakland. It was the pinnacle of Madden's ten years as head coach. It held the promise of vindication for the entire Raiders team and organization.

After losing to Green Bay in Super Bowl II (1968), the Raiders had lost six times in the AFL and AFC championship games, one step from the Super Bowl. They returned that year to beat the Vikings. It may still stand as the most impressive Raiders victory, one that established them as no longer just good but as a great team.

* * *

A blocked punt provided the memorable call. The referee is responsible for calling the play. When a punt is blocked, there's confusion everywhere. Players are scrambling for the ball. Nobody knows what's going to happen. Anything can.

The most dangerous and exciting plays in football are kickoffs, punt returns, interceptions, and blocked punts. Players do things that they don't realize they're doing, including inadvertently breaking the rules, because the unusual play breaks their concentration. It goes against the grain. Each player is supposed to be blocking or tackling, but suddenly the whole play is deprogrammed. Everyone's scrambling.

This puts pressure on the officials. You've got to think and react quickly. You must sort it out immediately. If you see the ball batted, you've got to be able to know instantly which player hit it and in which direction his team is going.

If a ball is batted, it may only be batted backward, not forward. Ruling decisively and accurately on a play like that gains the confidence and trust of the coaches, players, and fans. You have to decide what happened in what Madden calls a "neo-second." I like that.

On blocked punts, some officials tend to get as close to the play as possible. That's the worst thing you can do. What you want to do is back off from the play so you can keep the play in front and away from you. If you are too close to the play, the ball can come squirting out behind you. Then you are forced to turn your back on the players to follow the ball, which is a cardinal sin in officiating.

Officials can't rehearse a play like that, but we talk before the game about the possibility of a blocked punt and other unusual plays, always emphasizing that we should keep our positions in order to observe the play at all times. Then you just watch, let it happen, and don't anticipate which team will recover the ball. If you hurry the call and blow the whistle, you can be sure that the ball will pop out and you will have blown the play.

* * *

Stabler had a good day, but once when he was sacked, he dusted himself off and said, "Jim, can you count their players? I think they got fourteen guys over there."

Tarkenton earned my respect for showing strength in adversity when he threw a completed pass to Willie Brown. That was a problem, because Brown was a defensive back for the Raiders and he returned it 75 yards for a go-ahead touchdown. As Tarkenton left the field after that interception, he turned to me and with calm self-assurance said, "I'll be back."

In spite of making a serious mistake, Tarkenton had enough inner focus to prevent the dismay that he shared with his team and coaches from pulling him off his game. His belief in himself and his ability were strong enough to sustain his commitment. That kind of emotional durability is what prevents one big setback or an accumulation of minor ones from overwhelming your sense of purpose.

Since Tarkenton has retired, I've kidded him about that many times, telling him he should have learned by then that he was supposed to throw it to the players with the same color shirt he had. He takes the tease in stride.

The game was special in yet another way: it would be the last game Lou Palazzi and I worked together. When I was a rookie referee in 1967, the league had assigned Palazzi to work with me as umpire. A former player with the New York Giants and an experienced official, he worked the famous 1958 championship game between the New York Giants and Baltimore Colts, the one the Colts won in overtime. He was as good as they come or we're likely to get again.

The crowd of 103,438 set a record that year. I helped punch the numbers up there with tickets for fifty or more of my friends and relatives. As I always say, "Celebrate your victory."

All in all, if I had designed the game, I couldn't have planned it any better. I wanted it to last a month. Somehow, one of the game balls found its way into my bag. I don't have any idea how that happened, but I still have it.

Since then, I have felt that any time the Super Bowl was played in the Rose Bowl, I should work it. Unfortunately, the league office hasn't seen it that way. I guess the darts don't always stick where you want them.

9

We Get Grades

Our crew for Super Bowl XI (1977) was sitting in the Sheraton-LAX, Thursday before the game. We were with our boss, Supervisor Art McNally.

"We want you to know," he said, "you are the six best officials in the NFL. You each ranked number one in your position this season."

That blew my dartboard theory. I asked McNally later, "You mean to say that the top officials are selected each year for the Super Bowl?"

"That's right," he said.

"Then my goal," I said, "is to work Super Bowl XII."

And I did. Dallas versus Denver, January 16, 1978, the first Super Bowl to be played in the New Orleans Superdome.

To make it even more special, I brought my sons, Michael and Mark, to the game. They could enjoy the week before the game more than our crew could because officials aren't allowed to get involved with all the hoopla.

We were cloistered like nuns for the week, in a separate hotel from the teams and the media. We couldn't eat at Brennan's or Antoine's. We couldn't do Bourbon Street. It was room service and the hotel coffee shop for us. Even the commissioner's party, attended by 5,000 of Commissioner Pete Rozelle's closest friends, was off-limits to us.

A significant side issue of the game (the playing of it being the most important) was that I was the first referee to work two consecutive Super Bowls, which is the only time this has happened.

This precedent caused some concern in the league office, with good reason. There are too many thoroughly competent officials in each position among the fifteen crews to give the ultimate assignment to the same man each time.

I'll be honest with you. I would be delighted to work every Super Bowl for the same reason any coach would like to have his team win it every year: It proves you're on top. But if you're trying to motivate people, good management says spread the reward among all who deserve it.

For years in baseball, umpires were given the World Series based on seniority. All you had to do was live long enough. I disagreed. If you have the best baseball teams in the World Series, they deserve the best umpires. For the same reason, the two best football teams in the world deserve that year's best officials in their Super Bowl. But "best" is a broad term.

There's been some debate, for instance, on the question of whether the Super Bowl crew should be composed of the top person in each position or whether the overall top crew of the season should be selected as a unit. When you work together as a crew, camaraderie and teamwork skills improve. You know where each one will be on specific plays and how each man adjusts to various game situations.

Here's an example: The two toe-touches of a pass receiver on a sideline catch of a forward pass. The back judge and line judge see it from different angles. On an all-star crew, you might get the back judge signaling that the receiver was in bounds, whereas the line judge, from his angle 20 yards away, thought he was out. The result: a crew conference. After a crew has worked together awhile, you get less of that, because eye contact and communication between each of them keeps them on the same page. Experience counts.

Yet crews will have a rookie or a second-year man nearly every year. They are supported by stronger, more experienced officials. In a Super Bowl, when the intensity is highest, every official has to be able to make the big call. An inexperienced official is usually less able to handle the pressure and commotion that come with the Super Bowl.

During the regular season, the league seeks consistency from its crews. Supervisor McNally tries to balance inexperience with experience on each crew.

On our crew in the 1987 season, for instance, my twenty-eight years exceeded the experience of four others put together. We had men in their second, fourth, sixth, and seventh years. All competent men and we had a great year, but the second- and fourth-year men weren't ready for the pinpoint accuracy you need for the Super Bowl. With this as perspective, my vote is to continue selecting the best individuals from each position for the playoff games and the Super Bowl.

A team in the playoffs for the first time usually doesn't play its best game. Human nature works the same way with officials, which is why some have expressed concern in years when no one assigned to the Super Bowl had previous Super Bowl experience. It's better to have someone on the field who knows how to ignore all the hoopla. Experience helps transcend distraction.

In terms of game situations, regular-season games are often more demanding than the Super Bowl. All three Super Bowls I've worked were lopsided: Dallas 24, Miami 3; Oakland 32, Minnesota 14; Dallas 27, Denver 10. None of them presented especially tough play situations or any of the fierceness that any Raiders-Steelers game does, or any game between traditional rivals.

The hoopla, attention, and commotion that come with the Super Bowl are very real factors. They add pressure of their own kind. You can count on an overflow crowd in the stadium and a 100 million plus in front of television screens.

In recent years, because the game is televised throughout the world, we have the foreign press at the stadium along with all the American sportswriters and analysts. In 1988, there were 2,200 people issued media credentials. Whatever your feelings about whether it is justified, the Super Bowl inspires more media attention than any other event in the world. For two weeks before it happens, the event is debated and mined for every odd fact and bit of trivia the best sports reporters in the world can uncover.

If we conclude from this that the Super Bowl deserves the "best" officials, how do you choose them?

Officials are graded on a seven-point scale, seven being the best and one being the worst. A tough call made correctly rates a seven. There are only a few calls that pull a seven. Good calls, normally a five or six, are many or few depending on opportunity. Poor calls or noncalls (when a foul should have been called) rate a one to three. Because they mean nothing statistically, fours are traditionally not given.

A major call—pass interference, holding, roughing the passer—correctly made, is usually a six, but the rating distinctions are never cut-and-dried.

Take running into the kicker, which is the referee's call to make. If it's made correctly and the video shows it as clear, the call would pull a six. If the video shows that the kicker wasn't contacted but fell, then it's a poor call and would rate a three. If it wasn't even close, the rating may drop to two or one.

A five is given for routine calls like false start, offside, illegal motion—fouls that people in the cheap seats can see. Five says you did it right but it wasn't hard to do.

Some plays happen so fast you don't see all of the action. I had one of those in the 1987 season, Philadelphia at Dallas.

I thought the punter was contacted as he kicked the ball. The ball went out-of-bounds about 20 yards from where he kicked it. I was sure that the defensive player had touched the ball, causing it to go only 20 yards, so I did not throw the flag. The rule states that contact with the punter is legal if the defensive player touches the ball first.

On Monday, when our assistant supervisor reviewed the tape, he couldn't tell if the defensive player touched the ball or not. To get another view, he ordered the NFL highlights from Philadelphia and reviewed them on Tuesday. The NFL film showed that the defensive man did not touch the ball. The punter had just shanked it.

If I'd been right, the call would have pulled a six. It took three days to discover I was wrong, and I got a three.

I don't have any problem with that; that's what film review is all about. I thought I'd made the right call, but the third camera angle proved me wrong.

At other times, the call turns more on judgment than on line of sight. Consider this play: An offensive guard reaches out to grab the nose guard, but the nose guard rips right through him. To me, the best call is a no call. If you see a foul you could call, but which does not affect the game, I say don't call it. Officials should not put themselves into a game unnecessarily. We're not there to slow down the game. Let 'em play.

This is not only a personal viewpoint: It is the league's philosophy. The supervisor goes to great lengths to communicate this, because if officials start throwing flags to pack their ratings bank with calls, the competition between officials intrudes itself into the game.

The ratings system is intended to provide a way to reward the best and cull out any official who stops performing to the league's standards. It requires thoughtful and consistent education from the supervisor's office to keep officials reminded that they are there to support the game in invisible ways.

The rules are there to keep a team from getting an advantage or putting the other team at a disadvantage. The game gains nothing if officials try to be too technical or to serve themselves rather than the game. A wide receiver, for example, might not be exactly up on the line of scrimmage, but if he's split several yards out, everybody knows he's a receiver and there's no advantage. So why call that? That's good game sense.

Or take this: a punt situation and a defensive player lines up five inches offside. If he doesn't rush the kicker, where's the advantage? It's a technicality. But if the head linesman or line judge are protecting their ratings, either one of them will call it for fear they would be downgraded for not enforcing the rule. If game pace and simple fairness are the goals, which they should be, it would be better in that instance to leave the flag in your pocket and keep the game moving. Let 'em play.

Good officials use common sense. If a defensive back bumps a receiver, say, and the pass is far overthrown, the ball is uncatchable and therefore not a foul. It isn't defensive pass interference if the ball is uncatchable. If the offensive team wasn't disadvantaged by the action, it shouldn't draw a penalty.

There are dozens of rules like this that are subject to interpretation. This is as it should be. Reverse the situation and consider offensive pass interference.

The rule on offensive pass interference begins when the ball is snapped, not when it is thrown. That restricts the offense from blocking the defense illegally before the pass is thrown. It makes no difference if the pass is catchable or not; the rule is enforced anytime the offense blocks the defense downfield during a pass play.

I can see the day in the near future when we'll be told to just pick up the flag on that call, too. As the game changes, interpretation changes. You can make a case for no advantage being gained by offensive pass interference when the pass is clearly overthrown.

Another fine point is the level of "help" the officials should give players on the field. Officials should not be in the business of "coaching" players, but good officials operate on what I call the theory of preventive maintenance. They help players with the mechanical part of the game to ensure that the game will move along smoothly, but that should be the extent of their involvement.

For example, before every game, I ask the quarterbacks, even veterans, if they want help tracking the thirty-second limit. The thirty-second clock is the last thing a quarterback thinks about when he's in the huddle. If a play is slow coming in from the bench, a quarterback risks a penalty for delay of game (5 yards). If the time is running short, I simply say, "Take a look at the clock."

Another situation: If the quarterback has released the ball on a pass play and an onrushing defensive lineman is still coming on strong, I say, "Leave him alone." That sometimes keeps the quarterback from being slammed to the ground. I could let the quarterback get hit and throw a flag—and I'd get a six for the call—but that's not good for the game. The objective is to prevent the quarterback from being injured by unnecessary contact and to keep the game moving.

Sometimes the sack happens too fast. I remember a time when Bill Nelsen quarterbacked the Cleveland Browns. I had refereed games he played at El Rancho High and at USC. One spring he worked for me as a substitute teacher at Fairfax High School. The next September, I worked a game between Cleveland and Detroit in Municipal Stadium. Nelsen got buried under a pass rush.

Lying in the dust, he looked up at me and said, "I thought you were my friend."

I laughed. "I can't block for you."

Players come to respect an official when they know he adheres to the preventive-maintenance theory. I surprised David Deacon Jones one day when he was playing defensive end for the Los Angeles Rams. The quarterback went down, and Jones had a chance to punish him, but Jones hurdled over him.

I said to Jones afterward, "Smart move, Deacon, smart move."

He was dumbfounded. "Nobody's ever complimented me like that before," he said, but I wanted to let him know that that was the kind of game I wanted to see. Hard-hitting, yes, but please, no unnecessary fouls, which only create an unnecessary number of calls.

As long as there are wide areas for interpretation, the grading won't be perfect, but one way in which the grading system, as of yet, makes no effort to rate excellence is on the skill of game control. Game control is the single most important aspect of pro ball officials must manage.

If the game is to be decided by the players, officials must keep it under control and be essentially fair. Fans, owners, coaches, and players judge officials primarily on game control. While it is the least definable of an official's responsibilities, it is the most obvious failure when a game gets out of hand.

Game control begins with sufficient poise and self-confidence that add up to command and presence. Knowledge and preparation help, but readiness alone cannot carry the situation without there also being a strong flow of respect between the officials and the coaches and players.

In addition, you must react calmly in heated situations, which demand a cool head and impartiality. You can't get drawn into the emotion. If you do, you become part of the problem instead of part of the solution.

If game-control elements are the most important, they should be foremost in the minds of the officials. When an official has his grades as the primary focus, the game suffers. If an official goes into the game thinking, I want to get a lot of sixes today, he is focusing on self-interest instead of game management.

With the use of computers to tally the ratings of the assistant supervisors and extensive use of videotape review, the grading system for officials' performance is more sophisticated than ever before. Still, I'd like to see more of the subtleties, particularly game control, added to the grading system.

The game changes constantly. It is admittedly a difficult task to develop a rating system that is comprehensive and fair in capturing the ordinary elements of an official's performance, much less the subtle discriminations in judgment and game control. This being the real world, the rating system is not perfect, but it is regularly reviewed and improved as ways are found to better attempt the impossible.

10

People Make the Game

The tension was thick in the Packers' dressing room before the first Super Bowl (Los Angeles Coliseum, 1967). Coach Vince Lombardi was pacing. His players knew this game meant more to him than any of the four NFL championships he'd won with Green Bay. Nothing other than a win was acceptable. The Packers had best defeather the Kansas City Chiefs that day or else. As Lombardi called his men together for the final team meeting, Paul Hornung asked if he could say a few words.

Lombardi was reluctant. Hornung had a well-deserved reputation as a playboy and for being unpredictable. Hornung worked hard but wasn't consumed by the game. He knew that 800,000 Chinese didn't know who he was and wouldn't care if they did.

Lombardi knew all this, but he also knew that Hornung was a great player, a veteran the younger players looked up to. Who more deserved to speak? So Lombardi agreed.

Hornung stood before the team and said, "Gentlemen, I came to Los Angeles for two reasons. I accomplished one of them last night. Now, let's go out there and get the second one done."

Everyone broke up in laughter. Coach even smiled. The Packers went out to win, easily, 35–10.

That's typical of the lighter side of pro football. The game is people. The saying is that football builds character, but it's also true that it builds characters—players who are not just funny but who approach their craft idiosyncratically, with their own combination of imagination and flair.

George Halas was a prime example. He had the vision to see what the NFL could be and the stature to rally support for his ideas. He was a founder of the league and had the leadership skills necessary to coordinate leaguewide changes. He was, for instance, primarily responsible for the adoption of the rule that prohibited NFL teams from signing players whose college class hadn't yet graduated. All the while, of course, his Chicago Bears were winning football games.

Paul Brown, first owner and coach of the Cleveland Browns, was an innovator and a man who would do anything he could to gain an edge. The most outrageous example is probably his famous appliquéd jerseys. They were brown, of course, and at one point he had a piece of brown leather in the shape of a football sewn on the front of the jerseys. When a quarterback faked a handoff, he hoped the defense couldn't tell which running back actually had the ball. His "innovation" was outlawed, but not before it confused a few defensive linemen.

As the league got organized, the competitive zeal got organized, too. The game started out as a running game—"three yards and a cloud of dust." As the game attracted the best talent, it developed dimension and surprises.

I didn't have a chance to meet Bert Bell, who was commissioner of the league from 1946 until his death in 1959. Once co-owner of the Philadelphia franchise, Bell gained a reputation as a strong commissioner who ruled the league with a fatherly fist.

I came into the league in 1960, Pete Rozelle's first year as commissioner. He had been general manager of the Los Angeles Rams just prior to being selected as commissioner.

Rozelle has distinguished himself for bringing football into our living rooms. His background in public relations is probably what told him to move the league offices from Bala Cynwyd, Pennsylvania, to Park Avenue. From there he could be in easy contact with television and radio networks, and he made it his challenge to send football live to worldwide audiences.

In the last three decades, Rozelle has put his leadership skills to work in disciplining coaches, owners, and players who deviated from the spirit of the game he is charged to maintain. Protecting the integrity of the game has been his number-one concern from day one of his tenure.

Rozelle coordinated the merger between the AFL and the NFL, a necessary step in protecting the game and one that came with enormous headaches. To conclude the negotiations required tenacity, sensitivity, diplomacy, and conviction.

His conviction is what I admire most. Few leaders could top his performance in persistently fighting off the government's efforts to bring the league under the constraints of antitrust legislation. More often than not the "glamour jobs" require guts and fortitude.

Rozelle has also shown a deft touch in dealing with the human element. He takes players' antics in stride but has demonstrated courage every time he felt a player's behavior violated the spirit of the league.

The suspension of Alex Karras and Paul Hornung for betting on their own teams is one example. But Rozelle has been as quick to put an end to player indiscretions of all kinds.

When the rumors started, he investigated "Broadway Joe" Namath's bar in Manhattan, "Bachelors III." When he became satisfied it was attracting the gambling element, Rozelle made it off-limits to all league personnel, including officials.

Sometimes a player's personality off the field isn't the same one he has on the field. Namath liked to provoke comment and reaction. It was part of his game strategy. His challenge to the

Baltimore Colts before Super Bowl III, when he "guaranteed" a Jets victory, is representative of how brash he could be; and he certainly encouraged the "Broadway Joe" image. On the field I saw a different Joe Namath.

You have to remember that Namath was a Bear Bryant protégé at Alabama. Bryant demanded a businesslike seriousness on the football field, and Namath lived up to Bryant's standard. The press gave us the idea Namath was with a different girl each night, but his coaches say he took game films home with him at night.

On the field it was always "Yes, sir" and "No, sir" in any discussion I had with Namath. He wasn't being facetious; this was the Bryant influence shining still.

Bryant fed a lot of star quarterbacks into the league. During my tenure, I've witnessed the skills of Bart Starr, Ken Stabler, Richard Todd, and Namath.

Stabler came out of Alabama straight to the Raiders and threw the ball for them for eight years. The Raiders were attracted to Stabler because of his flair for high risk. He wasn't afraid, in his words, to "throw deep." He was happy on the Raiders because it freed him to open up and tap the gambler's spirit in himself.

Different teams attract players who seem to share certain personality traits. The Raiders, who like a rough-and-ready game, attract feisty, aggressive ballplayers.

Defensive end John Matuszak, a free spirit, journeyed around the league before finding kindred spirits in the Raiders. Fans and many of his opponents would say he ignored the rules when he could. Ignoring the rules isn't the same as not knowing them.

After a preseason rules talk with the Raiders, during which Matuszak looked as he always did—restless and bored—he approached me and said, "Jim, that was one of the finest rules talks I've ever heard." His seriousness caught me by surprise.

Defensive players traditionally are not rules oriented. Guys like Matuszak, Lyle Alzado, Ted Hendricks, and Charles Phil-yaw, all Raiders at one time, and defensive players from any team, treated the game as a war. Wars are notable for their absence of rules.

Many defensive players reflect this defiant attitude in their housekeeping. Their lockers look like a teenager's bedroom—nothing hung up, everything messy and jumbled. That's the way they play on the field, totally without regard for self or safety.

Tough, fit Raiders linebacker Ted Hendricks. At 6 feet 8 inches, he looked more as if he belonged in the NBA than the NFL, but on the field it didn't take long to see he met the Raiders' criteria. He loved a good hit. A sure tackler, he was always ferocious and keyed up. He seemed on the verge of explosion, but he played with control and pride.

A Raiders teammate, defensive end Charles Philyaw, was even bigger. More than his size and skill, though, my favorite memories of Philyaw have to do with how easily he could be unintentionally funny. The first time he saw "Van Eeghen" on the back of the jersey of Raiders fullback Mark Van Eeghen, Philyaw went over to Coach Madden and asked him why he couldn't have his first name on his jersey, too.

Another time, when Philyaw was hurt in training camp, Madden told him to "go see the doctor." Philyaw went up to the room of defensive back Skip Thomas, who by that time had gained the infamous nickname "Dr. Death."

Some guys always stand out as the exception in temperament and style. Rams defensive tackle Merlin Olsen should have been on the other side of the line. Here was a guy you would like to have over to your house for dinner. Quiet, unassuming, he'd have FTD send you flowers.

Intelligent and alert, Olsen thought football all the time. At a rules talk to the Rams in training camp one year, Olsen raised his hand and began his question, "What if, indeed, a player should . . ." His teammates exploded in laughter and started making cracks like "Knock it off with the high IQ stuff."

One of Olsen's rivals in the league was St. Louis Cardinals offensive guard Conrad Dobler. He didn't fit the image of an offensive lineman. He was routinely as "off the wall" as most defensive players. I caught Dobler holding one time and threw the flag. He ate my flag.

Dobler, who played most of his career with the Cardinals before being traded to the New Orleans Saints, always gave the extra effort. He would block a guy to the ground, then give him an extra shove. He was even known to bite defensive players' fingers. I've seen the teeth marks.

His reputation as a famous troublemaker didn't prevent him from keeping himself and the game in perspective. When he was traded to the Saints, he proclaimed he was the only man who ever went from a Cardinal to a Saint without going through the rest of the chairs.

The ability to have fun on the field knows no position. Walter Payton, All-Pro running back of the Chicago Bears, gave us a good share of levity. "Sweetness," as he is rightly nicknamed, had fun playing the game. He'd get tackled hard, maybe unnecessarily so, get up, pat the tackler on the back, and say, "Nice tackle." He gets high marks from me for his sportsmanship.

What few knew, though, is how often Payton would pull little stunts on the field. During a time-out in the Chicago-Minnesota game last year with first place in the division at stake, I was standing near the Bears offensive huddle when Payton came by and rubbed the bottom of his shoe over the top of mine, untying my shoelaces.

That was not the first time he'd done that. After the first time, I would usually double-tie my shoelaces for a Bears game. That night I had forgotten, but "Sweetness" hadn't.

That was just one of Payton's ways of relieving tension. Another was his habit of giving the officials a little pinch on the fanny or thigh. Maybe he thought he was helping us stay alert, but the twinkle in his eye gave him the look of a little kid getting away with something.

As an official, you have to respect that players have different temperaments. Walter Payton, like many, could joke on the field; some never do. I remember learning this lesson while working a Seahawks game in the Kingdome.

Jim Zorn was the first quarterback for the Seattle franchise. His mother, Esther, was the cafeteria manager for one of our schools when I was a superintendent of the Bellflower Unified School District. One time she asked me to say hello for her when I worked a Seahawks game. I said I would.

During the game Zorn, who was the Seahawks' captain, had to elect a penalty option. I said, "Before I tell you what your options are, your mother says hello." Zorn and the others laughed, but Zorn forgot which option he should have chosen. I saw that the interruption had broken his concentration and vowed to be aware of that in the future.

Bum Phillips, head coach of the Houston Oilers and the New Orleans Saints, looked at NFL coaching as just another adventure in his life. I admired him for that. Many coaches treat the NFL as the core of their lives, as if there isn't anything better. Bum always could see beyond the field.

Another thing I like about Bum is that he is intellectually honest. Whenever he had a question about a play situation and I'd go to the sideline to talk to him, it never failed he had something legitimate to say. He might use strong vocabulary, but he always had a valid point. He wouldn't think of using these occasions to try to intimidate. What he had to say was relevant, and he wanted a response.

Sometimes, when a coach calls you over to discuss a play, you have to listen for a couple minutes trying to find a question mark. The coach just wanted an excuse to express his opinion. Bum could fire out pretty strong, but he always had a question mark.

Coaches are as different in temperament as players. Buddy Parker, coach of the Pittsburgh Steelers, for instance, seemed to hate officials. He let it show vigorously.

One time when the Steelers lost, Parker blamed the officials. In the postgame interview, he told the press, "I haven't seen this kind of theft since the great train robbers of the West."

The next day, the Pittsburgh *Press* morning edition carried individual pictures of the crew with the headline "The Great Train Robbers of the West." They had doctored the pictures to make the officials look like Western bandits in cowboy hats and bandannas up to their noses.

I prefer it when the players get the attention, not the officials. Officials aren't there to be visible. As much as possible, we should be invisible, except as needed to enforce the rules, so that excellence has an equal chance to come from either team. That's the only way for the victory to belong to players, and victory is their purpose.

It should be a standard rule for everyone, football player or not, to celebrate your victories. Too often we're in such a rush to move from goal to goal that we forget to recognize our accomplishments. Football players give us plenty of examples every Sunday.

A quarterback throws a touchdown pass to a wide receiver, and a guard will turn around and give a "high five" to the quarterback. It's a way of saying, "Hey, we did this together." That's healthy.

One of the "Three Amigos" will score a touchdown, and all three will do their dance. There's some show biz to that; sometimes the exuberance goes on too long. When it does, I think, Hey, act as if you've been there before.

A cool attitude and self-control aside, a team needs team spirit; it should feel and act like a family. Celebrating together is a recognition of shared effort toward a shared goal.

Team spirit rises above salary differential. It says that everyone is important because it takes eleven together to do the job. The running back who makes $600,000 a year is no more important than the guard who makes $250,000. The place kicker, on the field only a few times a game for a moment or two, is no less important than the center, who is out there every offensive play. When a team breaks apart and begins to value its members unequally, the teamwork falls apart, and the scoreboard will prove it.

Choose whom you want to ask from the league office or coaches or fans. There's always a divided opinion about whether strong personalities are good for the game.

One opinion goes "Shut up and do your job. Don't brag. Don't do those funny dances in the end zone. Play ball." The other side says visibility helps the gate and that's great.

The bottom line is that the game attracts strong personalities and builds characters. This has always been true, and it will continue. Some of the players' antics create headaches for the coaches, but the liveliness is good for the gate. Fans wouldn't want it any other way.

11

Strong Understandings

When I think about Vince Lombardi, I remember my dad. They were tempered very much alike.

July 5, 1965, was the day my dad died. Lombardi died five years later, on September 3, 1970. I remember those two dates. I couldn't tell you the date of anyone else's death in the world other than November 22, 1963, the day President Kennedy was assassinated.

My dad and Coach Lombardi were even close to the same age when they died. Dad was just 59 when he died of a massive heart attack. Lombardi was 57 when he died of cancer.

Lombardi influenced every player, every game, the fans, the history of the sport. He set a new standard of excellence, and because of his dogged insistence on perfect execution, he changed forever what coaches expect not only from their players but what they expect from themselves. Lombardi inspired your confidence in him and in yourself. As I said, my dad and Lombardi were a lot alike.

Jerry Kramer, the right guard of that magnificent Packers line, tells a story from his early years under Lombardi. Kramer got chewed out one afternoon for missing a block in practice. Kramer let it upset him so much that he couldn't do anything right from then on.

That upset Lombardi, who told him, "If that's the way you're going to play, turn in your uniform. You don't belong on the Green Bay Packers."

Kramer left the field and planned to turn in his uniform. He was sitting disconsolate in the locker room when Lombardi came in and took him aside.

"Somehow I want you to understand," Lombardi said, "you're going to be one of the greatest linemen in the NFL. That's if you practice every block, every move as if it counts, as if every play means the game. Get yourself ready. Practice starts at eight A.M. tomorrow."

Lombardi was tough, but he took the time to be sure he communicated, to be sure you understood he was only pulling for the best from you. That's what he expected from himself, so it was fair expectation.

Same with my dad. As I was growing up, everyone I knew admired him, partly because he had been a great college athlete but mainly because of his strength of character. I've had heroes and mentors all through my life, but my first and strongest role model was my dad.

He was a school administrator; I became a school administrator. He was a coach and a referee; I became a coach and a referee. You can't miss the follow-through.

A friend pointed out to me there might have been unconscious rivalry, too, because I set goals one step beyond my dad in everything. He was a vice-principal; I became a principal, then a superintendent. He refereed the Rose Bowl game; I've refereed the Super Bowl. He worked in the old All-American Conference; I made it to the NFL.

Dad was direct and simple. He always said, "Son, being an athlete means discipline. No smoking. No drinking."

He didn't allow himself the everyday bad habits or indulgences other people did. He expected the same of me. Even now I'm a bit surprised that his influence was enough to offset peer pressure, but it was.

Jackie Robinson (#66) breaking a tackle at the Rose Bowl, circa 1939, with my dad, Jim Tunney following the play. His intensity always matched that of the players, which, he taught me, was a prime requisite for every official, every game, every play.

Supervisor of Officials Art McNally doesn't seem to be enjoying watching the
"Raiderettes" before Super Bowl XI as much as (from left) Field Judge "Turk" Terzian,
Alternate Gene Barth, and yours truly. Team mascots and cheerleaders add to the fun
of football as a spectator sport.

Super Bowl XII (1978). Kneeling from left: Back Judge Ray Douglas, Line Judge Art Holst, Alternate Cal Lepore, Head Linesman Tony Veteri. Standing from left: Assistant Supervisor of Officials Nick Skorich, Alternate Frank Sinkowitz, Umpire Joe Connell, yours truly as Referee, Field Judge Bob Wortman, Supervisor of Officials Art McNally, and Assistant Supervisor Jack Reader. For trivia fans, this was the last game in which the referee wore a white hat. Beginning with the 1978 season, to make it easier for television to identify the referee, the league put its referees in black hats.

Super Bowl XI (1977). To my left are Umpire Lou Palazzi, Head Linesman Ed Marion, Line Judge Bill Swanson, Back Judge Tom Kelleher, Field Judge Armen Terzian, Alternates Pat Harder and Gene Barth. This game was particularly exciting because it was played in the Rose Bowl, a stadium that already carried great personal memories for me.

Since 1972 I have been privileged to serve as the model for the Official Signals section of the rule book, which is reprinted in all *Game Day* programs.

As referee, I announce the down and distance, and indicate ready for play with an extended arm signal. Washington Redskins running back John Riggins (#44, partially visible) never did pay much attention to me.

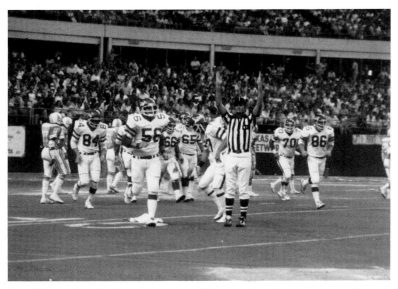

Touchdown for the Jets against the Oilers in the Houston Astrodome.
Part of the fun of every game is being out there with the "big guys." You
hope you don't get run over, even in celebration.

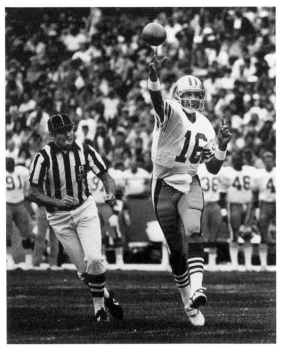

Running after the stars of
the game is one of the plea-
sures of being a referee.
Joe Montana (#16) of the
San Francisco 49ers is art-
in-motion here in the
NFC Championship Game
against the Dallas Cowboys
at Candlestick.

Almost as much as the game itself, John Madden loves the people who love the game. Before the 1986 NFC Championship Game between the Los Angeles Rams and the Chicago Bears, Madden (center) had time to visit with (from left) Line Judge Dick McKenzie, Head Linesman Burl Toler, yours truly, and camera shy Pat Summerall (partially hidden).

The biggest deal when I was a teenager was smoking cigarettes. I resisted. No one I knew was into marijuana or other drugs. Because of his influence, I've never had a cigarette or even so much as a beer. Never. Ever. The peer pressure was no less then than it is today, forty years later. Single-mindedness always meets resistance, in any era.

Dad was born in 1905. He was in his formative years when World War I came. He had no father at home, so he would bring his earnings from selling newspapers on the street corner home to my grandmother. Because of his background and Catholic training at Loyola High School and Loyola University, he developed a very strong work ethic, which thankfully he transferred to me. I haven't been without a job since I was 13.

He always encouraged me to do well in school. There was a threat in there, too. I went to St. Therese Catholic Grammar School. He warned me that if I gave any trouble to the nuns, he would double my punishment when I got home. He felt the sisters had a hard enough job without my adding to their burden.

I wasn't a model student. I threw chalk and erasers, talked too much, had too much fun. The sisters kept me after school sometimes. School was play for me. I enjoyed myself.

The sisters would call my mom, who very seldom punished me. She would say, "Wait till your father gets home."

Maybe the wait was her part of the punishment.

When Dad got home, he'd have no hesitancy in bending me over and using the "Board of Education." His method of discipline was carried over from his coaching style—immediate and specific.

One afternoon, some men were burning the grass in a vacant lot next door to our house. I took that board and threw it over the fence. My solution didn't last long. Dad produced another board before the smoke had cleared.

A privilege of being the oldest of four children, I was the one who got to go with my dad to his games. There's no way to overestimate the benefit of these early experiences. It was easy to absorb his standards because they were a daily routine.

I was hardly his idea of talent with superstar athletic potential. I was built like a stack of dimes. We were also different in basic temperament and natural-reaction style. He grew up on the streets. If somebody took one of his papers away from him, or his money, he was after them, fighting. I was not.

Because Dad was the playground director for the Alhambra Recreation Department, I always had a ball for any sport. Old baseballs, bats, and basketballs came home.

The benefit of this good fortune was not just plenty of practice with my dad. When I went to the playground, I always got to play. I might be chosen last, as in, "Oh, well, we've got to let Tunney play. It's his ball." But I got to play.

One time I came home in tears because five or six guys had jumped me and taken my basketball. My dad came home about the same time and said, "C'mon, let's go."

We went down to the playground and found the guys. He said, "Pick out one of them. Choose the one you want to fight."

I didn't want to fight. I was scared and right then wished Dad would be less strong-minded. But he wanted to make a point.

I picked out Jack Bates, a pretty tough guy. I don't know why I didn't pick somebody easier. I got whipped. Dad said he was proud of me, anyway. His point was "Stand up for what you believe in. Don't back down. Never run away."

This was a painful but good lesson for me. I didn't understand it at the time any more than Kramer understood Lombardi was helping him by chewing him out, but the lesson has never left me.

In football games, in a tough situation, somebody else might want to back away, but not me. I say, "No way." It can't get too tough for me. I feel in charge in a game.

I want the players to know that I'll run the game to my standards and according to the rules. That's possible only if you understand that you have to be in charge of yourself before you can be in charge of any situation.

This lesson in hardiness was the genesis of my understanding that personal power is more important than "position power." I have my dad to thank for that.

The bullies in life aren't really strong; they just put up a blustery front. Bullies are marshmallows with knives and guns sometimes, which makes them dangerous, but don't mistake being dangerous with intelligence, strength of purpose, or strength of character.

Dad was remarkable in another way. He had the kind of strength that said it was okay to let sensitivity show through. He was approachable. As strong-minded and stern as he was sometimes, I could always talk to him. I might be afraid to ask something, but once I gathered my own courage to do it, he was always warm and loving.

I saw the same kind of characteristics in Lombardi as soon as I met him. I immediately admired the strength he possessed, the determination he inspired, the respect he earned.

I came into the NFL without knowing much about Lombardi. He had taken over the Green Bay Packers in 1959, just one year before I came into the league. He had been one of the "Seven Blocks of Granite" at Fordham University in the 1930s, but that didn't mean much to me. I identified with the "Four Horsemen" of Notre Dame—Jim Crowley, Elmer Layden, Harry Stuhldreher, and Don Miller.

Once I had met Lombardi, it didn't take long to realize that he was special. You knew he would be revered by many and make history in the game.

There were other impressive coaches at that time—Buck Shaw, Clark Shaughnessy, George Halas. These men had certainly gained respect; they were recognized as leaders in the sport. Yet Lombardi had something even more special. He was destined to be one of the greatest coaches of all time.

Lombardi came into the NFL with an unlikely twist. He was a New Yorker. He was great at Fordham, then became assistant coach with the Giants and was with them during their great years in the 1950s.

Knowing Vince Lombardi, when he arrived at Green Bay, he had to be thinking to himself, I've only got one direction to go—up. It was his wry acceptance of this that allowed him, when teased by the press about his chances, to refer to the challenge as an "opportunity."

According to Bill Gove, a reporter quipped to Lombardi that "Green Bay is not the end of the world, but you can see it from there."

Lombardi inherited a team that had won only four games in the previous two seasons and was 1–10–1 the year before. Lombardi had never been associated with a losing team. One of his first challenges was to find something to do with Paul Hornung.

Hornung was a Heisman Trophy quarterback out of Notre Dame, but many in the pros considered him a man without a position. He could run, pass, and kick, and although he was a triple threat in college, some said that he couldn't throw well enough to play quarterback, or run well enough to play halfback, in the pros.

Lombardi disagreed. He designed an offensive strategy that used Hornung's talents. The secret was execution by the offensive line.

The pulling of the guards and tackles to lead the blocking on end-run sweeps allowed Hornung the option to run or pass. Because he was talented at both, the defense could not anticipate which he would select. With fullback Jim Taylor to do the inside running and Hornung to worry the defense about whether he was going to run or pass, Lombardi made a backfield to match his jewel of a line.

When Lombardi took over, none of the players on the Packers had shown exceptional talent or drive. Under Lombardi, they became winners. Lombardi relished the challenge of improvement.

I think that's why he loved Hornung. Nothing delighted Lombardi more than making a guy who wanted to "play" his way to stardom into a solid football player. Getting Hornung to make curfew was one of the most persistent tests of Lombardi's dedication.

Lombardi liked football because it typifies what he believed life should be. His approach to both was the same: get prepared and stay disciplined.

He was frustrated when his players couldn't see the fundamental importance of this attitude. To give him more opportunity to explain it to them, Lombardi started his "grading system."

Each player was graded on every play. Lombardi took note of the smallest detail, then he posted the "grades" on the bulletin board for all to see.

Lombardi saw his business as teaching football. The only way he knew how to do it was thoroughly. The players benefited. As they began to see this, they acquired a dedication to his deliberate methods and dogged insistence on careful execution on every component, every time. He gained the respect of his players by being consistent and evenhanded. As they improved their performance, they earned his respect.

Quickly, the spirit around the Packers changed. You could feel the energy. The light of Lombardi's inspiration was always shining. Every player reflected it. Rarely did a player not give open tribute to the change that Lombardi had made in his individual game.

Lombardi was firm and played no favorites. He treated veterans no differently than rookies. He expected every player to work equally hard. Real hard. Both mentally and physically.

He felt that if the Packers were in better physical condition than their opponents, this advantage alone could mean two to three more victories each year. He constantly challenged his players and kept his grading system going.

His eyes were always forward. He repeatedly told his team,

"The best NFL football game has yet to be played. When it is played, the Green Bay Packers will play in it and win!"

Lombardi claimed his winning teams were built on four principles: self-discipline, self-sacrifice, mental toughness, and teamwork. He believed in his formula. Without all four, he couldn't reasonably count on his players to focus hard enough and long enough to outexecute the opponent in any circumstance. That was the goal he set for every game.

He tolerated no slack from his players. He coached hard to get what he wanted and expected his players to want it just as hard. Each one had to be the individual victor over his own uncertainties, confusions, and distractions. Lombardi knew that conviction is a private experience. It is self-made. The coach's role is to provide the atmosphere and conditions for each player to thrive, then the player himself must do his part.

I asked Lombardi one time what he was after in this quality he called *mental toughness*? Was it tenacity?

"Tenacity is just keeping at it," he said. "What I'm after is the self-control and focus to limit your efforts to only the ones that are effective. Mental toughness is the power to focus forcefully and do it right the first time, every time. That's what I'm after."

"Right, Coach." A good distinction.

Our discussion reminded me of an insight I had after I decided to improve my tennis game. Anyone who wants to win at tennis has one goal: not to lose more than one point in a row. If you never lose two points in a row, you will never lose a game or a match. But to play that tight, to control yourself carefully enough to not have a "bad streak," you have to focus on the *narrowest goal* that will assure success.

Lombardi used that same insight. His insistence on attention to every move was nothing more than dividing the components so you could concentrate on each one in the right sequence. A Lombardi maxim : "Perfection is impossible. Excellence is not."

* * *

This competitive zeal notwithstanding, I challenge you to find a person more ethical than Coach Lombardi. It offended him the few times he sensed that anyone thought his drive to succeed would prompt him to cheat or even consider anything bordering on the illegal. It infuriated and embarrassed him at the same time. Lombardi would rather lose a game than have anyone think he would cheat to win.

Lombardi is often misquoted as having said, "Winning isn't everything; it's the *only* thing." This is a gross distortion. What he actually said was "The *desire* to win isn't everything, it's the *only* thing." His goal was focus and conviction.

Lombardi believed no coach, player, or anyone should ever approach a task without the single-minded desire to succeed. He also believed no one should ever drop his honor or his sense of fair play.

Lombardi didn't reserve this attitude for pro ball. He felt to play to tie in any situation is ridiculous. It's no fun for anyone. Like kissing your sister, it's friendly, but doesn't contain the energy you want.

Playing to tie, or worse, playing to lose, is dishonest. How can your opponent feel successful unless he feels he won on his own merits? Even as parents we should not play backyard games with our children and try to lose so that the kids will win.

You don't have to beat the kid unmercifully just to show him what losing is like, but letting him win says more to him non-verbally and subliminally than we realize. It's destructive.

Winning gains importance only after a full and fair effort on both sides. The competition has to begin with conviction and proceed with fairness. The distinction between "fair advantage" and cheating is made by the standard of honesty you demand from your cleverness. The approach outweighs the score. The man outstands the game.

Lombardi had an aura about him, even with his family. I met his son-in-law, Thomas Bickham, after a speech I gave in Miami in the early 1980s. We had time to trade some stories about

Coach. (Everybody called Lombardi "Coach" or "Mr. Lombardi." I never heard anyone call him "Vince.")

Bickham had met his wife-to-be, Susan Lombardi, at St. Norbert's College in Wisconsin, where the Packers trained. They were both students. "I didn't type very well," Bickham said, "so Susan typed my term papers for me.

"One night we were down in their cellar working on a paper when Coach came home. It was about eight or nine o'clock. Late, not dinnertime.

"When Susan heard him slam the door, she said, 'I'd like you to meet my father. I think it's time.'

"We'd never met before. I was always going out one door as he was coming in the other. I was awed by him.

"Susan called out, 'Daddy, I want you to come down and meet Tom.'

"There was a pause. Finally, a voice came down like a clap of thunder. 'Tell him to come up here and meet me.' It was like the voice of God.

"A couple of preseason games after that, on a day when the Packers weren't playing, Coach was watching another game on television. I thought, What a great opportunity; here's a great coach. I'll ask him what's happening.

"He was sitting there with his arms crossed, eyes straight ahead on the TV. A couple of times I said, 'Coach, what do you think of that play?' He didn't say anything. I don't think he heard me. When football was on his mind, he was totally in another world."

That was Lombardi. The waters parted for Moses; in Green Bay, the streets parted for Lombardi. People would actually step aside when he walked down Lambeau Avenue. Not that he demanded it or expected it. If you stopped him and said, "Hey, Coach, how's it going?" he'd talk to you. He never thought of himself as someone special, but he was treated that way.

Prior to every game I worked for the Packers, Lombardi was solemn. He would give back a smile occasionally, but only for an instant before the solemn look sunk in. I don't know who created the term "game face," but Coach deserves credit. He had an awesome sense of purpose. He knew why he was there, and nothing was going to interfere with it.

There's the story about his preseason meeting with his team. As always, he went straight to the point. "Men, there are three things that are very, very important in your lives. Your God, your family, and the Green Bay Packers. And not necessarily in that order."

That's exactly the way he approached football. His family was important to him, but not on Sunday afternoons during the season. When game time came, his wife, Marie, and his children, Vince, Jr., and Susan, weren't on his mind. He never gave attention to any physical aches or weather inconveniences. He rose to a level of single consciousness. It's as if he thought, "If anything bad happened, right now, I wouldn't know about it, nor could I do anything about it. So I'm going to concentrate on the game. That I can do." I admire that level of self-control.

Lombardi was a straight play-it-like-it's-supposed-to-be-played coach. The most important elements of the game for him were blocking and tackling. He didn't have any idea what a flea-flicker was; he would never have considered winning with a trick play. Bones and guts and smarts were his game.

At the beginning of the season, at the first team meeting every single year, he would stand in front of his players, holding his favorite object, and say, "Gentlemen, this is a football." It was really that simple for him.

I have seen him chew out a player coming off the field for not making a first down because he saw the lack of desire in that player or the offensive line as a unit. He knew they had the power and strength to make that first down. They knew it, too.

His strength was the offensive line. He learned how it's done on Fordham's "Seven Blocks of Granite." He knew that if he had the right men tackle to tackle, the other team wasn't going to stop them unless a player did something fundamentally wrong. That was something he wouldn't forgive. Not executing according to plan was an individual act of forgetting. He didn't accept that.

He knew how the linemen were supposed to block and what happened when a block was missed. Jerry Kramer and Fuzzy Thurston knew he knew. They knew that he expected every single block to be made with their butts low and their shoulders high and driving, driving, driving.

You could hear him say to a player coming off the field, "That is not the way the Green Bay Packers block. If that's the way you're going to block, you're not going to be a Packer." He meant it.

There would be other times when you'd hear him yell, "What the hell's going on out there?" It might be something as simple as a bad handoff from Starr to Taylor. Whatever it was, if it offended Lombardi's sense of perfection, he let everybody know.

Lombardi would take his playbook and give it to his opponents. "You want to see this?" he'd say. "Take it and I'll still beat you, because we'll execute better than you will."

In Lombardi's playbook, like every other in the NFL, every play is designed to score a touchdown. You don't design a play to get 5 yards; even classic first-down plays like an off-tackle run or a sweep are designed to score. Once you're at the line of scrimmage, if everyone is doing his job, the arrow in the playbook goes right to the goal line, with the linebackers being blocked, and defensive backs being knocked out of the play.

That's why Lombardi worked so hard on execution. If the offense does its job perfectly, even if the defense does its job right, the offense should score, because it has the ball. The offense knows where the play is going; the defense doesn't. That was Lombardi's whole theory; execute right and you'll score, and scoring is how you win football games. Simple, but effective.

He drilled and drilled and drilled his players, because preparation was the backbone of his game. Nothing in Lombardi's book excused not being prepared.

* * *

Preparation is the key. I feel the same way.

While some rules have changed, the basic NFL rules have not changed since I've been in the league. Yet I spend more time reviewing rules now after twenty-eight years than I did in the early years—so I can execute properly every time. Maybe I want Coach to be proud of me.

In the off-season, at a speaking engagement or while traveling, if someone asks me about a rule, sometimes I have to stop a second and think. During the season, that must never happen. On the field, I have to know the rule in any situation instantly. Only constant, concentrated review will assure that.

Intentional grounding, for instance. It used to be 15 yards and loss of down. Now it's 10 yards and loss of down. However, if the spot from which the quarterback throws it is farther back than 10 yards, that's the spot of enforcement. So if the quarterback is 12 yards back when he grounds the pass, that's where the ball is placed.

Officials aren't allowed to carry a rule book onto the field. I'm glad. I wouldn't want it to be permitted. What would you think of an official who had to stop during a game to look up a rule?

I was on an airplane once when an emergency-landing situation came up. The flight attendants pulled out pink booklets and started reading. Fortunately there was time for them to check what they needed, but frankly, I was strongly wishing their training instructor had played football under Lombardi.

Not only do officials have to be right; we must be prompt and decisive. That's the minimum coaches, players, fans, and the league expect. When a call is made and there is a penalty, they don't want the referee to come on the mike and say, "Uh, holding. Uh, no, illegal contact. Uh . . ."

You can't do that. For an official to miss a rule, mark off the wrong penalty yardage, or place the ball at the wrong spot is, to me, inexcusable, just as not properly executing was unforgivable to Lombardi.

* * *

Lombardi had a brief life as a head coach, 1959 through 1967 with the Packers and one year, 1969, with the Redskins. That's a short time in which to become immortal, but he did.

He accomplished this partly because of his determination but also because he was superb at evaluating talent. He was exceedingly intuitive whether it was players on the team he inherited or players he traded for. Lombardi could read talent in a player the way Madden can read plays. There's no way to say how they do it better than anyone else, but you saw the results constantly in their work.

Lombardi could have been the president of any Fortune 500 company using the same basic management perspectives he used in building football teams. His genius was being able to evaluate people, position them properly, and then get them to perform to their top potential.

Players come to a team with a "résumé." They are known for what they did in college or other pro teams. Lombardi didn't pay any attention to history. He was solely interested in what a player could become with the Packers.

"Charlie Brown" complained to Lucy one time, "There's no heavier burden than the weight of a great potential." Lombardi knew how to ease the burden of his players' great potential by training them effectively and inspiring them to believe in the potential he saw in them. He provided both the training and the atmosphere that allowed them to play out that potential to the maximum. He galvanized potential into performance.

Every player cannot be a superstar, but when Lombardi saw something in a player that would make a contribution to the team, he found a way to bring it into play.

My father did that with me. Like Lombardi with his players, my dad sensed potential in me earlier than I did.

Lombardi was a master at inspiring teamwork. He consciously developed a sense of family among the team. He wanted the individual coaches and players to bind themselves into an amalgamated force. He thought of his team very much like a family, albeit an undemocratic one. If the players didn't share the spirit, he traded them.

After several years with the Packers, Hall of Fame center Jim Ringo showed up for an appointment with Lombardi to negotiate his contract. He brought his agent. Lombardi said, "How are you today, Jim? Who's this with you?"

"Coach, this is my agent," Ringo said. "He's here to talk for me."

"But Jim," Lombardi said, "you and I always dealt one-to-one before."

Ringo said, "I know, Coach, but now I only talk through my agent."

Lombardi said, "Fine," flat-toned and solid. He asked them to be seated, and left the room.

About twenty minutes later, Coach came back and said, "Ringo, tell your agent you've just been traded to Philadelphia."

That's the way Lombardi was. A one-on-one guy. He didn't want anyone interfering with the process. If a player didn't know his value to the team and couldn't articulate it, "Well, fine. You're outta here."

Lombardi and I see eye to eye on that. You can argue the value of an agent back and forth, but a good manager will always want to negotiate a fair deal for the player. If you go out the door feeling you didn't get a fair deal, you're not going to give your best. Coaches and managers understand win–win balance.

No one doubted Lombardi wanted the best from his players. He was known to give a player the benefit of the doubt on salary. He was realistic. He knew he wanted to be able to demand constant extra effort from his players. He didn't want salary negotiations to undermine that.

Ringo offended those sensibilities by not being willing to speak for himself and took a tour of duty with Philadelphia instead of playing out his career with the Packers. Direct and decisive was Lombardi's style.

Another aspect of Lombardi that I admired was his sense of fairness. He included how he dealt with officials in that.

He could go after officials pretty good. Every official who ever worked a Packers game must have a story to tell. As my experience with him grew, I saw that he left officials alone unless (1) they were out of position and not hustling or (2) they tried to bluff their way through a call or rule interpretation. If he saw either of these, he would come after the official pretty hard. The clue was seeing his iron jaw jutting out.

If you made a mistake, the best thing was to say, "I kicked it." If you were direct and honest, you had a chance he would shut up and walk away.

Lombardi didn't try to psych you out. He didn't try to intimidate you. He yelled when he was mad. Education was on his mind. Excellence in execution was unrelentingly his goal. As soon as he saw an official take responsibility for his own improvement, Coach exited. The situation was in hand.

He never tried to flatter you, either, as some coaches do. He just coached his game. When the game was over, it was over. His eyes were always forward.

I don't remember Lombardi ever claiming a bad call cost him the game. More than several coaches have taken this easy way out.

Lombardi would always go back to his premise about preparation and execution. He would say something like, "Well, yeah, but we had the ball first and goal and couldn't punch it across. I don't blame officials for a call when I can't get my own team to execute properly."

Lombardi demanded excellence from officials no more and no less than he did from his team. He was consistently tough, but fair. He maintained the winning attitude and went out of his way to inspire it in others. So did my dad.

12

Ode to a Teddy Bear

As a coach, John Madden was a showman, as demonstrative as he is on television. We've all seen him jumping up and down, on the sidelines, ranting and raving. That bothered some officials, but to me it was about the same as Halas stomping on his hat. Just an expression of energy; means nothing to me.

Madden knows football. He could interpret what strategies the other team had planned and tell if they were executing. He knew when the guards were about to pull, how they were getting the job done, and why. He has an uncanny sense of the game.

I've always liked Madden, then and now. More importantly, we respect each other. That stems from an incident in a preseason game I worked with him as coach of the Raiders. Early 1970s. Oakland at Los Angeles, in the Coliseum.

Something happened four or five minutes before the half that enraged Madden. I don't remember the play except that it was of little consequence. It wasn't a touchdown, for sure, but Madden was livid. You've seen the excitement he pours out. He was screaming on the sideline, yelling at me to come over there. He wanted me to just stop play and get into it with him.

Can't do it. I shook my head and went on with the game. The half ended. As I started off, he shot across the field, arms wild.

I put my hands behind my back and said, "Calm down, John, or leave the field right now."

A coach explodes for one of two reasons. He either gets pent-up because of an intense desire to win, in which case he has lost control; or he is working on the official, trying to influence a favorable call. Either way, there is no conversation there.

An official must never—and I mean NEVER—allow himself to be drawn into the low-level game of one-upmanship. He must see the "big picture." He must place poor behavior or poor judgment from players and coaches in perspective. We don't care who wins. Detachment is our rule.

In like manner, no official can be intimidated by a coach, player, or owner unless the official permits it. Intimidation is not what someone does or threatens to do; it is a showdown with your inner courage. It doesn't happen unless you give up your personal power.

When Madden came storming over to tell me a thing or two, the situation was first, "What does it look like?" As long as a coach appears out of control, I can't talk to him, and he's unable to listen to any sensible answer anyway.

Under control, any true issue can be discussed. That's part of my job—interpreting the rules in light of play sequence and explaining the consequences to any participant who doesn't understand or who may disagree.

A conversation wouldn't have been productive right then, so I said, "Calm down, John, or leave the field now."

Madden, still red with anger, continued to rant and rave. I said, "I'm not leaving the field until you get off, and if you don't get off now, you're not coming back."

I stood there, hands behind my back, until he left. He'd stop every few yards, yell a little more, walk a little more, stop, and yell a little more. He was still grumbling in the tunnel. Time would help him settle down.

When I came out to start the second half, I felt a hand grab me from behind. "Hey, wait a minute," he said. "I wasn't trying to intimidate you. I was just trying—"

I said, "John, let's understand something. If you want to talk about a play, let me know. But don't make a big scene about it. When you are visibly out of control, everybody watches to see if you are controlling me, and I won't have that."

"You got it," he said. We never had a bit of trouble after that. Mutual respect started with that confrontation. In the ton of games I refereed for the Raiders while Madden was their coach, the understanding established that day held fast.

Great rivalries in football are often built on intimidation. One that will forever stand out was the feud between the Oakland Raiders and the Pittsburgh Steelers during the 1970s.

That was as intense a rivalry as any. I'm not sure when it started. Maybe with the "Immaculate Reception" in 1972, when Steelers running back Franco Harris caught a forward pass that bounced off the shoulder of Raiders defensive back Jack Tatum and scored the winning touchdown.

I wasn't in that game, but I worked the game four years later when Raiders defensive back George Atkinson struck Steelers wide receiver Lynn Swann on the back of the head. Swann went down and was out of the game with a concussion. He missed the next two games.

The play was a simple pass pattern where Swann curled behind the umpire. We worked with a six-man crew back then. There was a blind spot in pass coverage. None of us saw the action.

The Steelers were outraged that such a blatant foul was not called. When we reviewed the films, we saw that our crew covered the play according to the current mechanics. We just weren't able to see what was going on behind the umpire.

The league had considered for some time adding a seventh official to each crew. This play may well have cemented its thinking. When the Competition Committee met in the spring, the Atkinson-Swann play was discussed. The result was the addition of a seventh official—the side judge. The Committee's proposal went to the owners, who adopted it the following season. Now, we have three officials in the deep secondary to improve pass coverage.

Oakland and Pittsburgh, along with the Miami Dolphins, were the dominant teams in the AFC in the 1970s. Every time Oakland and Pittsburgh played, there was a sense that the game would decide the AFC Super Bowl team.

Their rivalry with the Steelers escalated as the Raiders drafted some very tough players—guys like Jack Tatum and George Atkinson. At only 5 feet 9 inches and 180 pounds, Tatum had no business playing in the NFL. He survived at Ohio State by playing all-out aggressive. That was the only way he was able to play against guys so much bigger than he was.

Aggressive play was the order of the day on Sunday, and the Raiders practiced that way, too, from training camp on, every season. Their playing style fit, maybe even promoted, the Raiders' image.

On their side, the Steelers had the "Steel Curtain"—"Mean Joe" Greene, L. C. Greenwood, Dwight White, and Ernie Holmes. You needed a laser torch to get through that defense. "Mean Joe" Greene always made a difference. He not only played with intensity, but he lined up in his own style, cocked sidewise. He felt he got a better pass rush that way. Right behind the "Curtain" were Jack Ham, Jack Lambert, Andy Russell, and Mel Blount. They were tough, too.

Officiating that rivalry meant you were sitting on a powder keg. It could blow at any time. Game control started with getting the captains to be responsible for the behavior of their teams. I would tell Steelers captain Joe Greene and Raiders captain Gene Upshaw, "Keep your guys under control. If you don't, I will."

For the most part, they did.

Working with Greene and Upshaw proved to me that when the leaders are up to it, even when the competition is fierce, responsible and respected leaders can maintain direction in the midst of intensity. These two men were influential in the enduring success of those two teams. It's all a part of knowing that consistent management is a key element in effective teamwork. This is true for football teams, families, corporations, and teams of whatever kind.

The intensity of that rivalry meant the level of physical contact went up a notch. They played hard football. It wasn't illegal or mean, but strong. Because it was so rough on the bodies, some rules changes emerged.

Two major ones were implemented to protect the quarterback. The "in the grasp" rule was added to stop play before the quarterback is pounded to the ground, and they allowed offensive linemen to use their extended hands to push defensive players. The offensive line had always been there to prevent penetration; but a strong, stiff shoulder couldn't stop the "Steel Curtain." The "Curtain" moved right through.

It wasn't peaceful on the sidelines, either. Steelers coach Chuck Noll and Raiders coach John Madden were equally concerned about "dirty play." You'd hear them shouting, "Watch out for so-and-so." It started from the time we walked onto the field and didn't stop until we were back in the showers.

In the 1960s and 1970s, the unwritten rule was that if a guy took a cheap shot, he was going to get it back sometime during the game. The players had their own code of ethics that said, "Play the game hard, but play it fair."

In the Atkinson-Swann play, I don't think Atkinson had any intention of injuring Swann. It was a hard hit. Both teams hit as hard as they could, because when you came down to it, fierce effort would make the difference between winning and losing. Intimidation was a strategy of both teams.

Madden, during all that time, was always excitable and would call your attention to what was happening. He reads plays better than anyone I've ever known. He is amazing. He could see what the quarterback was doing, but he could also see the linebackers. He has a field of vision better than the best running back. This ability naturally meant more to talk about with the officials. It was just his level of emotion that made him harder to deal with.

Noll was no less intense. He was very quick to tell you, for instance, that Upshaw was holding Greenwood. Proactive coaches increase the energy and tension of the game.

I remember some contests that were so demanding, so continuously on the brink of explosion, that at the end of the game I was physically and mentally exhausted from working between two kegs of dynamite for three hours.

The Raiders-Steelers rivalry gave a big boost to the popularity of the AFC. When the AFL and the NFL merged in 1966, the AFC was regarded as the junior league. It helped when Joe Namath and the New York Jets beat the Baltimore Colts in Super Bowl III (1969), but that wasn't quite enough. A good intraconference rivalry, like Oakland and Pittsburgh, helped. It felt traditional right away, like the rivalry of the Chicago Bears and the Green Bay Packers.

Officials don't take much notice of a team's image. Each play is what counts. If the teams want to play rough-and-tumble, fine. Let 'em play. Just make sure there's nothing beyond the rules during the play and nothing at all between plays.

Sometimes when the contest is hot, I do more work between plays than during plays, dealing with tempers, complaints, and expletives and giving a few quick seconds of instant education on the rules.

The Steelers are now an AFC team, but they were an old-line NFL team until they agreed to move to the AFC after the merger, along with the Cleveland Browns and the Baltimore Colts.

That set up a power team from the AFL battling an old NFL team. Now there was a special feeling of rivalry that didn't exist when the Raiders were playing other AFL teams. It meant better gates, and better gates mean more television viewers. No avoiding it, football is competition, and rivalries are tops at that.

The Steelers were always a rugged, aggressive team, maybe because of the city they represent. A "steeler" is a guy who works in the mills, a tough guy. The Raiders represented a blue-collar town, too—Oakland. Their images were mirror-true. They were tough. The competitive zeal of those two teams made a natural match for rivalry.

Individual players have a lot to do with it. Quarterbacks Terry Bradshaw for Pittsburgh and Kenny Stabler for Oakland were very strong-minded players, both excellent leaders. Neither could be intimidated, but their reaction patterns were altogether different.

Bradshaw was the kind of guy who would take on a fight any time, any place. If he ran with the ball and got tackled and thought the tackle was a little rough, he'd get up ready to fight. Stabler, on the other hand, didn't draw fights, but he had plenty of teammates who were willing to bash an opponent for him.

Had the Raiders and Steelers of that era had different quarterbacks, maybe a Bart Starr or a Johnny Unitas, we would have had a different kind of game. Personalities intensify the game. All who watched Bradshaw and Stabler discovered that.

Take their running backs, guys like Rocky Bleier and Mark Van Eeghen. You couldn't punish Van Eeghen enough. Here's a guy from Colgate, as nice a guy as you'll ever see in pro ball, but boy, Van Eeghen would put his whole body into every play every game. He'd just keep coming back, time after time. Being in for the extra effort defines every great football player.

Bleier was no exception. Out of Notre Dame, he barely made the cut to stay on the Steelers because he was small and slow. Coach Chuck Noll liked how hard he worked, though, and gave him a chance.

The Vietnam War interrupted his career, and he came out of it with a shattered leg. It took months of rehabilitation before he could barely run. Everyone said his playing days were over. Everyone but Bleier, that is. He fought his way back, proved himself at training camp and won another chance with the Steelers. Retirement came after he and the Steelers had won Super Bowls IX, X, XIII and XIV. That's the level of extra effort opponents fear.

It's something you learn about intimidation. The threat has to be constant. If you come across as sometimes "on" and sometimes not, the fear level doesn't rise in your opponent. The gaps in the pressure allow hope and self-assertion to gain ground, and that's most what intimidation is supposed to undermine. You want the opponent to feel trapped, overpowered, maybe a little queasy from the anticipation of what he's about to face physically.

The Steelers and Raiders understood that. The Steelers wanted to rub your nose in it every time. So did the Raiders. They wanted to inspire you to quit. But neither side would quit. The backs wouldn't quit. Bleier wouldn't quit. Van Eeghen wouldn't quit. The line play became more and more intense as the game went on. The defensive rushers on both teams pressed harder. Nothing fancy. Just solid man-on-man true grit. Each player had the same thought: You're not going to get the best of me. There was no backing off on either side.

After the Atkinson-Swann play, Steelers coach Chuck Noll made the statement that there "was a criminal element in the game." I'm sure when he said it he felt justified. It wasn't hype. That was his perception at the moment. He'd just lost a game where everyone walloped anyone they could. If you look at it, you'd have to say that both teams played as if ignominy was facing the loser, but that was the only criminal element. Fair is fair, even when tough meets tough.

Atkinson sued Noll for $2,000,000 for his remark. The jury deliberated for four hours and returned a verdict of "No slander, no malice, no damages for Atkinson."

I wasn't called to testify, fortunately, but if I had been, I would have said that I didn't think Atkinson intended to injure Swann, just as I don't think Tatum intended to hurt Darryl Stingley a few years later in the Oakland–New England game. The Raiders and Steelers played with an intensity that said, "I'm gonna hit you harder than you hit me to win the game."

I don't remember Madden or Noll saying anything to me after the game, but they sure said plenty during the game and at halftime. Madden called me over to the sideline several times to talk about things. He'd look pretty agitated, but we both knew that was mostly for the fans.

One time I said to him, "You know, you're asking me a question that has nothing to do with flailing your arms about. Stop flailing so we can get this thing worked out."

Madden was cute in another way. Coaches are not permitted in the officials' locker room before the game. In the 1960s and 1970s, we would get together to synchronize our watches and to get the names of the captains. Even after that procedure ended, Madden would still come into our locker room, smiling, and say, "Just want to check watches."

He'd say hello to each official. "Hi, there, Burl. Hello, Pat. How ya doing?"

I'd tell him, "John, you're not permitted in this dressing room. You know that."

Every time he'd say, "Just came in to get the time right. Just trying to get ready."

Madden likes to make his own traditions. Nobody else did that. No one even tried it. Madden was friendly. He wasn't trying to intimidate us; he just wanted to imprint our awareness. He wanted everybody, the officials, the other team's owner, the players, the fans, the vendors, everyone, to know he was coaching the game, especially at home in the Oakland Coliseum. He loved coaching. He loves being John Madden.

Madden has this idea about how officials mark the ball. He thinks that you mark the ball with your right foot if it's a first down and with your left if it's not. Officials are consistent in the things there are rules about, but they don't care about which foot they use to mark the ball. You are too busy thinking about your responsibilities. You charge in and mark the ball with whichever foot gets to the mark first.

Over all these years, I haven't been able to convince Madden of this. I'm waiting for some sports commentator to study the tapes, chart the numbers, and prove I'm right.

I give John great credit for knowing where officials should be. He knows what they're looking for and which players they are observing. He knows when they are out of position. I don't know how you watch twenty-nine people all at once, but John seems to be able to do it. It's not so much a conscious study of the game as a special ability to feel what should be happening and seeing right away where the unusual is happening. He's as remarkable with football as Van Cliburn is with the piano.

Madden knows the rules, too. I've had the opportunity to give many rules talks to the Raiders over the years. The league office assigns officials to give rules talks to teams during training camp.

Madden didn't like to take time out of his "more important business" to have me in for the rules talk. He figured he could do that himself. He was always very pleasant, though, and would introduce me in a respectful way. It wasn't a matter of "Oh, well, we've got to get this lousy rules talk out of the way."

Madden would introduce me to the team by saying, "Tunney is a respected official in the NFL. He's here to explain the rules so we can be a better football team. I want you to give him your full attention."

But we'd always have to negotiate. He would invite me to dinner with the coaches before the talk. "Is half an hour enough?" he would ask.

I'd say, "No, John. I need an hour. I have prepared an outline, and I know I need that time."

"Thirty-five minutes," he'd say.

"No, John. I need the hour."

Every year we'd go through the ritual. Madden likes his traditions.

The rules talks were an experience. You couldn't miss the hugeness of the renegades, tough guys like John Matuszak, Lyle Alzado, Ted Hendricks, Matt Millen. Rules? What did they care about rules? They were just waiting for the season to start. Their minds were on the first Sunday.

All the defensive linemen would sit in the back of the room. The running backs, the intellects, guys like Willie Brown, Gene Upshaw, the quarterbacks, the ones who wanted to know the rules inside and out, would be up front.

I never stand behind a lectern during rules talks. I wander around the room. I knew the guys up front would be listening, so I'd spend some time in the back of the room with the renegades.

On the field you expect to see and feel their intensity. They look like they want to destroy somebody. Walking among them at the talks, guys too big for their chairs and already in game face, I understood in another way why they were "Raiders."

Madden never stayed in the room. He'd be in the hallway, just outside the door. One time I made a statement, and boom, he was in the room.

"Hey, wait a minute. That's not right," he said, animated and serious.

He'd caught me. I had misspoken and was embarrassed, but at the same time impressed again with Madden's knowledge of the rules. He knows football inside and out, and while his appearance suggests a lackadaisical manner, he was never loose about the game.

I learned from him because, after the rules talks, I'd stay over for the night and join John to watch some films. He loved to point out things. He'd say, "Hey, look at this play . . . look at this foul . . ."

He wasn't trying to intimidate me. He just wanted me to understand his thinking on what the officials should be calling.

Officials always like a coach who knows the rules. At preseason rules talks some coaches have asked me to diagram the officials' position on each play, discussing the responsibilities of each official. They're not trying to get away with anything. They're just trying to make their players aware of what they need to do. Madden was that kind.

He was always a players' coach. Players respected him. He knew what grunting and groaning was all about. At practice, he wasn't up in the ivory tower. He was right out there on the field going "bam," "bash," "wham!"

Officials are required to arrive at the stadium two hours before game time. Invariably, when officials get to the stadium, they'll put their gear in their locker room and go out to walk the field. I don't know why. The field is invariably 100 yards long, but we like to get a sense of things early.

Usually the stadium is empty, but never at a Raiders game. Madden would always be there, watching. He'd watch, not saying anything for a long time. Then, maybe, he'd see Burl Toler, our head linesman, whom he'd known from San Francisco years ago, and he'd yell, "Hey, Burl, how are ya?"

That's the way John is. He LOVES football, all its aspects. He likes the stadiums, the smells, the colors, the ambience. He doesn't know what "ambience" means, but he loves it, anyway. He understands that it takes all the people it does in their various positions to make it work, and if that's a little complicated sometimes, it's okay by him. He can handle it, and always with a mixture of good humor and seriousness. That I like.

I told him when he quit coaching, "You'll be back, because you can't be away from football."

It looks as if he won't return to coaching, but he hasn't left the game.

I remember a Los Angeles Rams–Chicago Bears championship

game I worked in Chicago in January 1986. The officials arrived at Soldier Field earlier than usual because we were worried about ice on the field. Madden was already there.

He was walking around, shoes untied, talking to the players, the stadium staff, anyone who was around.

His love of people is one reason he loves the train. (Fear of flying is the main one.) He could talk to people constantly when he traveled on the train. And dress any way he wanted to.

In 1987, Greyhound outfitted him with the "Madden Cruiser" to get to the games. He'll get to the league city on Wednesday or Thursday and start visiting with the coaches and players. Some coaches and players are afraid they're giving away secrets when they talk to sportscasters, but no one feels that way with Madden. They feel as if they're talking to a friend. He has that puppy-dog, teddy-bear image. You can tell him anything and he'll never use it against you.

These days, the thing I like most about John Madden is that he hasn't let success go to his—clothes!

13

Fans Want to Know

There's an old saying among trial lawyers: Don't ask the question unless you know the answer. I remember that when fans ask me questions about players or clubs. Many already have their own answers.

No one can help but be amazed at how strongly people can become attached to a team or players. There's a real live charge when you come out onto the field and 60,000 or 70,000 people are in full roar, ready for the game. Because fans make for better football, I love the fans.

Which brings us to the most requested question I'm asked: Do you have a favorite team? No.

Officials don't have favorite teams or players. Some root for teams in other sports, but we couldn't work in the NFL if we cared about the outcome of any game.

Fans don't understand this because they care so much. But when I walk onto the field, I'm concentrating on the responsibilities I have for controlling the game and making certain that it's played fairly. Fans don't think that way. They want their team to win, and when it comes to a decision, they want it to go their way.

Remember that Webster says a "fan" is short for "fanatic,"

someone with "extreme and uncritical enthusiasm or zeal, as in religion, politics, etc." When Webster wrote that, he didn't realize that pro football would replace religion and politics on Sunday in some cities, but that only proves how right he was.

People really do become fanatical. Which is fine. It's good for the game. But I'm not a fan of any team in the NFL or in any sport. I wasn't a fan before I joined the NFL, probably because my attitude was formed through my dad's eyes. I've always looked at sport from the viewpoint of an official.

Players? I'm impressed with great talent, but more importantly, with players who do something outside the game. Your work should be only one aspect of your life. This applies to players with big contracts, too. If all a player has is pro football, he doesn't have much. Family and a wide range of interests ought to be as important as the gridiron.

Because officials have no interest in a particular team, it makes no difference which games they work. Denver, as an example, has about as rabid a group of fans as there is in the league, but an official who lives in Denver doesn't get caught up in that. A game in Denver is no different from a game in Dallas or Miami.

Some officials have played in the NFL, but once they become officials, they lose their allegiance, or they don't make it. Pat Harder, for instance, played for the Detroit Lions, but when he officiated a Lions game, he considered them just another team. Lou Palazzi, a former Giant, and Joe Muha, a former Eagle, considered those teams just one of the twenty-eight, no more, no less.

Some officials are collectors. Johnny Grier, a field judge in Super Bowl XXII, came into the league seven years ago on our crew. From day one, he bought a souvenir of the home team for every game we worked. His collection is phenomenal by now, but that doesn't make him a fan.

I don't collect souvenirs per se. I do have some autographed game balls. The photographs add up. Working three Super Bowls gives you three desk sets. As a good dad should, I brought home a "Terrible Towel" from a Steelers game and some wrist-bands from some players that my kids enjoyed having. But none of this adds up to a "collection."

If I have a collection, it is the game programs I save. I have one from virtually every game I've worked in the NFL. It's just a habit. I take my official's game card, on which I write down the fouls called during the game, and put it in the program. It's more of a chronology than it is a collection.

Another frequently asked question is, who do I think the best quarterback or the best running back or the best this or that is in the league?

I turn those questions around and ask, "Who do you think is the best?" That gets me off the spot, for the moment, because people always have their own favorites, and they love to talk about them. They'll mention John Elway, Dan Marino, Joe Montana, Jim Kelly. I'll ask them, "What do you like about them?" and they'll talk about that for a while.

Then I'll ask, "What do you think of Doug Williams, Phil Simms, Warren Moon, or others?" That gets them to talking some more. By this time, they've forgotten they've ever asked me a question.

I do that because it's not my place to give my opinion on players. If I said, for instance, that I thought Jim McMahon was the best quarterback, the next time I worked a Chicago Bears game, there would be somebody who would accuse me of favoritism. I can't have that. I make no personal judgment on a player's ability.

There's another point, too: An official isn't looking at the game in the same way that a fan does. The official has a job to do. There are times when you're tempted to be a spectator because these players are the best in the world at what they do and that's fun to watch.

I remember one time I was so involved watching Bears halfback Gale Sayers sidestep and hurdle his way up the field that for a moment I forgot my job was watching the quarterback. That happens to you once, and you quickly learn what your job is.

When I look at players, I'm looking for different things than a fan does. Quarterbacks are a good example, because as a referee, I am directly behind them during the play. I see their abilities to throw and scramble, but the skills I admire the most have to do with leadership and poise under pressure.

To be a starting quarterback in the NFL, you have to be the cream of the cream. There are only twenty-eight of them, and sometimes the best college quarterbacks don't make it. Some Heisman Trophy winners didn't find tenure in the NFL: Terry Baker, John Huarte, and Pat Sullivan. Paul Hornung made it, but not as a quarterback.

The quarterback is asked to do everything, from being the team CEO to delivering the mail. He must hand off properly, carry out fakes, pass the ball accurately, call the plays, read defenses, and motivate, motivate, motivate.

In the old days, before computers, quarterbacks called all the plays. We referred to them as "field generals." That term is archaic now. Coaches and software call the plays. Quarterbacks still have to read defenses and be flexible enough to change the play if it's the wrong play for that defense. But being a field general implies more than that. A field general has to be in command, in control of his players and the entire game.

The huddle is not a democratic process. The quarterback doesn't say, "What shall we do now?" As I've learned in studying corporate management, the idea of sharing information and airing ideas in a teamwork situation is a great philosophical concept, but when it comes right down to it, one person makes the decision. That's why CEOs and quarterbacks get million-dollar salaries.

A wide receiver might come back to the huddle and tell the quarterback what play he thinks will work. A guard might say he can block his man to the inside better than the outside. The good quarterback listens because it makes sense to utilize the strengths of his teammates.

He listens for another important reason. The quarterback, as well as the CEO, will get better cooperation, enthusiasm, and team effort if the members of the team believe "the boss" is listening.

My doctoral study at USC and my observation of successfully managed organizations has proved to me that if a decision affects a person's job, that person has a right to contribute his opinion toward that decision. It doesn't mean that he makes the decision or that the decision reached includes his perspective. But it does mean that every person affected by a decision feels as if he is a participant in the decision-making process.

The execution is always with the quarterback, so when you get right down to it, that's where the decision is. He has to consider all the information he has, apply the knowledge to the game, and, most importantly, win. "Just win, baby," as the Raiders' management demands.

Football is not golf, where an individual can be judged strictly on what he alone does. It is a team sport. A quarterback needs someone to catch the ball, to block for him, and do the rest. Some years a quarterback has his "Three Amigos." Some years he has "Three Stooges." Some quarterbacks have good offensive lines; some don't. Some have a defense that can get them the ball; some don't.

I'll say it again: Any quarterback good enough to start in the NFL is a superior athlete. Even the backup quarterbacks are outstanding. Don Strock at Miami. Earl Morrall, who stepped in when Bob Griese was hurt in 1972 and took the Miami Dolphins to a perfect 17–0 season. Or Zeke Bratkowski, who filled in for Bart Starr in the heyday of the Packers.

To get to the pros, a quarterback has proved he is in the top 1 percent of the competitors. They're all good. So to say that one quarterback is the best, well, that's a tougher call than any I make on the field.

It's not my place to pick an all-time quarterback or even the best since I've been in the league, but I can tell you about some quarterbacks I've admired.

One was Tarkenton, Francis Asbury Tarkenton, to call him by his full name. You would have thought Tarkenton was too small to play in the NFL. He looked as if he were destined to be a lawyer or a doctor, or the motivational speaker he is today.

But his coach, Norm Van Brocklin, knew that, pound for pound, Tarkenton was as good as they come. There wasn't anything classic in his style, but he got the job done.

He'd wait until the last moment to throw to let his receiver get open. It meant he got knocked down a lot, but he connected on a record 3,686 passes. When he wasn't able to throw, he could run. He holds the record for the most yards gained in a career—47,003.

Some people criticized him because the Vikings never won the Super Bowl. How can you blame Tarkenton alone? Football is a team sport.

Another guy I like is John Brodie. For a long time, I thought Brodie was hard of hearing. He had all these great skills, but I thought the poor fellow was partially deaf.

In any game, before the start of a play, my job as a referee includes letting the quarterback know the down and distance. When I do this, the quarterback is standing at the rear of the huddle, looking over the opponent's defense.

I'd give Brodie the down and distance, and he'd always say, "What?"

So I'd repeat it louder the second time, and he'd nod.

After he retired, Brodie worked as an analyst for NBC Sports. We were seatmates on a plane one day going to a game, and after talking to him for a while, I finally said to him, "You're not deaf at all." I explained why I'd thought he was.

Brodie laughed. "I was concentrating on calling the next play and blocked out everything that wasn't important. You weren't important to me," he said.

Thanks a lot, John, but I could understand.

Brodie, like any top performer, CEO, manager, or anyone who cares about maximizing his efforts, has learned to focus. Concentration is a matter of refusing all other options, of holding tight rein on your priorities. Partly this requires preparation, the skill necessary to the job, but mostly concentration requires self-control. Brodie understood that. All top perfomers do.

Charlie Conerly and Y. A. Tittle were going strong when I came into the league. They were old-style quarterbacks: They just stood in the pocket and threw the ball. I wonder how they would do against the great pass rush today's teams have developed.

Johnny Unitas was in his prime with the Baltimore Colts, Bart Starr was beginning his best years with the Packers, and Roger Staubach came along to take the Cowboys to the Super Bowl. These three earned my respect because of their leadership. Here again you have examples of men who by the command of themselves had control of the elements. In the clinches, they didn't become flustered or lose their self-confidence. They could maintain focus, and their control inspired their teammates to pull together even stronger.

These three leaders personified the adage that when the going gets tough, the tough get going. It's a cliché only because it's true.

There have been some great quarterbacks who didn't win everything. A classic guy whose team didn't win a lot of games is Tom Flores. He was cool, had a thorough knowledge of the game, but more importantly, he had a great work ethic. The one thing he lacked as a quarterback was good luck: The Raiders traded him to Buffalo the year before they won their first championship.

The Raiders went from Flores to Daryle Lamonica to Ken Stabler, who finally got them a Super Bowl win. I really enjoyed

Stabler. He had the nerve and attitude of a riverboat gambler. No question. He could have been dealing blackjack on the *Delta Queen*. That's the way he played football.

He enjoyed the game. He wanted to win, but if he lost, well, that's the way the cards turned over that day. There was always the next game.

Stabler was a strong leader, the kind of field general I described earlier, and he always called his own plays. He earned the confidence of his players, just as Unitas, Starr, Tarkenton, Brodie, and Staubach did. An aura surrounded these guys. Their teammates knew they would find a way to win.

I admired Van Brocklin as a quarterback in 1960, mostly because I was amazed he could be as successful as he was given his rough edges. He was arrogant and "managed" his teammates by browbeating them. Van Brocklin played no favorites; he was tough on everyone. People have said that if his grandmother missed a block, he would have chewed her out, too.

Another quarterback I admired was Bill Nelsen. I didn't have the chance to see Unitas or Starr when they were young, but I officiated games when Nelsen was still in high school. He was All-State in high school, All-Conference at USC, then quarterback for Cleveland.

Watching an athlete grow through the ranks, from high school all the way to the NFL starting lineup, is a rare opportunity, even for career coaches. It was fun to see Nelsen mature and gain ground. He won't be found in the record books, but some of the best human dramas don't get written down there.

People ask me why I always mention the stadium, as if where is as important as who and what happened. The answer is that where matters. Home field advantage is nothing to disregard. Team morale and fan morale flow back and forth between each other. There's that.

But it's more than that. Football is a turf sport, grounded. It's contact, weaving between obstacles, sweat and directness. Officials, coaches, and players see it through its specifics, the play-by-play, the strategy and tactics.

These are individual units. The units mean one thing alone and something else when they all flow together. Each play decides one thing. All of them together decide something else.

Decisions are relative, in football as in life. Team characteristics, strategy, grass or artificial turf, position of the sun, a thousand things. Sonny Jurgensen threw a bomb differently at RFK Stadium than he did at Wrigley Field. Both outdoors, but situated differently in terms of wind, noise, and vision.

All these variables add up to a factor someone once nicknamed "air thickness." I wish I could remember who explained it to me: "The air is thicker on some days than on others. Kickers and passers know that. Fans probably do, too, since they're part of it. Maybe it's that the churning air from hot and noisy fans adds density. Intensity adds density."

Sounds OK to me. Don't ask me how it happens. I can only tell you that it does. I've never been able to define what creates magic, but when it happens, you know it. When it happens in a stadium and tens of thousands of fans know it at the same time, the air becomes electric.

I am not surprised that fans bother to come to the stadium, passing up the ease of their living room or a big screen television somewhere. Television may have instant replay and chalkboard diagrams, a refrigerator nearby and a cushy seat, but the real thing is better.

Energy flows between fans and teams in a loop. Place works its presence into it. Where becomes as real as who.

The most frequent question during the 1987 season was, would I referee a strike game? My answer was "Of course."

As officials, our contracts gave us no option. Even if there had been an option, I would have worked. Not having favorite teams, any two teams will do to make a football game. When a team puts eleven players on the field, I don't question whether these are their best players. That's not my job. I'm not their coach. If the league says, "Play ball," I work.

There were a lot of questions about the strike and whether the league should have sanctioned the replacement games. In a general sense, I always have reservations about strikes. I equate it with the playground. Anytime one player gets mad and takes his ball home, the game is over.

People often ask if officials are prejudiced, if they try to get even with coaches who have blasted them for a call. Not likely. Not only do officials have to be bigger in spirit than that; it's virtually impossible to do. Trying to get even is like trying to even up your sideburns; you never get them exactly right.

Officials accept the challenge to be fair. They have had years of experience proving they can do it before being selected by the NFL. Officials don't make the cut or survive if they are the type who hold grudges or take verbal abuse personally.

Fans often ask if a coach with influence or a particularly strong opinion about an official can prevent that official from being assigned to work his games. The answer is no.

Coaches fill out evaluations at the end of each game. These are reviewed by the supervisors, but coaches do not have a say in the assignments.

People ask, "Do you look at the betting line?"

I respond, "Do people bet on football games?" Of course, I know they do, but my point is that I don't pay any attention to the partisan fringes. As for paying attention to "picks of the week" and the pregame predictions, if sportswriters had to make their living by being right, we'd have a new level of unemployment.

On this issue of impartiality I can't emphasize too strongly that officials look at each team or individual players the same way. It doesn't matter whether the player is a star or a rookie. When an official calls a foul, it's based on the action, not who did it. As parents, we shouldn't punish the child. We punish the behavior. It's the same in officiating. I never say to a player, "Aha, I caught you."

A player commits a foul for one reason: He's trying to help his team win. Rarely is a foul premeditated. If an offensive lineman is trying to block his man and doesn't, he may reach out and illegally grab him. That's a foul, and it has to be called, but he was only trying to do his job.

In a preseason game with the Rams at the Los Angeles Coliseum, Tom Mack, an All-Pro guard, was called for holding. Mack was furious.

He said, "What the hell was that for?" The umpire told him he'd held a defensive lineman.

Mack turned to me and said, "Jim. I don't need to do that. I've been in this league for twelve years. I don't have to hold. I know how to block a guy. I can block anybody."

I didn't see the play, so I don't know if Mack grabbed his man or not, but later in that game, the defensive lineman did a loop and shot right by him, heading for quarterback Roman Gabriel. The defensive tackle would have knocked Gabriel into the cheap seats, but Mack reached out and grabbed him by the foot. I threw the flag and I said, "Well, Tom, how about that one?"

Mack smiled and said, "Well, Jim, sometimes you have to protect your quarterback."

Players don't walk on the field thinking about what they can get away with. Officials don't walk on the field thinking, I wonder who I can call a foul on today? Players do commit fouls, and officials have to call them. Nothing personal; it's all in the name of fairness.

As an official, you love games like the 1988 AFC championship game between Cleveland and Denver. There wasn't a disputed call in the whole game. Not a single line written afterward that questioned a call. That's rare. You come away from some games with an uneasy feeling that a coach or his players might think you had it in for them. If that happens, I like to be assigned their next game to demonstrate that I officiate games, not people.

Because we are often right in the path of one or several of those 300-pounders, people ask me if I'm not concerned about getting injured. The risk of injury is obviously there, but I don't think about that. If I did I couldn't do the job. My job is to focus on one thing and one thing only—the next play. You just watch closely, with a clear mind.

In this we're like players, who also have to be single-minded. In no-repeat situations, distractions diminish performance. Pro football is great for teaching you how to switch quickly into deep concentration.

People ask me all the time to make predictions: "Who's going to win the game Sunday?" They not only want to know who's going to win; they want to know the score.

My answer always is "If I knew who was going to win, we wouldn't need to play the game." The excitement comes with the unpredictability. There's no plot once you know who won.

The truth, though, is that I not only don't know; I don't care who wins, only that it is played fairly.

A perennial issue is the question of whether the league should go to full-time officials. My answer is "Why?"

The only reason to suggest that officials be full-time is on the assumption that performance will improve if they were. I am not convinced that having 107 officials "standing by" full-time in the off-season and 5 days a week during the season will improve performance.

Performance is influenced by knowledge and practice. This is true for players, officials, or any job. It is true on the field, on the assembly line, behind a teller cage, or in any job where specialized information is needed and practicing specific techniques makes you better.

I can support any policy which improves performance. For

this reason I emphasize rules study and game review at our crew meetings and during the off-season. My program accepts that officials must stay prepared throughout the year in order to be ready at the start of the season.

The league doesn't have to pay us to do this, though. The stiff competition to get into and stay in the NFL assures a steady supply of qualified and motivated officials who are willing to study on their own twelve months a year for a twenty-week season. Competition to be in the NFL keeps the motivation strong. This takes care of the knowledge aspect as a factor which affects performance.

The other is the issue of practice to improve skills. The teams play only one game a week during the season. Officials can't officiate without an actual game.

Some have suggested that officials could increase their skills by going to the training sites and officiating the practice sessions. The problem with this suggestion is that NFL teams don't scrimmage during the week. Team practices are restricted to fitness, weight training, and mock blocking and tackling drills. Even if a scrimmage is included, it is against their own players. There's no real hitting, no scoreboard, no intensity, no true game conditions.

At practice sessions, an official would either be an observer or an instructor on fouls and formations. His role would be confined by the practicalities to that of a less formal but longer walk-around kind of rules talk. There would be no judgment calls, no fan energy cross-over, no issue of game control, no pressure, no live action.

Coaches and players know that it takes actual game conditions to separate the merely skilled from the masters. Some players look great Monday through Friday. They're fast, they weave, they endure. But come Sunday, they don't hold up to the pressure. Every coach has had players whom he agonized over, guys who are great practice ballplayers, but, when it counts, don't come through.

It is the same with officials. For the league to know that officials can handle game situations, we need to work under actual game conditions. A good performance in a practice session doesn't ensure adequate performance under the pressure of game conditions. The rule holds: Practice doesn't make perfect unless it is *perfect practice*.

Money is another issue. While I don't know the exact figure, it's reasonable to guess that the average income of an NFL official from his "regular job" approaches six figures. We come from a wide variety of vocations. Currently we have a bank president, several lawyers, doctors, a number of vice presidents of major corporations, several insurance agents and branch managers, many who own their own companies, quite a few teachers from high schools and colleges, and even a full-time professional speaker. Would the league offer contracts which replaced existing salaries?

Major league baseball umpires and NBA officials work full-time because baseball and basketball have more games. These officials work four to six games a week during the season and both sports have longer seasons than football. The cost of full-time officials is spread over more games worked per man. Baseball needs four umpires; basketball uses two; the NFL requires seven officials. At whatever the assumed cost, 107 full-time NFL officials is pretty high arithmetic.

Another regular question is, do I get tired of the traveling? No, I love my work.

Every Saturday morning during the football season I board an airplane to go to a league city. After twenty-eight years, this is the same sweet change of pace I thought it was when I was in the school business. I love going off to do what others think of as glamorous and exciting. Besides, I love football.

As a professional speaker, I am on the road 200 days a year, anyway. It's a tough job. Sure it is. I've had to make presentations in Maui, in San Juan, in Acapulco, in Athens. Toledo, too.

* * *

One of the least-known aspects of pregame preparation for officials, coaches, and players is religion. Not many people realize how devoted the majority of those in the NFL are. Some travel with their own priests, who say mass for the Catholic players.

For years, the Giants had Father Donnelly travel with the team, and during the game the father would yell with the best of them if he didn't like one of your calls. I remember saying, "Calm down, Father. It's only football."

When a special team mass is held for players on Sunday morning, officials are often invited. Nothing wrong with that; it's a very open thing. All the years I've been in the league, no one has accused me of favoritism because we prayed together.

Another perennial question is "Do the players talk to players on the other team during the game?"

Many do, because they know each other from college or playing on the same NFL team previously. Often the conversation, if you want to give it that much dignity, is a not very subtle attempt at intimidation. We ignore all the finger pointing and razzmatazz. What counts is the play itself, not "So's your old man" or loudmouthed bullying.

When I played high school and college ball, I was told not to talk to the opponents because it would break my concentration. Players who talk across team lines are trying to distract their opponents. It usually costs them, too, and they wind up being less effective. A lot of coaches forbid cross-talk for exactly that reason.

As an official, I try to shut it off. If they just throw out a few lines, fine, but if they keep it going, I step in and stop it.

Yes, I talk to the players. It's an important part of the job for an official to be sensitive to the players. If a player tells me, "Hey, this guy is really holding me," it's better that I know that, because if I'm not responsive, that player may then do something to get my attention, retaliating or committing a foul. So I'll say, "I'll take a look at it."

The minute a player knows you'll listen to him, you establish a sense of fairness. One caution, though: You can't let a player control you. The same with coaches. If a coach discovers he can intimidate an official, he'll do it. There's a big difference between listening and capitulating.

If you miss a call, you can't dream up another to even it out. The league calls these "phantom fouls." For there to be a name for them means someone sometime didn't meet the challenge of impartiality, but with the number of angles being taped today, the foul had better be there.

While the league would get rid of an official who could be intimidated, it also wants cooperation between officials and coaches. If a coach needs to talk to an official during a time-out, the referee should grant the request.

I feel that directly and immediately addressing coaches' questions is a chief aspect of controlling the game. Coaches aren't always satisfied with the answers; they are partisan and only want their way.

Knowing the fine line between intimidation and cooperation is what I get paid for. To know the difference and keep the integrity of the game as the focus is the single most demanding aspect of administering fairness.

Next question?

14

What's So Tough about Being a Hero?

A lot of businessmen tell me they jump right to the sports pages, skipping the headline stories and even the business news, hurrying to get to the fun stuff. I've long been fascinated by the universal appeal of sports—to men, women, young, old, rich, poor, America, everywhere—but also the healthy way sports gives people a vicarious release from everyday frustrations.

The universal popularity stems from the reliability of sports to show in action the attributes people wish they had more of: the courage of confrontation (call it *guts*), the ability to summon extraordinary effort toward a goal (call it *drive*), and a passionate respect for the rules, (call it *honor*). Sports is guts, drive, and honor in action.

Fans like that. They watch and respond, get excited, feel satisfied and pumped with small doses of self-generated inspiration every time they witness a feat or finesse that gains their respect. They see in each lesson how they should confront their foes, summon their strength, and remember their honor.

A fan who understands the rules well enough to judge the relative tightness of the situation develops a natural empathy. By being able to judge the difficulty of a situation, the fans vicariously experience the achievement or disappointment of the players. That's the fun of sports: feeling involved. Caring.

Sports is inspiring dramas of excellence and pure effort. Winning is followed by a celebration of the victory, but a dark side has appeared in recent years. The sports section now routinely reports players being arrested or rehab'd for alcohol, cocaine, and other kinds of abuses. We read about bar fights, drunk driving, paternity suits, rape, and general bad behavior.

Athletes, the pros and the amateurs alike, have been fighting in bars for years, sort of a prerequisite, some say, to the battles at game time. I've set a different standard for myself. It hasn't particularly bothered me that others make different choices and let their physicality explode. When it gets to drugs, though, it does bother me. People should never give up control of their minds and bodies.

Perhaps partly because I've never smoked or drank, I have a hard time being sympathetic to someone saying he *needs* that kind of release. It's almost sacrilegious for a person of Irish descent to say he doesn't drink. My grandfather once said, "Show me a man who doesn't drink and I'll show you a man who would kick a dog." I guess I've proved my granddad wrong.

So I have a hard time with people who say they need drugs. How can a wide receiver, say, who uses his God-given talents to outdistance a defensive back and catch a touchdown pass to hear 77,000 fans get on their feet and applaud him, then go out and use drugs or alcohol to "take off the pressure." What happened to celebration of self and well-earned self-esteem? What's so tough about being a hero?

Somebody said that the trouble with living on a pedestal is that there's no room to move around. There's something to that; I don't know anyone who would prefer to live in a fishbowl, but I also don't know anyone who was drafted into the NFL who didn't want to become a hero, have his name in the paper, be given awards, and be paid lots of money and attention.

The game is full of stars, certainly. Quite a few stars are actual heroes.

I was assigned to referee a 1979 preseason game at Candlestick, Denver Broncos versus the San Francisco 49ers. The 49ers had acquired O.J. Simpson the year before from the Buffalo Bills.

About an hour and a half prior to the game, 49ers general manager John Ralston came into our dressing room and asked me if O.J. could use the phone because the one in the 49ers' dressing room was out of order. He said O.J. needed to call the UCLA Medical Center.

We couldn't help but overhear the conversation. As O.J. talked to the doctor, he learned that his 22-month-old daughter had fallen into a swimming pool, had been rescued, but was comatose.

O.J. changed to street clothes and flew to Los Angeles. A few days later, his daughter died. Devastating. Tragic. Rips your soul out.

Did O.J. quit? He could have. In April he had announced that 1979 would be his last season of pro football. His teammates would have understood. But quit due to tragedy? No, sir.

O.J. resumed his place on the team. He could not make those "jukes and jives" which were to earn him a place in the Hall of Fame; his knees were gone. But he made a great contribution. He kept the right attitude. He asked, "What can I do with my experience, with my expertise, to help someone on my team be better?"

When life has struck you a blow, the best thing to do is to reach out and help someone else. This will do two things for you. You'll be helping someone. More importantly, you'll be raising your level of self-esteem.

O.J. felt the toll of tragedy and chose a constructive, positive attitude. He chose not to let the emotional aftermath control his sense of self or diminish his sense of purpose. He didn't allow the pressure to swamp him.

I hear some say the pressure is too much, that they "have to" get some release. Others, and I believe them to be the majority, work hard, become heroes, and bear the pressure and fishbowl life with dignity and honor, and often with humor, too. They're my kind of heroes.

Everyone has the ability and the responsibility to choose his attitude. I call it mental management. Abe Lincoln said a person is about as happy as he makes up his mind to be. He drew a workable conclusion on that one.

Drugs never create happiness. Exactly the opposite. They eventually destroy your self-confidence by controlling you. In this way, athletes face the same problems as their peers. Athletes don't live in a vacuum. They're part of society, and a big reason for the current level of drug use is that drugs have been used extensively on college campuses for the last two decades.

Drug problems are in society at large, so there's no way to keep them out of sports any more than you can keep them out of the YMCA. There is an element of history repeating itself. In the 1930s and 1940s, sports faced big problems with alcohol. We looked back on it on the 1950s, amazed it had gotten so bad before it got better. Maybe by the year 2000 we'll look back at the 1980s and be astounded at what athletes and people in general did to their bodies. It would be prudent to allow history to inform us.

Doctors tell me that many kids who use recreational drugs, which includes "crack" and cocaine, two nasty ones, have the idea that they are invincible. They've heard the warnings that drugs can trap, even kill, but somehow they exempt themselves.

"Not me," they say. "Only the other guy."

I find athletes who use drugs routinely spout this line, claiming that because they're in great physical shape their bodies can take it. I tell 'em to call Len Bias and ask him, and if he's not home, call Don Rogers.

While we're on the topic of drugs, let's discuss steroids, which some athletes take to build muscle. Anyone using steroids knows he is walking a tight line. Steroids build muscle, but they may be physically harmful. Why do they take that chance? Reckless hope.

If we had longitudinal studies from 50- or 60-year-old ex-athletes who had taken steroids for years, players today could make an informed decision. All we know is that doctors say there is likely to be a high price paid in years to come for taking steroids now for a four- or five-year increase in playing size and salary. Some guys say they're willing to take the risk on the idea that four or five years of big money will get them set for life. I call that mental-midget thinking, and silly to boot.

Athletes are far more knowledgeable about nutrition and life-style habits than they used to be. They know their wheats and brans and grains with the best of them. They eat more red meat and ice cream than Dr. Ken Cooper would condone, but we all enjoy ourselves from time to time. Moderation, please. The secret is control, and most athletes do a great job of staying in control of their eating habits and training programs all year long.

When I first started in the league, you'd see smoking in the locker room before a game. You don't see that anymore. Smoking is nearly at zero.

Use of candy bars for quick energy is almost zip now, too. Athletes learned that sugar gives you a false sense of energy. About the third quarter it's gone, and like momentum, it's hard to get back. They've learned carbo-loading works better.

Weight control is an important issue with athletes. Ask "The Fridge." After retirement, a player's weight often becomes a health issue. Ask Merlin Olsen, who dropped from his playing weight of 265–270 pounds to his analyst weight of 230.

There's a higher level of health consciousness among the ath-letes. They know that it's important how they start their day, what they put into their bodies, and how they train. They take much better care of themselves in the off-season than most did years ago. The emphasis on year-round training has meant a steady increase in individual and team performance.

A bigger reason for improved stats is what we've learned about psychological training. Positive mental attitude, a concept in self-management, has been around a long time, but in recent years, study after study has proved its validity. Abe Lincoln was right, and so were all our grandmothers, who said, "Don't worry yourself sick. Cheer up."

The simple truth behind that maxim is learning to accept responsibility for your own thinking. Viktor Frankl, an Austrian psychiatrist who survived six years in a Nazi concentration camp, said in *Man's Search for Meaning* that the one thing no one can ever take away from you is the freedom you have to choose the attitude with which you approach any task, problem, or opportunity. No one controls your attitude but you.

So when I hear people say, "This is the way I am and I can't change," I know it's not true. People are the way they choose to be. No one controls you unless you give them permission to do so. It's your choice, just as with intimidation.

On the football field, players may appear in control, but many incidents have occurred where their behavior becomes childish. Football is intense, and intensity usually creates high emotion from coaches, teams, families, and fans. Sometimes it's ridiculous.

I've broken up plenty of fights between players by stepping in and saying, "Knock it off." If I've heard it once, I've heard it a thousand times: "He hit me first." That kind of dodge makes me feel as if I'm back teaching school. This is a minor level of the same kind of attitude that leads some to drugs. They refuse to take responsibility for their actions.

Part of the problem with accepting responsibility for your choices is this question of control. If the idea is to make yourself and your life what you want them to be, setting a goal becomes the first priority. If you choose, like Lincoln, to be happy, you will find plenty to enjoy in the process, and that's where we find the meaning in our lives, not in the outcome.

Take football. Seemingly, only the quarterback and the wide receiver have fun practicing football; they get to pass and run. Everyone else is grunting, hitting, and being hit, which can be drudgery. Unless players get satisfaction out of the process, they won't improve.

Hall of Fame center for the Oakland Raiders Jim Otto told me, "I like what I do. I like to fire out at the snap, to open holes for the backs. They couldn't get through without me."

That's the way it has to be. If you choose a positive attitude, understand the contribution you make, and have respect for the process, you are less likely to choose drugs.

There's a story I like about a kid building a sand castle on the beach. As he was building it, a wave would come in and knock the castle down. The kid would laugh and build it again. This happened over and over.

That kid had a great attitude: He was enjoying what he was doing; he liked the process of building better than the need to be done with it. He didn't mind that the waves kept wiping out his castle. It wasn't important that he finish building the castle. His fun was in the process.

The Russians have understood the importance of psychological conquest for a long time. For years they have included a sports psychologist as a standard component of the coaching staff.

You hear about Russian gymnasts training eight hours a day. Nobody works out on the parallel bars for eight hours. They practice for a few hours, then work with their psychologist on visualization and mental imagery, which is as serious a part of their workout as the physical training.

In the old days, coaches tried to be everything to their athletes. They took on the role of parent sometimes, best friend another; even bankers. They'd loan the players $50 when they needed it. Now players loan money to their coaches.

The coach-player relationship is much more stratified now, giving us another good reason to add sports psychologists to team organizations. We have improved our understanding of the technical aspects of physical training, but we're not giving players the help they need psychologically in either learning to deal with the pressures of competition or in the mind's power to improve performance. We pay a price for this neglect in both the quality of their lives and in the stats.

For some, success is harder to handle than failure. There's always somebody around to help a player out of his doldrums, but when a player is successful, everyone keeps pumping him up, and no one remembers to notice whether he's handling it okay.

I remember visiting with John Madden the summer after Super Bowl XI. I was at the Oakland Raiders' training camp in Santa Rosa. Madden and I had dinner, and I asked him, "What motivates you, John?"

"Fear," he said.

"What are you afraid of?" I asked, surprised. "You just won the Super Bowl. You are the most successful NFL coach of the decade. You weigh 260 pounds. What can you possibly be afraid of?"

"I'm afraid to fail." Then he thought a little longer and said, "Maybe it's pride. I just don't want to ever be humiliated."

Madden's answer is to just work harder and harder. He was looking at failure as a negative and used willpower and extra effort to drive him beyond it.

This works as long as you are strong enough to keep putting forth the extra effort, but those who get exhausted early can't last on such a long, hard pull. Some opt for drugs. Some just quit. Those who do quit have looked at exhaustion and the aches and pain as failure instead of seeing experience, whether good or bad, as part of the process.

We get into trouble with too narrow a focus. It's better to see ourselves as part of a bigger picture. It's healthier to feel that having something or someone outside ourselves is more important than the single effort we are pouring ourselves into.

Leigh Steinberg, a sports attorney, encourages his clients to set up programs that give money to the community or to the colleges they attended. This helps his players have a better balance and prevents their being so tightly focused on football that they lose a sense of themselves in the world.

How can we get it across to a pro athlete (or anyone) that there's nothing from outside that will help them make strong choices? Courage has to come from within. Until this inner courage is discovered and utilized, we'll always have drug problems.

Delvin Williams, a former All-Pro running back of the 49ers and the Dolphins, had a drug problem but broke the habit on his own. He founded and continues to manage a program called "Pros for Kids" in which pro athletes help youngsters learn the lessons he learned the hard way. Williams is proud to be a role model and is helping other athletes understand how important they can be in a kid's life.

Some athletes complain. They insist they're not in sports to be role models. I understand their feelings, but it comes with the territory. If you are good at what you do, and in a business that gets attention, you have to realize that with the visibility and the success comes the responsibility for leading your life in such a way that kids can look up to you.

Some would say this is little enough pain for the advantages success offers. I add that it's no more than we should do for ourselves, anyway. It is a question of mental management and attitude. Do you let events control your mind and emotions, or do you control them and from that inner courage make strong choices?

15

The Players' Code

Role models come in different sizes and from all positions. You can say all you want about athletics building discipline, about the opportunities sports provides the inner-city kids, the release and inspiration it provides for fans, but out there on the field the game isn't that theoretical. It's people. It's one man going inside himself and pulling out the extra effort. It's twenty-two guys trying to earn the game ball on every play. People make the game.

Merlin Olsen was one of these. As a defensive tackle, he played in the trenches, and played very tough. Always impressive, he didn't take anything from anyone, but his moral code kept him from doing anything illegal. I don't believe Olsen ever had a 15-yard personal foul or unsportsmanlike conduct penalty in the fifteen years he played.

I recall a game in which Olsen was playing opposite Cardinals offensive guard Conrad Dobler. Dobler's attitude was 180 degrees the other way; he'd do anything he could get away with. If Dobler were on Wall Street, you could cast him as a Boesky.

In this particular game, Dobler evidently did something to Olsen, a punch in the belly or something illegal. Olsen was mad. The officials didn't see it; no foul was called. Between plays, I saw they had some words.

The next play, something happened again. Dobler returned to his offensive huddle, and Merlin walked across the line and straight into the Cardinals' huddle. I was watching and I thought, Uh oh—trouble.

Olsen said to Dobler, "I don't believe I'd do that again if I were you," almost fatherly, like to a child. And Dobler didn't.

Olsen had a presence on the field. You could tell he was more than just a defensive tackle. I've yet to see any other player control Dobler with that inner strength I call "personal power."

There are lots of ways to manage others, but the more personal power we bring to any relationship, the more we reduce how vulnerable we are to events and the actions of others. Olsen understands that no one can intimidate you unless you give up your personal power.

If people could reduce the intimidation factor by one-half from where it is now in their lives, and then by one-half again, and then again, there would be strength of character and better communication all over—in work, play, in every relationship. This is terrifically fundamental and something everyone can do.

It's always been fun for me, out there watching Olsen and others show me how it's done.

Olsen was a good communicator. Everyone knew his code and that he didn't break it. The respect this generates is very healthy for a team, and for the game.

In Joe Namath's latter years, for instance, almost without fail a defensive lineman would help him up after a sack. They respected what he'd added to the game. He made it spectacular, and he never complained. He never berated his linemen if they missed a block. He didn't complain when he got hit after the whistle. He just did his job and kept on going.

Throughout history, there are guys who advance the game to a higher level of popularity. "Broadway Joe" was one of them. Some people didn't like his brashness, for instance the time he "guaranteed" the Jets would win the Super Bowl. Then they won. As Will Rogers said, "It ain't bragging if you do it."

You see respect regularly on the field. That's one of the most inspiring aspects of the game for me, to see genuine camaraderie among players—opponents as well as teammates.

Guys like O.J. Simpson never complained. Tacklers hit him hard because he didn't go down easily—one of the characteristics of a running back; they're always trying to get that extra yard. We call it "second effort." O.J. always gave a second, often a third, effort.

Every effort means a hit, or two or three. Some of them were hard hits; some of them were harder. O.J. never said a word. He'd get up and trot back to the huddle. That's the kind of attitude that earns respect: the harder they hit you, the quicker you get up.

When a player has earned that kind of respect, even the opponents step in to help when they can. I've seen Walter Payton being grabbed by an opponent after he's run out-of-bounds to slow him down and keep him from running into the bench or the Gatorade. That's respect. Players know what Payton has done for the game. No one, teammate or opponent alike, wanted him to risk unnecessary injury.

The best team leaders are the players who have distinguished themselves as tough and dedicated. "Mean Joe" Greene, defensive tackle for Pittsburgh, for instance, hyped himself up through self-talk and game-face preparation and could become extremely intense. He could hold that intensity for three hours solid. He was amazing.

"Mean Joe" was the Steelers' defensive captain for a long time. I learned I could count on him to be a strong leader. When his players would start to get out of control, I could go to him and say, "Either you settle them down or I will."

He would always say, "I'll take care of it," and he did.

Dick Butkus, linebacker for the Chicago Bears. He scared everybody. I called him "Mr. Butkus."

He admitted his intention was to punish players. "When that running back turns the corner," he told me, "I want him to look for number fifty-one. If I can get him looking for me, I've distracted him. His concentration is gone. Then, when I hit him, I want him to think, Wow, who's that guy?"

He explained it further, "I wouldn't ever set out to hurt anybody deliberately. Not unless it was, you know, important—like a league game or something."

But Butkus had his code. If he saw a player in a defenseless position and knew he could really zap him, he would avoid it. If that player was free and running, you could take it to the bank that Butkus would be hunting him.

In games where the code is working, officials don't need to use the whistle. We could play the game with a clock and scoreboard only. Players know when the play is over. They stop the hitting on their own when the play is dead. They're playing football, not survival of the fittest.

This is the modern game. Used to be that when you tackled a runner you had to hold him down. As late as 1954, the runner could advance the ball even by crawling along the ground until stopped.

Not the case today. Starting with the 1955 season, the ball was declared "dead" immediately if the runner touches the ground with any part of his body except hands or feet if he went down as a result of defensive contact. If a player goes down, he's down. Gang tackling is still legal as long as the runner is on his feet, but eliminating piling on a runner already down has reduced roughness and therefore injury.

Players are trained to "play the whistle." They know when a runner is down by rule and cannot advance the ball. They leave him alone.

When we get a late hit, it's usually just enthusiasm, not that the players are dirty. Coaches still teach players to gang tackle, to pursue the runner, but if the runner goes down as a second or third tackler approaches, the tacklers merge and go down, but together. They are all part of the play.

The spirit behind eliminating piling on was at work in the change to the "grasp and control" rule, as well. If the quarterback is in the grasp and control of a defensive player, the play is over. The quarterback doesn't have to be taken all the way to the ground.

The end of play is based on the judgment of the official as to what amount of "grasp" means "control" of the quarterback. The whistle does help here, because the defensive player will continue the tackle until he hears the whistle, but the code helps even more. It says, "I want to win, but I want to do so fairly." That attitude saves more injuries than whistles ever did.

Don't get me wrong. We couldn't play this game without officials. If there were no officials, there would be no code. It would be a wharf fight, one gang against another.

We do have to have officials, and we have to have rules. The coaches and players want both. The rules give them an opportunity to measure their excellence. In that way it measures skill, not just force.

All serious players, which automatically means the best, respect not only the letter but the spirit of the rules. To protect that value of having a way to measure their skill, the players develop their code. If a player is out of line, they'll take care of him. A player is treated as he treats others.

Johnny Unitas exemplified this. Nothing ever seemed to fluster him. His ability, his command, and his sense of the game were extraordinary. He was respected by opponents and teammates alike. He was never unduly critical of others. If a pass was intercepted or he was tackled particularly hard, he got up and went about his business. He was a quiet, skilled quarterback and quickly earned the full respect of everyone.

Joe Theismann thought self-confidence meant believing in yourself 100 percent—and then some more. During his years with the Washington Redskins, he was very self-assured and very businesslike. He understood that his job was to "direct" his team to victory. He knew that winning didn't happen unless someone guided the effort.

Most quarterbacks today think the same way. They're highly competitive, strung like John McEnroe's racket, and they don't let themselves be drawn into unnecessary battles, verbal or otherwise.

On the other hand, quarterbacks like Norm Van Brocklin and Billy Kilmer played with a different *modus operandi*. Van Brocklin wanted to get people upset; he used the old idea of getting the opponent's mind off the game by getting him mad.

Kilmer didn't appear to have enough ability to make it into the NFL, but he did because of his competitive spirit. His passes wobbled, and he wasn't much of a runner. In fact, after an automobile accident early in his pro career broke both legs, the doctors told him he'd never walk again. Not only did he walk, but he ran and played successfully several more years.

Kilmer got the job done, but he was unforgiving. If a receiver dropped one of his passes, he wouldn't let him forget. If a guy tackled him extra hard, he'd get up and start a war of words. If he could have, he would have taken the guy behind the bleachers and settled it right there. Opponents thought of him as a cocky guy and came after him with the idea to take him down a peg. Billy loved it.

To go the other way, my respect goes out to the ones who are strong enough to be gentle—the guys who are naturally soft-spoken and self-contained off the field but who drive the hardest and work the longest on the field.

Guys like Mark Van Eeghen, a Raiders fullback during the Madden years. Van Eeghen, like Rocky Bleier of the Steelers, seldom ran for more than 8 yards on a play. His yardage came hard. He hit with tremendous force, and tacklers would hit him back just as hard. He was a punishing runner who put as much force into the tackle as he took. He knew his purpose was to carry the ball as far as he could every time and never allowed himself to be distracted by verbal jousting and intimidation.

Coach Lombardi had it right when he said, "Football is not

a contact sport; it's a collision sport. You have to go knock some-body down."

Players who understood this—guys like the Packers' Ray Nietschke and Willie Davis, the Steelers' Jack Lambert and Mel Blount, the Bears' Doug Atkins and Bill George, and plenty of others—took more physical punishment because they gave more, fairly.

Skilled players know how to express intensity or physicality without being illegal. Not always and not all players. Sometimes players lose their focus and consequently lose control.

At the preseason rules talks, I tell them, "Don't retaliate. Even if you've been wronged, retaliation will cost you. All the swinging does is set you up for a personal foul. Odds are the officials will see the retaliation swing but not the original act."

Savvy players know you can punish your opponent in a legal way more than you can by punching at him after the play. Think about it: When a player takes a swing at an opponent, it's his hand against a helmet or a face mask or shoulder pads. Who's going to be hurt most?

With the emotional heat of a game, it's tough for a player to stay in control, but that's the goal. Enough tough guys do it to make it a reasonable standard.

Some guys have broken that standard often enough to have earned the reputation of being "dirty." In the eyes of many fans and sportswriters, Ed Sprinkles, a defensive end with the Chicago Bears in the 1950s, Monty Stickles, a tight end with the San Francisco 49ers in the 1960s, Johnny Sample, a defensive back with the New York Jets in the 1960s, and Fred "The Hammer" Williamson of the Kansas City Chiefs in the 1970s, fit that category.

These are individual players, but many felt that the Raiders won a team reputation for "dirty play." Raiders management encouraged it. They actively promoted the tough image with their colors, the patch over the eye, and their name.

A recent study concluded that teams in dark colors—the Raiders, the Steelers, the Bears—are perceived to be rougher, tougher, and often "dirty." If the intention of these teams was to promote a tough, don't-mess-with-me image, the psychologists say they did it right. For myself, I think it's only image. They play rough, tough football, and that's it.

If you were to ask me to name the "dirty" players of today, I couldn't do it. The attitude has changed.

What's made the difference? Some of it comes back to the officials. Having a seventh official in the game improves play coverage and reduces the opportunity for players to get away with illegal acts.

The rules changes make a difference, too. Most of them are designed to protect players from injury.

It used to be that defensive backs could contact receivers as many times as they wanted and knock them down anywhere downfield. The old "clothesline" technique meant the middle linebacker "owned" his area of the field. A receiver didn't come through that area; he went around. A receiver who didn't avoid that area would get "clotheslined" by the linebacker, who would wrap his forearm around the receiver's neck and drop him. Zingo.

That doesn't happen anymore. Changes in the officials' mechanics have improved play coverage, and this means better protection for the players. There are only two reasons behind rules changes—to protect players or to improve the game. Behind every rules change is a series of incidents the owners mean to eliminate.

Protection of the quarterback is a prime example. Pass rushers are trying to stop the quarterback, not hurt him. They may come in a little high, but that's not designed to hurt him so much as get his attention. All they're interested in is the sack.

If a defensive lineman does take hold of a quarterback and start to throw him down, I'll say, "No, no. Don't throw him." They listen.

When 49ers quarterback Joe Montana returned in 1986 after

back surgery, opposing pass rushers seemed to ease up a little. You could sense that no one wanted to be the one to put him back in the hospital. They wanted to win, of course, but not by breaking the code, which says, "The strong only go after the strong."

It didn't take long. As soon as Montana showed he was as strong as before, they played him like before. It's the code of the game.

The strongest players, and by strong I mean in leadership and ethics, are the ones who shape the game. They are the ones who write and keep the code. Football is played by individuals. On the field, as in life, leadership determines how much of the written rule is reflected in the spirit of the game. May the code be with us forever.

16

Standing Up to Your Dreams

Major corporations and businesses that I speak to throughout the world have a strong interest in winning, in being the best in their competitive arena. Athletics provides endless good examples of how individual performance and solid teamwork go together to make the win.

One reason sports illustrates my themes of motivation and achievement so well is that it's easy to see what works and what doesn't. Everyone relates to athletes. The scoreboard gives us the bottom line; it tells us clearly the winner and the loser. One thing you'll find is that a consistent winner has developed a winning attitude.

A winning attitude works from the distinction between human nature and human nurture. We all recognize human nature. Sometimes we give it too much leeway and abdicate control. That part of human nature aside, the thing to understand about a winning attitude is that it can be nurtured. The lucky ones get the right start through parents and teachers who emphasize positive options and the "You can do it" attitude from the earliest consciousness.

Unfortunately, while we build systems to train athletes to run faster, jump higher, and throw farther, we give too little concern to the psychological aspects of developing emotional durability.

Roger Staubach tells a great story that highlights this. He and baseball great Steve Garvey work with prison inmates to develop a sense of the future for them.

At the start of one of his talks, Staubach asked the inmates, "How many of you had parents who told you that someday you'd wind up in jail?" Almost all of the hands went up.

Garvey was amazed both at Staubach's question and the response. Staubach said he asked Garvey, "What did your father say he expected of you, Steve?"

Garvey said, "My father told me someday I would be a major league baseball player."

The importance of positive affirmations can't be overstated. You nurture a person by building a winning concept, right from day one.

Success begets success. Success is to living as sunlight is to a stained-glass window; when the sunlight comes through the window, every bit of window lights up. This happens for human beings, too.

In all my years in education, I never knew a kid who *wanted* to fail. We crave success. Once we achieve a little, we see how it lights up our lives, and we want more. If the will to achieve is lacking, it's because someone starved the natural hope that would have developed into the spirit of "I can."

No matter what kind of nurturing you have had, achievement is an individual act. You must want it. If you don't, you won't.

It's not enough to only think "I ought" or "I should." Saying "I really should be successful" doesn't engage your initiative. The willingness to make the effort comes from your feeling inseparable from your goal. "You gotta wanna," for yourself.

I live not far from the "Lone Cypress" on the Monterey Peninsula in California. I watch that tree growing out of sheer rock, nobody watering it, but continuing to grow, indomitable. Human beings are a lot like trees; as long as there's life, there's growth. As long as we're alive, we can grow and change and continue to strengthen our attitudes.

To grow, you have to change. Not all change is growth, but growth doesn't come without change. With the willingness to accept or even speed up change, you have to believe in yourself.

If you say you can't, you won't. If we become comfortable with the idea of defeat, self-defeat—our own self-limiting beliefs—becomes our purest enemy.

Self-talk is a self-fulfilling prophecy of the best kind. But it isn't a matter of just saying it should happen. You have to understand you are the one who must make it happen.

Some players never quite reach their potential. One reason is that they're afraid of failure at a higher level. To grow, you have to be willing to leave your "comfort zone." It's a risk some are not willing to take. Only the pioneers see the vistas first.

We all tend to put limits on ourselves. We get started with this form of self-protection in school. Kids will say, "I'm only a C student," as if to exempt themselves from the effort it takes to go on to a B or A.

Sometimes teachers reinforce this when they decide a student isn't capable of good work. If the teacher believes that, the student comes to believe it, and then they both are stuck. The self-fulfilling prophecy works again.

Jack Lousma, one of our astronauts who space-shuttled beyond the skies about ten years ago, says the question everybody asks him is, "What does the earth really look like from space?"

He explains, "Sure, it looks like a globe, as we can imagine from pictures and models we have seen for a long time, but the thing that strikes you in space is that there are no boundaries. All is related; nothing contained. Someday I hope we can look at each other with the same perspective, that there are no boundaries."

I say, "Try it. You'll find you like it."

If we imagine boundaries around us, we will find them. If we imagine open, limitless possibilities for ourselves, we will discover that, by the natural consequence of the self-fulfilling prophecy, our lives improve, going in the direction we imagined. But this can happen only if we give up the self-limiting beliefs which prevent imagination from working.

The important first step is a willingness to change, a willingness to accept risk as an everyday opportunity for growth. Nobody likes to fail, but with a healthy sense of purpose, you can handle the risk. If somebody tells you, "You're not going to make it," with a sturdy sense of yourself you can say, "Yes, I am."

A curious example of this was Walt Disney. When Disney had a new project in mind, he would ask people around him what they thought. When he had collected ten "no's," then, for Disney, it was time to do it. Talk about a healthy sense of purpose!

The opposite of this is Billy Loes, a pitcher for the Brooklyn Dodgers in the 1940s and 1950s. He once said that he didn't want to win 20 games in a season because people would then expect him to win 20 every season.

Here was a guy who was a top-flight pitcher, a Hall of Fame candidate if he'd fulfilled his potential. His poor self-esteem limited him. In a curious but common reversal, fear of success held him back. He wasn't willing to take the risk. While athletic success has a lot to do with physical talent, the action always happens in the mind before it happens in the muscles.

Of every 10,000 kids playing high school football, only one makes it to the NFL. Of the thousands of college players who finish their eligibility each year, only about 336 athletes are drafted and only about 200 or so survive the cuts. What makes the difference in the special 200? A lot has to do with belief.

When New Orleans Saints field-goal kicker Tom Dempsey was playing football at Palomar Junior College, he was told he could never make it in the pros. A deformed foot and a withered arm might get him by at Palomar but never in the NFL. Yet he played six years in the pros, and his 63-yard field goal record still stands.

You'd have to say that his self-esteem, his belief in himself, and his courage to risk failure were very high. He could overcome the doubts of others, their negative beliefs, by the strength of his own winning attitude.

I see that in a lot of pro athletes. Johnny Unitas had been cut by the Steelers and was sitting at home when he was called by the Baltimore Colts after their quarterback, George Shaw, was hurt. Unitas not only made a spot for himself but wound up in the Hall of Fame. He says it happened because he never stopped believing in himself.

If you look at the physical skills of Vikings quarterback Joe Kapp, you'd have said there's no way he could make it. His throwing accuracy was spotty, and he was clumsy when he needed to run out of the pocket. His success was supported by the strength of his belief in himself, and he kept working at improvement. His payoff came when he quarterbacked the Vikings to Super Bowl IV.

People felt Baltimore Colts running back Buddy Young was too small to survive in the NFL. Only 5 feet 4 inches, he made Cardinals running back Stump Mitchell look like a redwood. He turned his size to an advantage. He escaped would-be tacklers with his quickness and agility.

Eddie LeBaron was another. Only 5 feet 7 inches, he wasn't tall enough, it seemed, to get a pass by a defensive lineman, but he routinely did. While with the Dallas Cowboys, he baffled the defense with his peculiar quarterback spin. Like Young, he used his small size as an advantage. He was a successful quarterback and later became general manager of the Atlanta Falcons.

High self-esteem is sometimes misread as brashness or cockiness. The sureness and decisiveness of a belief in yourself may appear similar to arrogance, but it's distinguished by its emphasis on inner strength and silent reward. Arrogance always assumes superiority and seeks outside reward.

* * *

If you haven't seen the movie *Chariots of Fire*, go out right now and rent the cassette. It presents a classic example of the winning attitude.

The story centers on Harold Abrahams, who won the 100 meters in the 1924 Olympics. In an early scene, we are introduced to him as he meets Aubrey Montague while boarding the train for Cambridge. Montague is loaded with athletic gear for every sport known to Englishmen, and Abrahams asks him, "What do you do?"

Montague replies, "I'm a runner."

Abrahams asks him, "Do you like it?"

Montague answers, "I love it. Only trouble is, I don't like getting beat."

He turns to Abrahams and asks, "How about you?"

Abrahams says, "I don't know. I've never lost."

That was literally true for Abrahams, and only because he intended with full heart to win every time. That's the winning attitude.

Bobby Layne, Hall of Fame quarterback for the Detroit Lions, was quoted as saying, "I've never lost a game; I just ran out of time."

The issue of time is critical. We never know how much time we will have to accomplish what we want to get done in this life. It's practical to have a sense of readiness, to get going now.

We must not let ourselves be dissuaded just because something takes more than a day. I'm reminded of the Harvard professor who believed the Bible had some inaccuracies in translation and that it should be interpreted differently in several areas. His colleagues warned him that people's beliefs about the Bible were fixed and it would take 500 years to change those attitudes.

As he began his lecture on the first day of the semester, he said to his students, "I've been told by my colleagues that it may take five hundred years to change some of the attitudes toward the Bible. Let the record show that we are beginning to do that today."

That's the right perspective. Change begins from a starting point, and now is the best time to start to look ahead, to begin the preparation.

O.J. Simpson had that vision as he grew up in a poor section of San Francisco. He attended Galileo High School, near Fisherman's Wharf, where graffiti covered the walls, the windows were broken, and the fences were torn.

He grew up when Jim Brown was having a great career with the Cleveland Browns. One day, at Kezar Stadium, Brown ran through the 49ers pretty good (of course, in those days, it wasn't hard to run through the 49ers), and hundreds of kids clustered around him when he came out of the dressing room. He signed autographs until O.J. was the only one left.

"Hey, kid, you want my autograph, too?" Brown asked.

O.J. looked up at him and said, "No, sir, Mr. Brown. I just want you to know that someday I'm going to break all your records."

Arrogance? Maybe a touch. But mostly, self-confidence. He was standing up to his dream. This was the first of many times that O.J. would put himself on the line and commit himself. It takes commitment and a strong self-confidence to convert a dream into 2,003 yards rushing (1973—most yards gained in rushing).

The football field at Galileo High School is now named O.J. Simpson Field. Dreams came alive on that field, but only because O.J. believed in himself, enough to risk the odds. He stood up to his dreams, ran with the ball, and won.

What dreams steam inside you, trapped? Wouldn't standing up to them be more fun?

17

Every Day as Game Day

Athletics teaches a valuable lesson about the natural sequence of achievement. This is true partly because the idea of training, of improving your skills until you can meet some outside standard, is part of sports goal planning from the outset.

No athlete pulls on sweats without a conscious readiness to struggle through some pain. He comes to the task knowing he's not yet good enough and is going to make himself better. All training is premised on the idea that you are better today than you were yesterday, but not as good as you will be tomorrow.

Athletics, like life, builds from a series of events; it is a sequence. One goal is met, another naturally appears. Excellence is the quest, but as soon as you define it as a goal, then meet it, it moves forward to another goal, another level of excellence. Excellence is an attitude, not something stationary that can be captured.

In high school, if you are chosen as an All-City player, that means you are excellent, the best at that level. On to college and you are playing with a whole team of All-City players. You're back in the pile again. If you struggle through hard work and pain, you may become All-Conference, even All-American. If you're drafted by the NFL, you're back in the pile again, with a lot of All-Conference or All-American players.

Say you make the Pro Bowl. This says you're the best in your position that year, but there's still the Hall of Fame to strive for. The definition of excellence moves forward as you do. It grows as the quester grows. Your standard of excellence measures nothing more than the strength of your commitment.

Until you break the habit of placing limits on yourself, until you stop trimming your dreams, you will not sense how much dedication helps in accomplishing your dreams. Still, what gets you there is action, hard work, actually doing what's necessary. That can come only from having specific goals in the right sequence.

What if you were on an airplane and the pilot came on the intercom and said, "Well, folks, I wonder where we'll go today"? Would you feel comfortable? I want the pilot to know where he is going and to have a plan on how to get there.

That's what I like about football. There's always a goal and a game plan. We should prepare no less for life.

A common reason that goals aren't accomplished is that they are not clearly defined. If employees don't understand their company's goals and its game plan, these goals won't be achieved. Plenty of organizations fail for that very reason. Football doesn't make this mistake. Its goals are always clearly defined.

At the end of the field is a goal line. Why do we call it a goal line? Because eleven people on the offensive team huddle for a single purpose: to move the ball across it.

Everyone has a specific task to do. The quarterback, the wide receiver, each lineman—every player knows exactly what his assignment is.

The defensive team has its goal, too: to prevent the offensive team from achieving its goal. Each is a direct obstacle to the other. It is intrinsic to the game that only one team will make progress toward its goal. The next attempt is just as basic. The principle of sequence—one down, one attempt after another—is a matter-of-fact component in goal planning.

Time after time, I've seen a guy like Jon Arnett or O.J. or Walter Payton or Franco Harris or Floyd Little or Gale Sayers get knocked down and get right back up. They didn't cry about it; they said, "I'll be better next time."

Players are conditioned to the "try and try again" attitude. Maybe it was their heroes or their coaches when they were young who told them to get back up after they were knocked down. They understand that getting up again is how they continue the effort toward their goal. Getting knocked down may hurt, but it's of little consequence. Goal planning in football accepts that setbacks are an inevitable part of the process of winning. Life is no different. Failure isn't in getting knocked down. Failure comes from not getting up again.

Abraham Lincoln failed many times, but he was undaunted. He tried again, using a new strategy. He succeeded. Lee Iacocca was fired by Ford before finding the challenge that would distinguish him as one of America's visionary executives. Neither Lincoln nor Iacocca would assert that a positive mental attitude is enough.

The discipline of optimism is only part of it. Without it, you limit yourself, you bench yourself before the game gets started. Achievement is developed from specific goals, a game plan, and the willingness to work hard and endure interim defeats without relinquishing your goal.

The margin of difference between the draft choice who makes it and the one who doesn't is usually in how hard the winner works. When talent is uniformly high, extra effort makes the champion.

I've yet to see anyone endure in the NFL without constant dedication and pure hard work. I'm not talking about the hotshot who comes in and has one great year, or even two, and then fades out of the picture. I'm talking about the champions who become the bones and guts of their team, who are there year after year. The sport is built around those willing to work.

John Brodie, for one. Brodie had all the skills a quarterback needs. His touch and his intelligence gave him the quickness that made you believe he could do almost anything. Brodie didn't just show up; he worked at it. That commitment and work ethic allowed him to make the transition into a second successful career as a professional golfer.

Walter Payton, the record-setting running back for the Chicago Bears, was asked recently when he first realized that he had more physical ability than his peers, whether it was in high school, in college at Jackson State, or with the Bears.

He answered something like this: "I never assumed I was better than anybody else. I believed I could succeed only if I worked harder than everybody else."

That's very important. While Payton had an underlying belief in himself, he also knew he would have to work very hard to achieve the kind of success he wanted. That's a winning attitude.

On the other side of it, there have been players who had the physical ability to play in the NFL but who washed themselves out because they didn't pour on the extra effort. Chuck Muncie bounced around the league as a running back. Several coaches saw talent, but none of them saw enough commitment.

Floyd Little, running back for the Denver Broncos, used a ritual that points to the truth about effort. Little was the third in a string of four great running backs who came out of Syracuse: Jim Brown, Ernie Davis, Little, and Larry Csonka. He was the smallest of the four, which made him realize he would need to make an extra drive to succeed.

Every time he carried the ball, he reminded himself, "Floyd, this may be the last time you will carry the ball." His self-talk prepared him for total effort on every play.

Off the gridiron and into swimming now. Patricia McCormick, four-time gold medalist in the 1952 and 1956 Olympics, was angry at me when as the M.C. I introduced her to an overflow crowd at a 1949 diving exhibition. I said, ". . . a woman who was not good enough to make the 1948 Olympic team. She missed it by four-tenths of a point. That tells you how good she is."

I meant it as a compliment, but she was striving for excellence and didn't like a reference to an interim defeat. Her success four years later proved her irritation was valid.

From that shaky beginning, we became good friends. During a conversation in March 1984, as her daughter, Kelly, was getting ready to compete in the 1984 Olympics, I asked her, "How many hours of practice and preparation will it take Kelly to be an Olympic champion?"

Without hesitation, Pat said, "Eighteen thousand hours."

I thought, My God, it takes only a few seconds to do the dive that wins or doesn't and so much effort to have the chance. Kelly won a silver medal in 1984, and is going back for the gold in the 1988 Olympics.

There's no substitute for preparation and training. You can't substitute talent, because there may be ten competitors as talented as you. You can't substitute hope. Hope isn't active.

What makes champions, what makes dreams come true, is the willingness to do what you do well even better, and accomplish that again and again and again.

If it's as simple as that, why don't more people accomplish their goals? Why is there rampant burnout?

Focus is the answer. Focus is why champions get up again, why silver medalists come back for the gold, why Iacocca was able to bail out Chrysler, why Neil Armstrong walked on the moon.

You could ask the question Why in the 1980s have there been no back-to-back Super Bowl champions? Again the answer is focus.

Concentration and dedication require enormous and consistent effort in refusing to be distracted. After the biggest win of the year, the champions are subjected to more hoopla than ever before. Somebody wants you for a commercial or for a book, a talk show, a speech, or a video, or you want to go spend some of that money you made.

Distractions and excuses for easing up on the work take their toll. That undermines individual preparation, and that diminishes team performance. More dangerous than distraction, though, is that you now think of yourself as being "The Best." You break Payton's rule.

A champion can never assume he's the best. There is always someone willing to work harder to claim the title.

For the last several years I've adopted a policy of off-season rules study to help maintain my focus. All officials take the preseason rules exam and a shorter weekly test during the season. To bridge the gap from season to season, I make up a monthly rules test and send it to each member of our crew. Each one answers the questions and returns the test to me. I review their answers, adding comments and corrections. Teaching is a great way to learn.

Players and coaches don't wait until the season to get in shape. A professional cannot afford to lose his edge. Rules study in the off-season, along with physical training, maintains that edge.

The better you know the rules, the more you can concentrate on the play. If you have to think about a rule, you cannot give undivided attention to mechanics, crew coordination, and unexpected play situations.

There's nothing more satisfying to your self-esteem than to feel in control of a tense situation. That's one reason I love being a referee and the reason that at age 50 I learned to fly.

The first time I soloed, I was fully aware that my life was in my hands alone. Knowledge and practice had prepared me, but only focus and self-control would get me down safely.

The value of focus and self-control was made real to me in a similar way by my friend Charlie Plumb. Charlie's book, *I'm No Hero*, tells of his experiences as a POW and what it was like to contain all your human hopes and dreams in a 6-by-8-foot cell for six years. Surviving that says a lot about Charlie's ability to keep it together.

His job as a navy fighter pilot led to his being captured, and the skills that requires served him well during his ordeal. He described for me one time what it's like to bring an F-4B Phantom roaring in at 150 knots onto a flight deck with a landing area of 300 feet at night on an undulating sea.

"It's not all that tough," he said. "You just have to know you have to do it. You get into final approach, and they turn on the runway lights. That's all you have to spot to. Watch the lights come your way and watch your instrument panel. Those are your only reference points. If you don't maintain your focus, you get awfully wet."

Dramatic situations make it easier to see what excellence requires. Out of drama we get heroes and champions. Excellent performance is recognized and more often rewarded in dramatic situations than it is in everyday life. Society in general tends toward this, but as individuals we do, too.

How do most of us wake up? The alarm goes off, and bingo, we hit the deck running and don't stop to think about what our game plan is. We get off to our first appointment and let the day evolve from there. It's the ready-fire-aim theory, which is just one off from being right, but that's all it takes to miss the target.

Take a look at pro football. From Monday to Saturday the team has already spent fifty to seventy hours preparing for a sixty-minute game on Sunday.

In the locker room prior to the game, some players pray, some players sit quietly, some are stretching and getting taped, but everyone is pulling in their focus for an opportunity they won't have ever again—today's game.

In this, winning teams are as single-minded as Charlie was when landing his Phantom on the Kitty Hawk: Do it right and you get to do it again, *once* again; then again, if you did it right. Each landing, each game, each day is a no-repeat situation. Treat every day as game day.

18

It's Their Ball

Each summer the league publishes a new version of *The Official Rules for Professional Football*. For the first ten years I was in the league, about the only difference was the color of the cover and the season schedule. The rules themselves stayed pretty much the same. What changes there were, were minor editorial improvements and not a change in how the game was played. Fans and commentators weren't aware of most of them, and to be frank, most coaches and players weren't, either.

In the early 1970s, the velocity and importance of the changes increased. The merger of the NFL and the AFL created the need to eliminate a series of differences. This took a couple of years of discussion and spread changes throughout the rules.

If this makes it sound as if the rules for professional football are made by a committee and its work is as cumbersome as the federal government's, you got it. No one intends it to be that way; it just is.

The owners, in their sole discretion, determine the adoption of any new rule or policy. After all, it's their football.

A special committee of five elected representatives of owners and coaches, called the Competition Committee, meets in March each year to discuss suggested rules and policy changes. The committee in 1988 was composed of Tex Schramm, president of the Dallas Cowboys, as chairman; Paul Brown, owner of the Cincinnati Bengals; Miami Dolphins coach Don Shula; San Francisco 49ers coach Bill Walsh; and Cleveland Browns coach Marty Schottenheimer. The Supervisor of Officials, currently Art McNally, serves as an adviser on rules and officiating.

The committee is the major policy review board for the owners, but the final decision on all matters is by full vote of the owners.

There are two reasons why rules are changed: to reduce the chance of injury and to make the game more exciting. The Competition Committee is quick to shape a rule when it feels a better balance can be created.

The owners want the excellence of players to determine the outcome of a game. This happens as long as the rules, by staying as they are, don't end up inadvertently favoring either offense or defense. The balance between offense and defense constantly shifts as coaches devise better strategies within the old rules and players become more talented. The game evolves as the people playing it do. The rules must correspondingly change.

In 1978, when the owners adopted the rule that allows an offensive lineman to use his hands to block, defensive strategy changed. The defensive linemen used to try to go around offensive blockers to get to the quarterback. Now the onrushing defensive linemen routinely try to engage the offensive linemen in a close physical encounter. It's called the "rip-up" technique.

If a defensive lineman can rip his arm up under the offensive lineman's armpit, he has reduced the ability of the offensive blocker to use his hands. The logical question is, what does that do for the defensive man? He's supposed to be on his way to the quarterback. Does he, by locking himself up with the offensive man, delay his route to the quarterback? No.

Defensive linemen are very strong. Most can bench press 400–500 pounds. They are being blocked by an offensive man who weighs roughly 270 pounds. Their intention in the rip-up is to lift the offensive player off his feet in order to take away his control. The offensive lineman wants to avoid the rip-up so that he can use the force of his hands to delay the pass rusher more effectively.

To the uneducated, it appears that the offensive blocker is "holding" the defensive rusher. To the educated eye, the defensive player caused the entanglement of arms and is able to escape from it when he chooses. Should the offensive blocker restrict the movement of the defensive lineman by pulling him to the ground ("take down") or by not allowing him to escape from the "rip-up," the official is empowered to call holding by the offense.

The change in the holding rule came about when it became evident that the increase in size, strength, and speed of the defensive linemen made shoulder-blocking techniques ineffective. Inadvertently, the chance of injury to the quarterback increased as the defensive linemen more and more routinely got through.

The offensive linemen could no longer adequately protect the quarterback. The owners changed the rule to allow offensive linemen to use their hands in pass blocking. This change was limited to blocking in the pocket area.

Offensive-line coaches started training their linemen in the new techniques. They had to reprogram the conditioning of the linemen so they would react instinctively.

On running plays, the linemen were still restricted to shoulder and arm blocking. Programmed with the new pass-blocking techniques, many forgot to make the switch on running plays. They didn't pull in their hands and, as a result, drew a lot of flags.

The number of illegal-use-of-the-hands fouls increased to the point that the owners changed the rule again, in recognition that the two blocking techniques were confusing the players. Beginning in 1987, blockers could use their hands anywhere on the field to push an opponent.

Another improvement in line play was the prohibition of the

"head slap." Prior to that, on his initial charge at the snap, the defensive player could strike an offensive player with his open hand on the head. Rams defensive end David "Deacon" Jones perfected this technique. He and other defensive linemen found that if you control a man's head, you can control his body.

From the perspective of the umpire, allowing a direct strike on the initial charge was a nightmare. It meant he had to observe simultaneously all defensive linemen, tackle to tackle, as the ball was snapped.

Personally, I objected to the head slap ever being a part of the game. I felt allowing a direct strike from one player to another at any time is counter to the spirit of the rules. Besides, it rings your bell.

In the early days, not many linemen used the technique. "Deacon" showed them how to do it. Others followed. Pretty soon the technique was universal; injuries increased.

The owners responded. In 1977, they changed the rules to prohibit the head slap. The next year, they initiated the use of hands by offensive blockers. Both changes were directed at rebalancing offense and defense.

Unquestionably the most difficult aspect of an official's job, veteran and rookie alike, is to stay current on the changing philosophy of the game. The coaches and players have to learn the new rules, of course, and they are constantly trying to find new ways to play the game within the rules, but they are less concerned with the fine discriminations than officials are.

The official, as a monitor of the rules, must know not only as much as the coaches and players but more. His challenge is not only to know them well enough to tell when teams are playing by the rules as literally written but also to use judgment that is consistent with the spirit of the entire body of the rules. How you do this is more complex than most fans, coaches, and players understand.

For example, the spirit of professional football says that a personal foul shall never go unpunished. When fouls occur by both teams during the same play, they are called "double fouls" and usually offset, meaning neither team is assessed a yardage penalty. The offsetting of fouls has been in the book for years.

A consensus among coaches, players, and officials interested in the spirit of the rule said that this didn't seem fair. Clipping is a personal foul (15-yard penalty) and by the spirit of the rules should not go unpunished. Offside is a common foul but not personal (5-yard penalty). In many cases these two fouls offset. The concerned consensus insisted this needed to be corrected.

Thus entered the 5 and 15 rule, which says that in most cases the minor foul is ignored and only the major foul is penalized. The words "in many cases" and "in most cases" are used advisedly. The rules contain numerous exceptions and variations to the 5 and 15 rule.

In a game as complex as professional football, it is difficult to balance the rules so that all foul situations are treated fairly. Then again, our social justice system has the same challenge.

While the owners enjoy total authority over final adoption of rules and policy, neither they nor the Competition Committee work in a vacuum. They recognize that coaches and players have a strong interest in seeing that the rules are written to match the contemporary style of play. Coaches and players get their say through coaches' representation on the committee.

Proactive fans who write the league office with suggestions also get heard. Fans want the game wide open, with lots of scoring. Fans like to get excited about touchdowns and their team winning. That means offensive drives and lots of running, passing, and scoring, not tough, defensive struggles at the line of scrimmage.

They also have amazing ideas on how to "improve" the game. A recent suggestion was that the league allow a means to reward bull's-eye accuracy on field goals. The suggested procedure would be to place a ring between the goal post uprights. On field-goal attempts, if the ball went between the posts, the field goal would be worth one point, two less than it is now. If the kicker's expertise sent the ball through the ring, his precision would be worth three points. The fan who suggested this idea didn't specify the size of the ring or what the "ring shot" would be termed.

The idea was sent to the Competition Committee, which discussed it and decided the league wasn't ready for this innovation. But fans keep thinking, and sometimes the ideas are accepted.

Fans expressed concern over the awarding of the ball when a fumble occurred that went in and out of the end zone. They felt there should be a distinction between a fumbled ball that went out of bounds in the end zone and one that the defensive team recovered in the end zone.

For years the rules considered the situation this way. If a runner fumbled the ball at the opponent's, say, 3 yard line and the ball went into and then out of the end zone, it would be ruled a touchback, and the opponent would take over the ball at their 20 yard line. This meant a gain of 17 yards with no effort on the part of the defense. Fans shouted this isn't fair.

Prompted by a fan's letter, the Competition Committee studied the issue and recommended that the distinction be recognized. The owners agreed.

Beginning with the 1986 season, the rule was revised to state that when the ball is fumbled from the field of play and goes out of bounds in the end zone, the defense will take it over at the spot of the fumble. Yea, fans.

Officials, of course, have an interest in the rules. Matter of fact, we are encouraged to offer suggestions for rules changes. I faithfully submit my recommendations each year.

Last year my list included twenty suggestions for either a new rule or changes in the wording of existing rules. As the complexity of the rules increases, the language of the rules and how effectively they are cross-referenced to related rules become not only more important but more difficult. One of my objectives is clearer, more concise language. The other is player safety.

One of my perennial suggestions is to eliminate clipping everywhere on the field. Clipping is defined as "throwing the body across the back of the leg of an opponent or charging or falling into the back of an opponent below the waist after approaching him from behind, provided the opponent is not a runner or it is not close line play." I would like to see the words "or it is not close line play" struck.

Close line play is that area on the line of scrimmage from tackle to tackle and 3 yards on either side. Linemen have been given the privilege to clip in this area because of the intricate stunts and blocking maneuvers involved in close line play.

If the center's assignment is to block the nose guard, instead of the center blocking him straight on, he may allow the nose guard to slide by him and then block him from behind below the waist (clip him). The force of a 260-pound center falling or throwing himself onto the back of a player's legs is as likely to tear up knees and ankles in the clipping zone as it is in the open field.

When it became legal for offensive linemen to use their hands in pass and run blocking, this eliminated, to my way of thinking, the necessity for a legal clipping zone. The Competition Committee, at this point, doesn't see it my way.

Another change I feel should be made to prevent injury concerns receivers when they jump to catch a pass downfield. As it stands presently, the defensive player may contact the receiver as soon as the receiver touches the ball. Often, the receiver is in midair and concentrating on catching the pass. The defender, watching the flight path of the ball and the receiver simultaneously, can time his contact so that just as the receiver touches the ball, whambo!

My suggestion is to change the rule to prohibit the defender from contacting any receiver until that receiver, after catching the pass, has both feet clearly on the ground.

By rule definition, a pass is not complete until both feet are clearly on the ground. Often a receiver is in full control in the air, gets hit, the ball flies loose. That's an incomplete pass, not a fumble. There's no pass completion unless the receiver is in possession with both feet clearly on the ground, in bounds.

The suggested change I offer is designed not only to prevent injury to receivers but to open up the game. When a receiver lands on the ground after catching a pass in midair, he'll be off and running with the defensive back in hot pursuit. It runs counter to the spirit of the game to allow a defender to take advantage of a player who is concentrating on the ball and has his back to the defender.

The clipping rule, in saying that no player in the open field can be blocked from behind, is centered on the same philosophy. The owners' thinking is that a player is placed at a disadvantage, and risks injury, if opponents are allowed to take aggressive action on his blind side.

It seems consistent to extend that to treating contact on the receiver when he's in midair and with his eyes on the pass as a personal foul. The penalty would be 15 yards added to the end of the run if the pass is complete. If the pass is incomplete, the penalty would award the ball to the offensive team at the spot of the foul (same as defensive pass interference).

Although I have submitted these suggestions several times, the committee has so far concluded that these changes are not warranted. They'll hear from me again.

These two points address safety. Of the two reasons for rules changes, the committee and the owners consider safety paramount. Every year they study ways to reduce player injury.

The other aspect considered in all rules changes is balance of the game. Owners, coaches, players, and fans discovered in the mid-1970s that the defensive units of many teams were overpowering the offensive scoring potential. Pittsburgh's "Steel Curtain," Los Angeles's "Fearsome Foursome," and Minnesota's

"Purple People Eaters" were three of many defenses that had begun to dominate the game.

Back then, a defensive back could make contact ("chuck" or "jam") with an eligible receiver anyplace beyond the line of scrimmage before the pass was thrown. This meant that a 220 (plus or minus) pound defensive back could "chuck" a 150 (plus or minus) pound receiver anywhere, slowing down the passing offense.

In 1977, the "bump and run" rule was changed to permit legal contact by a defender once within 3 yards of the line of scrimmage or once beyond that zone, but not both. A year later, the rule was changed to permit a defender to maintain contact ("chuck") receivers within 5 yards of the line of scrimmage, but no contact beyond. Now the receivers were free to run their pass routes without threat of contact beyond the 5-yard zone until the touching of a forward pass.

The high scoring games and all-time passing records in the 1980s are evidence of the efficiency of well-targeted changes in the rules to make dramatic shifts in the balance between offense and defense. Games with 400 yards passing have become commonplace. Talented quarterbacks have something to do with it, of course, but if their receivers can't get downfield, their arms don't help their team.

Punt returns, another exciting part of football that fans like, almost became extinct with the improvement of the kicking game. Punters had become too good. They learned how to get better loft ("hang time").

Until the rule change in 1974, it had been legal for any or all offensive players to go downfield as soon as the ball was snapped. The poor return man was often buried. The owners acted. They wanted to give the return man a better chance to run with the ball.

That interval of three to four seconds may mean a 20-yard gain by the return man. Football is a game of seconds.

The new rule specified that only the two widest men (no, not their girth) on the line of scrimmage are permitted to go down-field on the snap. The others must wait until the ball is kicked.

Even though you probably couldn't find 10 fans out of a 100 in the stands who would say so, football is a game of subtleties. When the owners change a rule, whether on the issue of safety or in order to rebalance a shift in offensive and defensive strategies, many other aspects of play and rule enforcement become affected.

The committee spends a great deal of time trying to anticipate all the variables. This is complex and difficult, made more so because coaches and players are inventive. With every rule change comes a concurrent change in strategy as coaches and players constantly try to gain every advantage permitted. This creates an almost impossible task for the committee. As Captain Yossarian would say, "It looks like a Catch-22 to me."

The grasp-and-control rule is a good example. Joseph Heller would love it.

The owners decided to add the grasp-and-control rule for quarterback safety. The rule is designed to keep quarterbacks from being thrown to the ground ("stuffed") by a defensive player. With the bigger, stronger defensive lines getting through the offensive blockers, even with the blocking rule changed to allow use of the hands by the offense, the quarterbacks were still routinely in the dirt.

Sacking the quarterback is legal if the defensive player observes the limitations of a normal tackle or the grasp-and-control rule. The referee is responsible for enforcing this rule. He blows his whistle when, in his judgment, the defensive player has control of the quarterback's movement ("taken his feet away").

Today's quarterbacks are far more mobile than those of the 1960s and 1970s. Fran Tarkenton being among the exceptions, quarterbacks like Johnny Unitas, John Brodie, Sonny Jurgensen, Joe Namath, Joe Kapp, Don Meredith, and Jim Hardy were statues compared to the scrambling quarterbacks of today.

The balance between offense and defense had shifted by the time the bump-and-run rule was added in 1977. It allowed the offensive receivers to run more, so now the defensive team recruited and trained faster defenders who could run with the receivers. This meant the quarterbacks now needed more time to throw because the receivers needed more time to outdistance the faster defenders and get downfield far enough to be open.

Quarterbacks today hold the ball longer to allow their receivers to get more open. Use of the bump and run and changes in offensive blocking techniques give quarterbacks more time in the pocket. While the grasp-and-control rule is meant to protect them, the quarterbacks are still getting injured.

The action of the defensive rusher to sack the quarterback becomes so fierce at times it is misread as intent to injure. To give protection to the quarterback, the roughing-the-passer rule was refined in 1987 to restrict the defensive rusher to only one step after the quarterback has released the ball.

The defensive rusher never thinks in terms of "steps." He is covering ground on his way to the quarterback, trying to get there fast, fending off blockers, and often does not know when the quarterback releases the ball. He has difficulty in adjusting his momentum once he sees the ball has gone.

League policy is clear in putting the responsibility on the defensive rusher. It reads, "Coaches should put their players on notice that it is incumbent on pass rushers to be aware of the position of the ball during pass plays. Professed ignorance about whether the passer had clearly released the ball will not be accepted."

This doesn't make it easy on the referee. My responsibility is to watch the action of the passer to determine pass or fumble. I watch the quarterback's action, for legal use of hands by the blockers and the action of the pass rushers. All this makes for a busy Sunday afternoon.

In this series of examples, we see that through rules changes a dominant defense style of play was rebalanced to open up the offensive passing game. A strong offensive game normally means a faster moving, more exciting game. Fans like this, and because that means good gate, owners tend to like it, too.

In response to the rules changes that eliminated certain defensive strategies, the coaches' response was to find players to match the new style of offense.

Football is constantly evolving. Coaches and players change the style of play to create an advantage. When a real shift takes place, a disadvantage is created. Owners then step in to change a rule when one style of play clearly dominates the other. For the same reason, the owners adopted the current draft system so that parity is constantly being reestablished.

Most rule changes create a shift in balance for the style of officiating, as well. We have to learn the new rules, of course, but more importantly, we have to make judgments and interpretations on the field that match the owners' intention in trying, through rules changes, to balance the style of play. In this we are supported by a good deal of communication and assistance from the league office.

When I officiated in college during the 1950s, we had a crew of four—referee, umpire, head linesman, and field judge. At one time, the NFL had four-man crews. The NFL added a fifth official, the back judge, in 1947, when the passing game became more prominent.

In 1960, when I joined the league, we still worked with a five-man crew. In 1965, the sixth official, the line judge, was added. This came about because of increased shifting in the offensive line and backfield. This offensive style of play was intended to create confusion for the defense. More "man in motion" and double shifting of the entire offensive unit not only meant problems for the defense but increased the coverage expected of officials.

The line judge was added to assume responsibilities that had overloaded the umpire and back judge. As the game opened up, five men could no longer cover all the play situations created by the expanded rules. In addition to his responsibilities for play coverage, the line judge became responsible for keeping time.

The bump and run, which opened up the passing game, led to the addition of the seventh official, the side judge. Offensive strategy was to have as many receivers downfield as they could. By rule, the maximum is five. These five receivers are covered by at least five defenders, sometimes as many as six or seven. The addition of the side judge now gave us five officials to cover the five receivers and their defenders. He joined the back judge, field judge, head linesman, and line judge in pass-coverage responsibilities.

The incident that may have prompted the owners to make this change was the injury to Pittsburgh wide receiver Lynn Swann in the 1976 game with the Oakland Raiders. The pass route that Swann ran resulted in his being contacted by Raiders defensive back George Atkinson just behind the umpire in the secondary.

At the time, the officials' field mechanics did not adequately cover that area of the field. A foul resulted in injury, yet the four officials responsible for pass coverage, while in position according to the then current mechanics, were unable to see it. The owners responded.

Even with seven officials, the changes in the rules and the style of play continue to create challenges for the officials. One is a simple thing: to count the players.

While counting the players has always been a responsibility of the officials, this is now a lot tougher. In the past, the same linemen would play all four downs. Today coaches use more sophisticated play variations and cover each down with specialists. Coaches commonly send in three, four, or five downlinemen or pass rushers on every play. The same number of players should leave the field. To prevent extra players on the field, the field judge and back judge are responsible for counting the defensive players, and the side judge counts the offense.

Although the multiple changes are handled satisfactorily with a seven-man crew, coaches came up with "lingering," a strategy intended to confuse opponents. Hank Stram, coach of the Kansas City Chiefs, is often credited with the invention of this technique.

What Stram would do is send three defensive substitutes onto the field while the offensive team was in the huddle. He'd have fourteen men on the field. At about the time the offense would break the huddle to take their positions, three defenders would quickly exit. Trouble was, the offense didn't know which eleven defensive players were in the play until just before the snap. This gives the offense no chance to adjust the play to the defensive strategy. This technique can be used by the offensive unit, as well.

As often happens when an innovation occurs on the field or in training procedures, other teams quickly adopted the "lingering" technique. When too many teams were doing it, the owners concluded this created an unfair situation. They changed the rule to make lingering an unsportsmanlike-conduct foul (15-yard penalty).

The official spotting this infraction warns the offending coach that when sending in substitutes, the replaced player must leave the field immediately. If the infraction is repeated, the official calls a foul.

Most fouls are unintentional. Unsportsmanlike-conduct penalties are reserved for those situations in which a player or coach overtly takes advantage of the rules. Lingering fits in that category, as does the "hide-out" play.

Coaches have attempted the hide-out play ever since they pumped up the football. Occasionally it is cleverly done; most often the officials are alert to the possibility.

Coaches use the hide-out play when the ball is near their bench. They send in only ten men for the offensive huddle. The eleventh man, usually a wide receiver, steps onto the field near the sideline just as the other ten break the huddle. Usually, the defense doesn't notice him. When the ball is snapped, the wide receiver goes flying downfield faster than the defense can react. The quarterback hits him with the "bomb," often resulting in a long gain or a touchdown. Surprise, surprise, surprise.

It is legal for that receiver to be near his sideline if he comes from the huddle. Whether he comes from the huddle or not, he must be at least 5 yards from his sideline at the time the ball is snapped.

In the 1980 NFC playoff game I worked, Minnesota at Philadelphia, the Eagles attempted the hide-out play. Fourth down, Eagles' ball, with punter Max Runager in position to punt. Runager had been a quarterback as well as the kicker in his playing days at South Carolina. The Eagles had only ten players in the huddle. This is legal, so no action was necessary by the officials. The Vikings hadn't counted.

Just as the punting team broke the huddle, Eagle John Sciarra, playing as wide receiver, stepped onto the field about 4 yards in bounds. The ball was quickly snapped, and Sciarra took off. Runager faked the punt and threw a pass to Sciarra at the sideline for a first down. Some 70,000 Eagles fans at Veterans Stadium broke the sky open with cheer.

I hadn't noticed Sciarra enter the field, but when he caught the ball, I remembered that he hadn't come from the huddle. I called an officials' time-out and quickly conferred with Line Judge Dick McKenzie, who had been in position on the line of scrimmage at the Eagles sideline.

I asked McKenzie, "Where did number twenty-one come from?"

McKenzie, an accountant during the week, replied, "Twenty-one usually comes after twenty."

I said, "No, no. Where did Sciarra come from?"

McKenzie reported, "He came directly from the bench onto the field."

I asked, "How far in?"

McKenzie, pointing to the ground, said, "About here," indicating a spot about 4 yards from the sideline.

I said to McKenzie, only in his third year with the NFL, "You know that's a foul. Throw your flag." He did.

As the flag came fluttering down from about fifteen feet in the air, Eagles coach Dick Vermeil screamed, "What's that for?"

Stepping a few feet over to Vermeil, I said, "You know what that's for. You can't hide out. That's been in the rule book as long as your dad's been operating his auto shop in St. Helena."

As I went back onto the field to announce the call, I looked up to the CBS TV booth. Pat Summerall and Tom Brookshier, the network announcers, were looking at the monitors, reviewing the play. I could see Brookshier saying to Summerall with hand gestures, "He got it. He got it. It's the hide-out play, and he caught 'em."

Whether it's the hide-out play, bump and run, grasp and control, or the number of points for a field goal, the Competition Committee and the owners constantly wrestle with new issues. Few are aware of how much time and thought they give to small changes to improve the game.

Football has as many faces as the people in it. It is malleable. It evolves first inadvertently through natural changes in coaching and playing variables, then by intention, according to the will and understanding of its owners. All who love the game suggest ways which they think will make it better. It is a tribute to the committee that it accepts ideas from anyone who is interested.

I love football in part because it is complex and constantly evolving. It is also basic. It is sport. It is entertainment. It is business. Unwritten rule number one is: "It's their ball."

19

Instant Controversy, or What "God" Does on Sunday

What do fans, owners, coaches, players, officials, and the media have in common? They've all spent the last two years debating the pros and cons of instant replay. Did they ever have fun!

Instant replay was implemented during the 1986 season to bring into the game the power of video technology to verify certain calls that have traditionally been the most difficult. After years of having television viewers enjoy the luxury of seeing the play from three or four different angles, the league decided to experiment with this prospective advantage.

Television developed the power to do split screen and slow motion of the action on the field in the early 1960s. We have Hal Uplinger and Tony Verna, CBS Sports producer and director, respectively, to thank.

They envisioned the excitement that being able to get into the mechanics of sports would add for viewers. They were after better entertainment, and a competitive coup. They didn't foresee that instant replay would become a formal way to judge an official's call.

Fans and commentators quickly did. The die was cast. You don't turn back technology.

Rumblings that instant replay was coming began among the owners. The question was "How *exactly* do you do it?"

In the mid-1970s, while I was waiting for my luggage at DFW airport, the day before a preseason game in Dallas, my eye caught Art McNally and Norm Schachter zipping through the airport. Why are they here? I thought.

The game agenda didn't list either of them as assigned to observe this game. Moreover, it would be highly unlikely for both to be assigned to the same game.

As I got out to the curb, I saw them again, so I asked, "I'm surprised to see you two here. Did I get the wrong game sheet, or did you?"

Both smiled. McNally said, "We were going to call you at the Marriott tonight and tell you we're here. We're staying at another hotel." Now I was really curious.

Officials, including the observers, stay at a hotel separate from the players, but all of us are together, for convenience in having meetings and for security reasons. It was unusual that McNally and Schachter wouldn't be with the rest of us at the Marriott.

McNally continued. "The league has decided, Jim, to test the mechanics of instant replay in your game tomorrow. We prefer not to tell the other officials. We don't want to shake 'em up. We wanted you to know; you're in charge of the game."

"How will it work?" I asked, wondering how our crew would be involved.

Schachter inserted, "The crew won't be involved at all."

McNally picked it up. "CBS has set us up in a separate booth with four monitors. We will be able to review any play we want to see if the television angles could help to get a better look at the play. It's an experiment. We'll report to the Competition Committee; they're looking into it."

The idea of experimenting with instant reply didn't bother me. The supervisors' use of game films to review officials' accuracy of calls and mechanics had been going on since the late 1960s. I was accustomed to having my performance inspected and considered this simply an extension.

The Dallas game went along well. On the field we were unaware of what McNally and Schachter were doing. We didn't know if they were reviewing every call or only special plays. Nothing was said to us after the game, and I didn't ask.

This test game gave the Competition Committee some preliminary information on how instant replay might be used, but it didn't slow the debate about the philosophical and psychological consequences of adopting it.

The purists didn't like the concept because they see football as a game that's played by people. They accept that mistakes have always been part of the game. They say it's folly to try to science-your-way-out of it.

If a quarterback throws an interception, that's a mistake. You're not supposed to throw the ball to the other guys. If a guard forgets the snap count, that's a mistake. If a defender doesn't cover his man because he's working man to man and the coverage called for zone, that's a mistake. If a coach elects to go for the first down on fourth and short, instead of punting, and doesn't make it, either he made a tactical error or his team didn't execute properly. Either way, someone's going to say they made a mistake.

Coaches want to make the right decisions. Players want to execute perfectly. Officials want to be 100 percent accurate. But coaches, players, and officials are people. People make mistakes. The game is played by people. Purists feel they support the realistic viewpoint.

Others knew that television technology is as imperfect as people. Dazzling as it is, the screen has only two dimensions, height and width. It can't see in depth, as the human eye can. Television creates illusions. It looks real, but it doesn't show what actually happened.

Hollywood uses this "defect" to its advantage. It thrives on illusion and spins out to us fantastic fistfights, car chases, and other special effects by expertly using the fact that cameras do not accurately see what happens.

As Rocky Balboa fought his way to the championship, we cheered. We were drawn into the action, feeling his courage and pain because the bleeding cuts and the action were so believable. We "saw" him take the blows and give them back. We "saw" the hits flatten his nose. Sweat visibly flew off his face from the force of the blows.

What we didn't see was Sylvester Stallone walking off the set each day without anyone having laid a glove on him. There would be no Sylvester Stallone today if he had had to actually take and retake those *Rocky* scenes daily.

In a fight scene, an actor can swing at another and miss by as much as one foot and the camera angle can show it as a landed blow. Knowing how to use the limitation of the camera to make it look real is a movie and television cameraman's art.

Sports cameramen don't intend "art." They aren't protecting players from violence the way special-effects directors protect actors. They want to capture the real action, not make simulated action look real.

The fact that cameras don't capture the third dimension is an advantage in Hollywood and a disadvantage on the sports field. The networks' solution is multiple angles.

The networks brought up another issue. Why us? We don't want to be deciding games. If the league wants a camera on every play from every angle so that any call can be reviewed, you figure out how to do it. We can't do it with only the nine-camera crews we use. How do you predict where you'll need to be? Who's going to pay for this? Television insisted that it was in the entertainment business, not in the business of officiating football games.

Fans added to the upswell. Fans in the stands have the same disadvantage as officials and coaches: The play happens once, and fast. As soon as portable televisions were available, fans started bringing them to the stadiums. Fans loved being able to watch the action again in slow motion and from different angles.

Fans loved it so much the owners had to fight back with

Diamond Vision. They spent big money to install gigantic television screens on the scoreboards to offset the lure of the living-room television. They knew they had to be aggressive in keeping the entertainment value in the stadium high.

Uplinger and Verna hadn't intended it, but there was no way to deny that the technology of instant replay on television meant a new era in officiating. It wasn't done by seven men alone anymore.

The league sent out a questionnaire to all game officials, asking for our opinion. Some officials were adamant against it because of the possibility of embarrassment in front of millions of people. Officials are accustomed to having their performance reviewed, by supervisors and by fans alike, but it draws on another level of personal esteem to have a decision reversed in a public forum. How would you like to face the prospect of being publicly corrected in a situation where you were doing your best but turned out to make a wrong decision?

Some officials said they didn't care. Some responded that if one wrong call was corrected and saved a team from losing a score or game, it was worth the effort.

I felt it was inappropriate to seek advice when the response wasn't going to be considered. I was fully persuaded that the owners would base their decision to use instant replay or not on the value it had for the game, not on whether the officials liked it or not.

I work for the NFL. If the twenty-eight owners decide they want to make the field 99 yards long instead of 100, if they want fifteen players on the field instead of eleven, or if they want to count replacement games, I will do my job. It's their ball, their game.

As everyone had come to expect, the owners couldn't resist the possibility that this new technology could be used to do something about "bad" calls. The gun was loaded. Then came two events that pulled the trigger.

In a New England–Baltimore game near the end of the 1977 season, a controversy arose that cost Miami its chance to make the playoffs. The referee blew the whistle because he thought Baltimore quarterback Bert Jones was stopped. New England recovered the ball, but the whistle had made the play dead, and the ball reverted to Baltimore. Baltimore went on to score a touchdown and won the game. The film later indicated Jones had fumbled.

Two weeks later, in the playoffs, an almost identical situation arose. Denver running back Rob Lytle fumbled the ball at the line of scrimmage and Oakland recovered. The head linesman blew the whistle, believing Lytle had been stopped. The ball was given back to the Broncos, who went on to score and win the game, 20–17. Film later showed that Lytle had fumbled. The ball should have gone to Oakland.

These two experiences so close together prompted the Competition Committee and the owners to activate their plan. The league selected seven 1978 preseason games to work out the mechanisms of the system. Will it hold up the game? Which calls should be reviewed? How do you communicate between the booth and the field?

During the 1978 experiment, means to communicate with the officials on the field hadn't been worked out. The supervisors could not overrule a call even if the replay showed that the official had made an error. They were connected to the live feed and could recall any play they wanted. They were working on how long it took to sort, rewind, and review. The critical question was would the television cameras give them the angles they needed. In the test game I worked, we had no calls reviewed.

This series of tests indicated that the mechanical problems could be worked out, but the philosophical split among the owners had not been resolved. The debate and considerations continued for the next six years. League policy requires the owners to have a majority vote of twenty-one or more for adoption of any new rule or policy. They weren't there yet.

Then, in a regular-season game with Pittsburgh at Los Angeles in 1984, Raiders wide receiver Dokie Williams caught a pass in the end zone for a touchdown. Television replay and league film later showed Williams's second step was clearly out-of-bounds.

It was a blatant error, and that caused more owners to feel that the time to try instant replay had come. The decision was made. The league would use the 1986 season as a full-year experiment in using instant replay "as an aid to officiating."

The experiment was limited to officials' calls involving the ball and lines. Was the pass caught or trapped? Did the receiver catch the pass with both feet inbounds or not? Did the ball break the plane of the goal line with the runner in possession? Was the runner's knee down before he fumbled? The reviews were to be restricted to what I refer to as "sight calls."

Fouls weren't included. Calls such as holding, pass interference, intentional grounding, offside, false start, grabbing the face mask, clipping, illegal blocks, and all other penalty situations involve an official's judgment. Whether a team was advantaged or disadvantaged by the foul is a "judgment call." There are many situations in which some action could literally be considered a foul but which in the judgment of the official doesn't affect the play.

The league suddenly needed fifteen instant-replay officials (IROs). Where do you find them? The five assistant supervisors could be used, or you could draw from the dozen or more observers, but doing either would leave a void somewhere.

To increase the ranks, the league encouraged early retirement of older officials. A few chose to. The league also looked over the ranks of retired officials who might be called back to become either an observer or an IRO. It was a scramble, but McNally found them.

Operating the instant-replay monitors and communication equipment in the booth is more complicated than operating your VCR by remote in your living room. The next scramble was to crash-course the new crew of IROs in the latest electronic gadgetry.

The complexities were more than the owners and the league had anticipated. They discovered the networks were right when they said, "This isn't going to be easy."

The procedure is that the IRO views the game and the monitor simultaneously. When he sees a call or play that might be questionable, he immediately reviews it on the "A" tape, which is the live network feed, the same as the viewers saw at home. The IRO reviews it quickly as play continues.

If he needs another view, he can request a replay of the "B" tape, which may or may not include the circumstance in question. The networks choose how they follow the play, trying to capture the most action, but that doesn't mean they always have multiple angles on the play situation being reviewed.

If the IRO believes a call or play needs further review, he communicates by a wireless Telex to the umpire, who serves as the liaison to the referee. The IRO says, "Stand by. The play is being reviewed."

The umpire responds with "Standing by," and he calls an officials' time-out. Play is stopped. Officials who may be involved in the play tell the umpire what they saw or called on the play in question. The umpire relays this information to the IRO.

For example, if the IRO is reviewing a sideline catch of a forward pass and observes that the receiver did not get both feet down inbounds, the IRO would normally rule that as an incomplete pass. If the game official on the play determined that the defensive back pushed the receiver out-of-bounds before the receiver had a chance to get both feet down, the game official would rule that as a completed pass.

This is just one type of situation where the information conveyed to the IRO by the umpire from the officials on the field becomes essential. Judgment calls take precedence over sight calls. The IRO doesn't overrule if a judgment call is involved.

If, after review, the IRO decides that the call or play should stand, he says to the umpire, "Continue play. Continue play. Continue play." Always three times. League procedure.

In a Los Angeles at Kansas City game early in the first year of the experiment, there was a play in which the game officials ruled a complete pass for a touchdown. When the IRO reviewed the play, he saw it as incomplete. He relayed his decision to the umpire on the field by saying, "Pass incomplete."

The umpire heard it as "Pass is complete." The touchdown stood.

The next play happened almost immediately. The IRO had no chance to stop play to correct the misunderstanding. As a result, the league issued new instructions on what terminology to use and initiated the procedure that each instruction shall be repeated three times.

If, after review, the IRO decides that the call was in error, he says, "Reversal. Reversal. Reversal." The umpire repeats the message back to the IRO exactly as he heard it.

If it is a reversal, the IRO informs the umpire as to the disposition of the ball and down. The referee, having received the IRO's decision from the umpire, makes the public announcement.

Assisting the IRO in the booth is a league official who handles the communication between the IRO and the media. As a backup system, the league has installed an instant-replay telephone located behind the home-team bench. When necessary, the referee can speak directly to the IRO.

Although the primary responsibility for recalling and reviewing plays is with the IRO, the referee has the prerogative to request a review if he or any of the game officials have any question. Many proponents of instant replay feel that coaches and players should also have the opportunity to request review. The owners determined that for the experimental period the decision to review a play should be confined to the officials only.

In its initial season, 1986, there were approximately 35,000 plays in 224 regular-season games. There are dozens of possible calls in every play. Of the hundreds of thousands of possibilities, the IROs reviewed 374 play situations involving a call or no call that appeared to have the prospect for being wrong. Of those, thirty-eight calls were reversed.

The owners extended the experiment for the 1987 season. In 210 games (one week lost in the strike), there were 490 contacts to the field. Of those, 57 calls were reversed.

In 1985, before instant replay, the average game time was 3:09.20. In 1986, the average length increased to 3:11.40. In 1987, the average game time was back to 3:09.49, which rather busts the idea that having instant replay automatically means longer games.

The debate continues. The owners decided (23 for, 5 against) to extend the experiment for another year. Prior to their vote at the owners' meeting in March 1988, the speculation was that instant replay was doomed. The persuasion point seemed to be the change, beginning with the 1988 season, to making the IRO a regular member of each officiating crew, rather than his being assigned at random.

This change is designed to improve communications between the field officials and the IRO, but it should not have any effect one way or another on officiating, not if the goal of the field officials is to give "God" nothing to do on Sundays.

From my perspective, I feel instant replay provides game officials with an extra incentive to perform even better. This is as reasonable a goal for us as it is for any major corporation which is continually trying to improve its products and services. The goal is "zero defect."

If Chrysler Corporation builds 1,000 cars and 999 are perfect, that good track record means nothing to the customer who bought the "lemon." Officials feel this way, too. We strive for 100 percent accuracy, but we have to recognize that we work with variables we cannot control. Perfection is rarely possible, but it is constantly the objective. Owners, coaches, players, and fans wouldn't have it any other way.

20

Call Me Sentimental

Maybe it's only that I'm a traditionalist, but I loved the old parks: Yankee Stadium in New York, Wrigley Field in Chicago, Franklin Field in Philadelphia, Griffith Stadium in Washington, D.C., Kezar Stadium in San Francisco, Sportsmen's Park in St. Louis, Metropolitan Stadium in Minneapolis, the Orange Bowl in Miami, the Cotton Bowl in Dallas, and old Tulane Stadium in New Orleans. Many may not have been built for football, but great football happened there.

Their replacements are more comfortable and maybe more convenient for fans, but the new stadiums also lack character. Like franchise hotel rooms, when you've seen one, you've seen them all. Without their nameplates, you can't tell whether you are in Riverfront Stadium or Three Rivers or Fulton County.

Not so with the old parks; each had its own ambience. Most of them were old baseball parks, converted during football season, which meant they had inadequate dressing rooms, dugouts too close to the field, and end zones that ran right into the outfield walls.

In many, the first-base dugout would be in one end zone, and the field would stretch out to the left-field wall. Many times a receiver would catch a pass in the end zone and fall into the dugout. Pretty soon they learned to put a padded wooden slab over the dugout so when the receivers hit it, they'd avoid some bruising.

Speaking of a receiver hitting an inanimate object, I remember a game in Pitt Stadium in the early 1960s. Mike Ditka was playing for the Chicago Bears against the Steelers in what was kind of a homecoming, because Ditka played college ball for Pittsburgh.

In those days, the goal posts were right on the goal line. Ditka had outrun the strong safety, and was wide open on a "post pattern." He forgot the Steelers had a twelfth defender—the post itself. As Ditka reached up for the ball, he never saw the goal post coming. He hit it head-on and was stopped cold. He slid down the post like melted butter.

Ditka was always a tough guy as a player, and now as a coach. He refused medical attention, wobbled off. He returned later and played a heck of a game. Since the Bears won, it didn't matter that he couldn't hold on to that one. Incidents like that were one reason the goal posts were finally moved back to the end line.

When an architect designs a stadium, the dressing room for the officials is like a Christmas gift for your mother-in-law: something you think of a little late. For instance, at Lambeau Field in Green Bay, they converted part of a boiler room into the officials' dressing room. They stuck some lockers against the wall that must have come out of Yale about the time Albie Booth played; only Billy Barty's clothes would fit in there.

Yankee Stadium was great, the greatest, except that our dressing room was as big and busy as Grand Central Terminal. It was right next to the ramp, and everybody who came through the press gate had to walk by us. Every old-time ballplayer came in to say hello. The Giants' crew had been there for years and knew everybody, every athlete, every sports celebrity, so they all stopped by. It was slow getting dressed, because you were always having to shake hands with somebody and say hello. I prefer not to have distractions before the game. I want to concentrate on getting ready. No choice at Yankee.

* * *

I was disappointed when the Giants moved out of Yankee Stadium to the Meadowlands in 1976. The feelings were a repeat of when the Chicago Bears moved from Wrigley Field to Soldier Field in 1971. Wrigley Field could seat only 37,000 people, but it seemed like much more because everybody was right on top of the field, in the middle of the action.

The end zone backed up to the left-field wall. There was no more than three or four feet from the back of the end zone to the wall. When a receiver caught a ball going into the end zone, he'd run right into that ivy-covered wall.

I was then a field judge, and my position was behind the defensive secondary. When a team moved down near the goal line, I'd be right up against that wall. Of course, there were fans there, and if it happened once, it happened a dozen times: A guy would pour beer right down on me. Another distraction to disregard.

George Halas, then owner as well as coach of the Chicago Bears, was always looking for ways to cut costs. In the early 1960s when the media first started postgame interviews, most team organizations were willing to renovate an existing room, or even add a new one, to make the media comfortable. Not so with Halas.

A man of direct action, he strung a wire down the middle of the officials' already too small dressing room, and threw a painter's drop cloth across the wire and presto! The press room was ready.

After the game, the media would crowd in for the interviews. If there had been a controversial call, we could hear Halas on the other side of the drop cloth giving his opinion. He knew we couldn't help but hear. He loved it.

The first game I worked at Kezar Stadium was a 1960 pre-season game between San Francisco and the Philadelphia Eagles. I was the field judge. Norm Van Brocklin was the Eagles quarterback. He took them to an NFL championship that year. This game was memorable not for what Van Brocklin did but because of a brawl sparked by a racial epithet.

A black wide receiver caught a pass and was tackled by a white player with a little more enthusiasm than was necessary and who swore at the receiver, calling him a "black so-and-so."

There's very little of that now. Players with ability are respected regardless of color. Performance has finally won over prejudice, but racial tensions were high in the 1960s. Everybody was wound pretty tight. The black player got up and punched his tackler. Players from both benches poured onto the field. I remember San Francisco running back Hugh McElhenny kicking a big lineman and then backpedaling all over the field to keep away from the guy. He was faster running backward than the guy was chasing him. It was a real donnybrook.

There was another game at Kezar in which nothing seemed to go right. It was the first year Jerry Bergman came into the league and was the head linesman in our crew. Bill Schleibaum was our line judge. The players were scrapping and bickering. Many calls, even the simple ones, were debated, and the fans were booing at us.

During a team time-out in the third quarter, a lady ran onto the field and up behind Schleibaum. She yanked his flag out of his back pocket and hit him over the head with it. Then she ran back into the stands. A cop watched the whole thing and did nothing, just laughed. I couldn't blame him. I was laughing, too.

That was harmless enough to be funny, but something that happened after the game certainly wasn't.

Kezar had a tunnel at the east end that led to the dressing rooms, with bleachers on each side of the tunnel. Both players and officials had to go through that tunnel to get to their dressing rooms. There were always fans up above yelling at the coaches, players, and officials, and sometimes throwing things. Players would keep their helmets on, but coaches and officials didn't have that option.

I always run off the field after a game. That day, as I was

running up the tunnel, I heard Bergman yelling, "Jim, Jim!"

When I turned around, I saw him staggering up the tunnel, blood all over his face. A fan had thrown a sack of bottles and hit him on the forehead. He looked like a Civil War veteran. He fell to the ground, and I picked him up and took him into the dressing room to get stitched up. He recovered with no ill effects, but it was a scary moment.

The fans were in control of that game, and we weren't. When officials have control of a game, I think the fans sense it and respond to it.

Next year the 49ers' management put a wire netting over the tunnel to prevent objects from falling through, although a net didn't stop them from pouring beer on us as we ran into the tunnel.

A couple of years later, Dallas was playing at San Francisco, with John Brodie quarterbacking the 49ers. Dallas was ahead, 31–27, with less than two minutes to play. The 49ers needed a touchdown to win, and they were moving pretty well.

Brodie threw a long pass, about 40 yards, to about the Dallas 20. Our field judge, Joe Gonzales, called offensive pass interference against the 49ers, which took a long gain away and penalized them 15 yards. Brodie was unhappy about that but came back and threw another long completion.

Our rookie umpire, Barry Brown, called offensive holding, another 15-yard penalty. The fans were ready to riot. Their next play was unsuccessful. Time was gone. The 49ers lost.

As we left the field, I stuck close to Brown, mindful of the assault on Bergman. It was the right thing to be thinking about, because a fan ran onto the field, straight at us. He chose me instead of Brown, and down I went.

Before anything else could happen, Bob Lilly and Leroy Jordan of the Cowboys' defense picked me up and escorted Brown and me into the officials' dressing room. Nobody was going to mess with Lilly and Jordan, so it was a one-punch event. The next day some reporters had it that I punched the guy back, but I didn't.

This sort of thing doesn't happen much anymore, fortunately. Officials take a lot of verbal abuse, which you can't take too seriously or at all personally. I notch it down by remembering my definition of a fan is a guy who sits in the sixtieth row, yells at the officials for calling holding in the middle of a line play, and then can't find his car after the game. Let them say what they like; I've learned not to let it bother me.

We worry less about violence because the league office assigns a security man for every game. He knows our exact route to the stadium, and when we get there, security guards meet us and take us to our dressing room. They are with us as we go on and off the field. They wait after the game until we're dressed and sometimes escort us to the airport.

The NFL takes these precautions only because there have been enough individual acts of violence by fans in the past to warrant continuous caution. The increase in violence from fans is no greater than that of society in general. It's a problem that we all face. The gridiron is no exception.

Fans have a right to make as much noise, cheering or booing, as they want. Sometimes crowds get so noisy that a visiting quarterback can't be heard. Some say the home crowd should be penalized. I disagree.

Let fans shout as loud and as long as they want. And the wave. It's pretty much died out now, but there was a time in the early 1980s when fans were doing the wave for everything. If the peanut vendor made a good toss, they'd start the wave. That's fine with me. When the fans are into the game, the game is better. But fans belong in the stands. The price of their ticket doesn't give them the right to a piece of the turf, or the goalpost to take home in victory, or the right to be physically destructive by venting their disappointment in defeat.

Working in Memorial Stadium at Baltimore was like working a domed stadium because of the din. Horseshoe-shaped, fans curved around the upper deck, looking almost straight down at the field. The Colts fans had healthy lungs. They also had great players to cheer about—Johnny Unitas, Ray Berry, Lenny Moore, Alan Ameche, Gino Marchetti. A Colts game in Baltimore guaranteed some fancy football.

Memorial Stadium had been built for baseball. Some evergreen shrubs grew in the area behind the goal posts. When Unitas would connect on one of his famous long bombs, Berry or Moore or whoever caught it, would usually end up in the bushes.

The locker-room attendant at Memorial Stadium gets my all-time award for thoughtfulness. For years he brought us crab cakes. If you've ever had a Maryland crab cake, you know why our crew loved to work in Baltimore. Forget who was playing.

There are other teams that year after year had the benefit of dedicated fans. Oakland, for instance. They get my prize for being "well dressed." They had more hats, pennants, T-shirts, jackets, pom-poms, horns, and all kinds of getups than ever you saw. Oakland Raiders fans really got into accessories.

The Colts fans, or the Giants and Bears fans, for instance, were more into the game itself. They didn't carry a lot of stuff into the stands, but they could bring their teams along with noise and support. The fans had a basic rock-'em, sock-'em style that matched their teams.

Before the Saints had their Superdome, they played at Tulane Stadium, the old Sugar Bowl. The New Orleans fans were so excited in 1967 about having a team at last that they would start stomping their feet so fast those old metal bleachers would begin to sway. Several times, I thought it was an accident about to happen.

A great Saints game happened on November 8, 1970, at Tulane Stadium, against the Detroit Lions. With about a minute to play, the Lions scored the go-ahead touchdown to make it 16–14. They figured they had the game won.

On the kickoff, New Orleans ran the ball back to about the

20. Billy Kilmer threw a sideline pass down about 7 yards to Danny Abramowicz. With about thirteen seconds left, Billy came back with another sideline pass to Abramowicz, complete, and with a quick step out-of-bounds, to stop the clock, the Saints were still in their own territory with six seconds left.

It was decision time for a rookie Saints coach. Tom Fears, coach since 1967, had been fired earlier that week, and J. D. North had assumed command. Within seconds of the time Abramowicz stepped out-of-bounds, everyone heard North yell, "Field goal team," and even faster, everyone turned around and looked stunned. North was sending Tom Dempsey in to try a 63-yard field goal. I wasn't alone in thinking North was crazy.

I had seen some great kickers in the NFL—guys like Lou Groza, George Blanda, and Jan Stenerud. Back then, more than 40 yards was exceptional, and the record was only about 54.

Lions defensive tackle Alex Karras asked me, "What's he doing, Jim?"

I told him, "The Saints are going to try a field goal."

"You've got to be kidding me," Karras said. "They're going to be kicking from their own territory."

I shrugged. "I don't make these decisions, Alex."

Dempsey had a deformed right foot. His foot ended about where the arch is. He wore a piece of leather over the stub of that foot. Some opponents complained because he didn't wear a standard shoe. He didn't wear a standard shoe because he didn't have a standard foot. Officials look for instances of unfair advantage, but I couldn't see any here.

Dempsey looked as surprised as the rest of us but trotted onto the field with full confidence. The snap was perfect; Kilmer set it down right on the mark, and Dempsey took his normal step and booted it. Everyone was really surprised.

Straight as could be, the ball split the uprights as time went to zero. I gave the touchdown signal and ran off the field as the Saints cleared the bench to congratulate Dempsey. The Lions hardly moved, stunned and immobile.

The New Orleans *Times-Picayune* played it up the next day·

as "Dempsey-Tunney, Dempsey kicks a wonder. Tunney calls it good," with a picture of Dempsey just finishing his kick and my touchdown signal behind him.

That same year, St. Louis and the Saints, we were in an injury time-out, with several trainers on the field attending an injured Saint. One of them, a young guy in a white turtleneck sweater, started berating our umpire, Lou Palazzi, because he thought the player's injury had been due to a foul.

I wasn't about to allow anyone to start a harangue, so I stepped over to him and told him to shut up and leave the field, which he did. The Saints' general manager, Vic Schwenk, a classmate of mine from Occidental College, came over to me and said, "Do you know who that is, Jim? That's our owner, John Mecom. You just ran the owner off his own field."

I was embarrassed that I hadn't known. Mecom was a very young man, surely the youngest owner in the league. Since that time, we have become friends.

That same year I met a friend of Mecom's, Jim Nabors. Leaving Minneapolis after a Vikings game, I took a late flight out to Chicago, where I would connect to Los Angeles. Our back judge, Jack Nix, was traveling with me. On the connecting flight out of Chicago, we were the only ones in first-class. Nice. Just before they closed the door, two other passengers came in, Jim Nabors and his agent, Dick Link. For privacy, they had stayed in the Ambassadors' Club until just before departure.

As the pilot started the engines, the power went out and everything went dark. It took ten or fifteen minutes for them to activate the emergency power. It took two hours to get the problem fixed, and in that time Nabors and I became good friends. Nabors is a great football fan and was as interested in what Nix and I did as we were in his work.

Back in Los Angeles, Nabors invited me down to see the taping of his television show; the studio was just a couple of blocks from

Fairfax High, where I was then principal. I was glad to do that. He did his show live, and watching from backstage was fascinating. He treated me then, as he does now, like a brother. I was his guest many times and became friends with many of the stars he had on the show.

I thought it only fair to reciprocate, so I invited him to Fairfax High for lunch. "Gollee," if he didn't drive that Rolls-Royce right up in front of Fairfax one day. Talk about being a hero! I was walking around campus with Jim Nabors and had football to thank for that.

At Metropolitan Stadium in Minneapolis, I became aware that stadiums take on the personality of coaches, if the coach is special enough. It happened at Wrigley with Halas, at the Oakland Coliseum with Madden, at the Orange Bowl with Shula, at Three Rivers with Noll, and at Metro with Van Brocklin.

I first met Van Brocklin when he was quarterback of the Philadelphia Eagles. In a game at Kezar in 1960, I was the field judge, and Bud Brubaker was the referee. Van Brocklin threw a pass that went off one receiver's hands and was caught by another. I signaled first down; it was an Eagles 40-yard gain.

Brubaker came running down the field and said, "Didn't another receiver touch it?"

I said, "Yes."

"Then it's an incomplete pass," Brubaker said, "because two receivers from the same team can't touch the ball." (The rule has since changed.)

Right behind Brubaker was Van Brocklin, and he said, "Wait a minute, Brubaker, let the rookie call the play."

From that time on, he never let the tease go. When Van Brocklin became head coach of the Vikings, he would yell at me constantly. He was quite clever with his use of vulgar language, though I won't use any of it here. His sense of humor came through even though he was often nasty and vicious. He seemed to hate everybody. Talk about game face. He seldom smiled;

he stormed at his players, assistant coaches, and the officials.

Van Brocklin was totally dedicated to winning. I don't think he ever cheated, but he certainly went after what we call the fair advantage. He wanted everything to go his way and felt the only way to make that happen was to intimidate everybody he could. A number of officials were afraid of Van Brocklin, but not Brubaker.

After the Kezar game, Brubaker gave me some advice. "Just see Van Brocklin in terms of his value to the game," he said, "and ignore his style of language."

I understood what Brubaker meant and remembered. I would smile when I would see Van Brocklin yelling at other officials. I knew what he was trying to do.

In his home park, Metropolitan Stadium (another stadium built for baseball and seasonally converted for football), both team benches were on the same side of the field to ensure the view of the fans in the box seats. The Vikings team bench area extended from the 50 yard line to the Vikings 20 yard line.

This was ideally suited to Van Brocklin, who preferred to ignore the rule about coaches staying in the bench area. To give a better earful, he would roam the entire sideline, as far as he wanted, to yell at officials.

Frankly, I find strong personalities are easier to take than strong elements. I remember one time I woke up in Minneapolis to see the temperature sign across the street reading minus two. We went to mass, breakfast, our crew meeting, then, all bundled up, to Metropolitan Stadium. We walked, we were so close. The sign still said minus two. The sun was out for the one o'clock kickoff, but it was still minus two. Days like that test your commitment to your job.

The game that day was against the Lions. As we came out on the field half an hour before the game, the Lions were warming up, and had on their blue jerseys. The Vikings came out soon afterward, and they were wearing their purple jerseys.

Blue and purple aren't a whole lot different, so Brubaker got

Van Brocklin and George Wilson, the Lions' coach, together with the team captains—Alex Karras for the Lions and Jim Marshall for the Vikings.

The rule book says that if there's a conflict about uniforms, the visiting team is supposed to change. This has always seemed ridiculous to me, since visiting teams don't lug around two sets of jerseys.

As you might expect, the Lions said blue was all they had. The Vikings said their white jerseys were in a cleaners in St. Paul.

I was witnessing two coaches, two captains, and the referee trying to decide if the game can be played or who should wear what. It was minus-two degrees, and 50,000 hardy fans were rubbing their hands and swearing. Brubaker was suggesting that we go ahead and get the game started and as soon as the Vikings can get their white jerseys over from the cleaners, they can change.

"No way," said Karras. "I'm color-blind. I'll be tackling my own guys."

We were forced to hold up the game another forty-five minutes until the Vikings' white jerseys arrived.

I didn't mean to slight Texas when I gave the prize for being "well-dressed" to Oakland fans. Let's not forget the Texan women, who fan for fan wear more rhinestones, furs, and boots than Dolly Parton's ever dreamed of. That's only one reason it was fun to work in the Cotton Bowl, particularly the week of the Texas-Oklahoma game, which always coincides with the Texas State Fair, filling the town for a triple-event weekend.

In those days, we didn't have as many films to look at or meetings to go to before the game, so we had time to go to the state fair, for the rides, the midway, all of that. On Saturday afternoon I'd try to take in the Texas-Oklahoma game. That was college rivalry at its best.

When the Cowboys left the Cotton Bowl, they left behind a stadium filled with memories, but since their success came on so fast at Texas Stadium, I'm sure they feel the price was right.

Texas Stadium is unique, with a roof that covers the stands but with a hole cut out of the area over the field. Texans say this is so God can watch America's team.

When I first walked onto the field and saw that hole, I asked Bob Fuller, the stadium's electric-clock operator, "How big is that hole up there?"

He said, in a slow Texas drawl, "Oh, about seven-eighths acre." I think he's about right.

The stadium that is most like home to me, where I feel as comfortable as if I were in my own backyard, is the Los Angeles Coliseum. As a kid, I went there with my dad for college games. Later, I worked a lot of games there as a referee for high schools and colleges. One was a high school "jamboree," with sixteen teams playing twenty minutes at a time. I can't imagine having sixteen schools in the Coliseum today; the chaos would threaten World War III.

Best of all, the Coliseum is where I worked my first game as an NFL official—the Rams against the Bears, 1960. Even now, when I work a game there, the memories flood back. Call me sentimental.

21

Everyone Needs Mentors— I've Had the Best

There's no single way to become an official or to grow as one. There are a lot of different routes. If I had to choose one, however, I'd like every official to journey the route I did.

My dad was my first role model, and I couldn't have had a finer one. He was a true professional and taught me why to care about the standards that define a professional.

I was lucky in another way, too. My uncle is Bud Brubaker. I grew up watching him officiate high school and college games, and about the time I started officiating, he had moved up to the NFL. He was an NFL referee for twenty years, 1950–70. I worked with him his last ten years before he retired.

When I started officiating high school games in 1951, Bud was coaching one of the teams. My dad was also there to watch me for the first time. Talk about feeling the pressure!

Bud had an instinctual understanding of the game, but what marked both Bud and my dad as real pros was their strong sense of fairness. Rules knowledge and game mechanics are essential, but they are rather easy skills to acquire. The more difficult ingredient to acquire is the impartiality that is necessary to fairness. Impartiality is as much a skill as concentration or any acquired habit of mind.

Another lesson I learned from them is the attitude of giving.

In a sense, officials compete against each other for advancement through the ranks and playoff assignments. Bud and my dad were consistently teachers first, competitors second. They were willing to share their insights and to help you when you made a mistake.

Most officials are willing to be teachers. Sports began in our schools, first as physical education exercise and then as intramural competitions. When officials were first needed, teachers and coaches were the immediate answer. They still are.

Two other men helped me along. Jay Settle gave me my first job officiating in the Alhambra Summer Basketball League while I was still playing ball at Occidental College. Jay thought it would be a natural supplement to my future coaching career.

The next boost came through Bill Lopez, supervisor of athletics for the Los Angeles Unified School District. His confidence in me probably outpaced my own, because suddenly I was being assigned to a lot of big games where I got to work with veteran officials. This speeded up the learning curve and taught me to trust in myself. If I had a tough game or the coaches were unhappy about some aspect of it, Bill would send me right back to those teams the next week. This toughened my mettle.

One game he sent me to was the Los Angeles City Basketball Championship final between Jordan and Manual Arts. Johnny Wooden scouted the game, and that led to my being asked to officiate major college basketball games. My partner for that game was Norm Schachter.

I'd known Norm for several years previously and had watched him work in the NFL and college games. It was great to work that game with a veteran. Over the years we became good friends. I've known Norm now for almost forty years. There's nothing I wouldn't do for Norm Schachter, and if you were to ask him, there's nothing he wouldn't do for me, so for forty years we've done absolutely nothing for each other.

Norm has a cellular understanding of rules balance. He taught me that only if an official conscientiously studies the rules will he learn the philosophy and spirit behind them. You can have a fundamental understanding of the rules without mastering how one rule balances another. Only with the deeper knowledge will you be effective on the field and be able to grow in officiating.

An exciting situation involving Schachter developed in the officials' clinic in July 1971. The issue was punts. The group couldn't agree on the enforcement spot for fouls during punts, and as the discussion dragged on it developed some heat.

Mark Duncan, then supervisor of officials, finally said, "Time out. Norm, you and Jim go out in the hall and stay there until you have written a rule that we can all agree on." Out we went.

That was the birth of the "postpossession foul," which is a foul that occurs prepossession but is enforced postpossession. Football in the NFL is a very precise sport.

The one thing Schachter can do he didn't teach me was how to have a photographic memory. He can cite the page number and location for any rule. With his years of encouragement, I have mastered it with many rules, but not all. Schachter knows every one, but then, he writes the book.

During my early years in the league, I worked with some giants of the cra—Bill Downs, Dan Tehan, Ron Gibbs, and Dutch Heintz. While none of them was a mentor as such, I learned valuable lessons by watching them do their jobs expertly.

Bill Downs, a 5 feet 7 inch referee, had great poise and presence on the field. He could easily control players who were a foot taller. He was avid on rules knowledge and set an example for us all.

Dan Tehan worked in the league for forty-five years, thirty-three as a head linesman and twelve as an observer. Tehan taught me the value of a sense of humor as a part of your job mind-set. That was a good lesson for me, because as a young official, I wanted to be right all the time and to establish myself as competent.

Tehan worked a game in Baltimore with Ron Gibbs. Gibbs, as the referee, was solely responsible for the passer. Tehan, as the head linesman, was responsible for acts at the line of scrimmage.

In one particular play, Gibbs threw his flag because he thought the defense had jumped offside. Tehan didn't. Just about as the penalty was being enforced, Tehan asked Gibbs, "What did you call?"

Gibbs said, "Defense offside."

Right then Tehan threw his flag and said, "I have intentional grounding. Penalties offset."

Today's system of video review doesn't allow that kind of "rules balancing." Well, maybe if Tehan were here.

In one of his last years as a referee, Gibbs was working a game in the Los Angeles Coliseum. I was the field judge. Elroy Hirsch was general manager of the Rams at the time. A call came up that was important, and Hirsch thought we had kicked it. After the game, he came down to the dressing room, fuming.

Gibbs sat Hirsch down, very calmly saying, "Let me explain the rule."

Hirsch seemed ready to listen. I moved in closer, knowing I was about to learn from the master.

Gibbs started in on such a line of double-talk, going from some fictional history of why the rule was in the book straight through what effect it had on other plays that I'd never heard of. He was smooth and convincing, but what he was saying made no sense at all.

I looked at Gibbs. He knew I knew it was all air.

Hirsch took it all quietly, and when the chance opened up, he stood and said, "Thank you, Ron, for explaining it all so carefully. I'll go now and explain it to my coaches."

Gibbs was a true master at game control, and masterful in his own way with rules exposition.

Dutch Heintz exemplified the adage "strong enough to be gentle." He was quiet, unassuming, yet always in control and possessing the steady kind of courage that gives confidence to his colleagues. He was immune to intimidation.

When I entered the league, officials didn't yet work as crews that stayed together for the regular season. This practice was instituted in 1964. Then a field judge and still in the days of the five-man crew, I was assigned to work with referee Bud Brubaker, umpire Tony Sacco, and back judge Stan Javie. Several other officials came in and out of the crew as head linesman during the three years the four of us were together.

Under Brubaker's leadershp, crew unity both on and off the field came about naturally. Javie became my Sunday mentor. He was a hard taskmaster. He would challenge me on rules knowledge, asking questions about play situations for which the rule book gave no direct answer. His persistence in pointing out to me that football doesn't get simple, not if you care about its complexities, taught me that you can't study enough.

Sometimes to his personal detriment, Javie would sacrifice his own playoff chances to help young officials develop. During a game, he might allow another official to make a call that he, too, could have made and taken the credit for, thereby enhancing the other official's record and playoff chances. Not all officials care more about building the league than building their own careers.

By working with Schachter and Javie, I came to understand that rules interpretation was the most subtle, most challenging part of officiating. Since the referee is primarily responsible for rules interpretation during games, I knew that was the position I ultimately wanted. In 1967, this dream came true when Mark Duncan called me and said, "We're going to make you a referee next year. Is that all right?"

"Absolutely."

Art McNally was one of the two assistant supervisors of officials that year. I had known and admired Art from my first year in the league. He has consistently been a supportive colleague, as he has with so many officials. He deserves a great deal of credit for the growth of the officiating program in the last twenty years. His strongest attribute is his honesty. I would play poker over the phone with Art McNally.

From McNally, Javie, Schachter, and Brubaker I learned the importance of giving time and attention to younger officials. Maybe it's because I was a teacher and a coach when I entered the league, or maybe it's because I enjoy the process of developing talent, but McNally has told me he never hesitates to give me the rookies.

In this respect, a mentor is like the lamplighter who makes his way through the village lighting each lamp. You can always tell where he's been. He leaves the light shining.

22

They Buy Their Ink by the Barrel

The league has a policy of secluding the officials from the time they arrive in the league city to the time they depart for home. I agree with this practice because it protects the integrity of the game. Before the game, the media is dealing in conjecture. Conjecture and anticipation are none of our business.

This is why I was surprised the week before Super Bowl XII to get a call from Art McNally requesting that I give an interview to Bob Oates, Jr., of the *Los Angeles Times*. McNally explained that Oates had called for permission to interview the referee of the Super Bowl, promising that the story would not appear until the day of the game. McNally said he had hesitated because of the league's policy, but after conferring with Commissioner Rozelle, they decided to make an exception.

The opportunity for fan education was too good to pass up. Controversial calls in the New England–Baltimore game and the Oakland-Denver playoff game had created a lingering debate. The commissioner felt that an article giving the viewpoint of the officials might ease some of the discontent.

In a telephone interview lasting about two hours, Oates and I discussed officiating procedures and the prospect of working a Super Bowl under a cloud of controversy. Oates was well prepared and understood that officials are in a fishbowl. His approach was inquisitive but supportive.

The article succeeded in educating readers about the training and preparation of officials and the types of game situations that pose the most difficulty. It also resulted in my being pinned with the nickname the "Dean of Referees."

Super Bowl XII was also the first game in which reporters were allowed to interview the officials after the game. This was a second deliberate step in opening dialogue between the media and officials, but neither pregame nor post-game interviews are commonplace.

I agree with the league's thinking on pregame seclusion. Officials shouldn't be concerned with what may happen, what players may do, what team strategy might be. Our preparation ought to be on our individual and crew performance.

After the game, events are history, and that makes some discussion acceptable, but the wiser officials are guarded in any situation. However, as the public demands more information, I foresee the day when officials will be routinely interviewed live after a game, particularly if there's an incident that needs to be explained.

When a pool reporter asked me after Super Bowl XII about the dispute over Dallas wide receiver Butch Johnson's catch of a touchdown pass, I turned to the field judge, Bob Wortman, and said, "Bob, will you explain what you saw on that play?"

Wortman described what he saw: "Johnson caught the ball, rolled over and then the ball flipped out." It was a judgment call, that's all. The video replay had raised questions, but when Bob explained it, the reporters understood.

Post-game interviews reduce the need for inquiries to the league office about unusual calls and quell the likelihood of controversy or a lingering debate. Timeliness means a lot to media and the fans. When confusion is allowed to persist or goes unanswered, assumptions are made. These assumptions take on the face of gospel and become difficult to change.

Some guidelines are necessary. Officials shouldn't be sitting in newspaper offices and talking to reporters every day, but when a question arises involving officials, the ones involved should be accessible in the same way coaches and players are after interesting play situations. As it stands, a reporter's only recourse is to call the supervisor's office for an explanation.

To his credit, McNally never attempts to alibi. If the officials messed up on a rule or call, he'll say so. Even so, if I'm involved, I would rather he have the option of saying, "I'll have Tunney call you. He was the referee in the game. He can explain the call."

Questions arise constantly. Fans and media are often confused about the rules and with good reason. The rules change every year, and there are different rules in the pros than in college. The league's interpretation is constantly evolving. If officials were able to talk about a new rule or unusual call when situations arise in games, it would speed the education process and make better sportswriters and fans of all these interested people.

The league and many officials become upset when announcers and reporters criticize officials. I try not to. Like anyone else, I don't like to be criticized, but you have to shed any irritation fast. In the first few years as an official, any questioning of my competence was a bitter pill. I had to concentrate to maintain a positive perspective. Criticism is tough to handle for anyone, but the job of an official automatically includes it. The ones who last learn to handle it.

The tendency is to roll the mental tape, protecting your ego, "Why are they trying to hurt me? Why are they saying that? Are they trying to get to the officials?"

If you persist in reviewing negative thoughts, your mind begins to think in the negative. Self-doubt is created. It is demoralizing because a superior-inferior tension comes into your feelings.

With experience, I learned that no reporter is superior to me unless I allow his criticism to intimidate me. On the other hand, neither am I superior to him. If I allow either of these thoughts to form, I have cast it as a superior-inferior standoff. Right then a win-lose situation gets created.

I have no desire to be the intimidatee; in like manner, I have no desire to be the intimidator. Criticism should be treated as a questioning of the action or behavior, not as an attack on the individual.

Fans come to the game to get involved. Part of the excitement of sports is being allowed to yell at authority if you feel like it. The first time I put on the black-and-white stripes and heard the boos, I wondered, Why are they booing me? I made the right call.

I came to realize that the fans were not upset with Jim Tunney. They are partisans, yelling at the authority that has punished them. I happened to be that authority.

"Molly Meter Maid" comes to understand this, as does Judge Wapner. The anger arises from the situation, but because you can't call a parking ticket a name, you say something to Molly.

Sociologists and psychologists tell us that it can be healthy for people to vent their frustrations on something as innocuous as an official making a call in a football game. Booing is a vicarious expression of anger at authority that arises partly from the excitement of the game but is largely a residue from daily living.

So why should I let their booing affect my performance? More importantly, why should I allow their booing to affect how I feel about myself?

If I believe, as I say I do, in the positive effects of nurturing— that is, that the feedback my parents and mentors have given me has helped me gain self-confidence—then I must accept responsibility to nurture myself. I must choose positive perspectives. Choosing to be responsible for yourself in this way is a mandatory part of self-management and self-control.

* * *

The old story about the two Manhattan businessmen buying a newspaper applies here. On the way to the train at the end of the day, they stopped at the corner newsstand to buy a paper. One of the men handed over a five-dollar bill.

The vendor yelled a vulgar remark and slammed his fist, adding, "I don't have time to make change. Come here next time with a quarter."

The businessman accepted the angrily passed over change and said, "Thank you."

The other businessman, embarrassed by the public attention the vendor's loud remarks had drawn, asked as they walked on, "Why did you take that from him? Why didn't you tell him a thing or two?"

The first man said, "Because I didn't want him to control my behavior."

A simple story, one that is repeated endlessly in modern life. It speaks to the issue of who's in charge—the situation or the individual. The vendor allowed a five-dollar bill to control him and lost his temper. The businessman consciously refused to allow the vendor's behavior to control him and kept his dignity.

While anger is natural and sometimes justified, trying to rebuke anger with anger is futile. Exciting, maybe, and one way to release tension, engaging in verbal battle is no more than low-level one-upmanship. Your attention is locked in the skirmish. You give up self-control and lose the ability to move forward.

The embarrassed businessman felt involved even though the situation had nothing to do with him. His friend, while apparently involved, understood that he wasn't, that the vendor's anger was the vendor's problem, not his.

The ability to maintain self-control in "skirmishes" comes from an understanding of what I call "personal power." Being an official has taught me how to distinguish quickly whether the issue is "me" or the "situation." Is the anger directed at me as the one in authority or at me as a person?

The reverse distinction is equally important. Personal power is inherently within me. Only I can abdicate it. No one can take it away from me, but neither can I add any by putting on a uniform.

Indeed, even in uniform and with a clear position of authority, unless I apply my personal power, I will not be able to do the job expected of me. Only personal power has strength.

The businessman who wouldn't let the vendor control his behavior showed true personal power. On the field, if I cannot keep my head while others about me are losing theirs (thank you, Kipling), I don't deserve the "position power" given to me as the one with the whistle.

If I choose to allow criticism to undermine my confidence and performance, I have abdicated personal power. Bitterness usually follows. Why? Because you can't be bitter without self-pity. Who is to blame for that?

Reporters and announcers are paid to be critical of authority. They are not paid to be "vanilla." Their job is to add excitement even when the action is dull. Officials need to remember this.

Color commentators in pro football are usually former coaches and players who weren't fond of officials when they were on the field. They are hired because "they know the game." Their experience as a coach or player supports this conclusion. What the networks and the commentators themselves often overlook is that their expertise is in playing strategies, not necessarily in rules knowledge.

The challenge is to add excitement and provide critical analysis, and still be intellectually honest. "Call 'em as you see 'em," as Howard Cosell often said. Questions draw fire and that's what media wants. Reaction means ratings and market share.

CBS sports analyst Dick Vermeil is one of the nicest guys in the business. When Vermeil was head coach of the Philadelphia Eagles, he was intense. If I made a call he didn't agree with, he would let me know it. That's okay. He was fighting for his team.

When Vermeil left the field to go into the booth, he translated his proficiency in game strategy into skillful technical analysis. He converts the action, using graphs, charts, and numbers, into a clear explanation of the strategies being used on every play. There's no question he knows football.

As to his style, his network bosses felt he was too kind in his comments about officials, glossing over a call that was wrong. They wanted a more critical (read, aggressive) approach. Vermeil heard them; he changed his style. He now comes across as much more severe (read, less "vanilla"). People said, "He's really changed."

Vermeil as a person hasn't changed. His level of knowledge of the game hasn't changed. He simply adopted a different style, adjusting to circumstances.

Howard Cosell is generally regarded as one of television's most acerbic commentators. He brought a new style to sports commentating, much as a new coach brings a new playing style to a team.

Cosell didn't pay much attention to officials. I don't believe I ever heard him make a derogatory statement about officials other than a passing comment such as "It didn't look that way to this announcer." He used the third person a lot, effectively defusing the personal attack by avoiding the "I-you" confrontation.

Cosell has a photographic memory. In the booth he could recall facts and statistics faster than his support staff could provide them. He dotted his commentary with an amazing array of information, which earned him a loyal following. He also used five-dollar words to talk about football, something no one else had done.

These skills notwithstanding, ABC wanted Cosell to spark controversy on *Monday Night Football*. It was clear that the well-placed controversial remark was a job requirement. He would say things on the air, often not because he believed them, but to incite reaction. The network wanted the phone to ring on Tuesday morning. It did.

Off the air, his natural personality is much different. I found him to have a balanced perspective and to be considerate. He inspired my trust and confidence.

I worked with Cosell when I was associated with ABC's "Battle of the Network Stars," a sports contest (of sorts). The "Battle" pitted the athletic skills of television personalities from each of the major networks against each other. I was the referee for the football passing-only game, one of ten events. Cosell interviewed the stars before and after each event.

There is a lot of waiting time in any television production, and Cosell and I had a lot of time to talk. We developed a strong camaraderie.

During the filming of "Battle," spectators on the set or in the stands would often call out derogatory remarks to him to see if he flared. I watched him handle it.

On the air he often shot from the hip. Now, spectators were shooting comments at him. Nasty ones, sometimes. To his credit, he never responded to the catcalls. Cosell had self-control. Officials need to have the same self-control in dealing with the media.

My dad's advice rings in my ears: "When it comes to dealing with sportscasters and sportswriters, there isn't much they can say or write that can hurt you if you do the job you expect of yourself. You can transcend their criticism."

As an official, if I respond to a sportswriter who wrote something inflammatory or that was based on a misunderstanding of a rule, the only thing I achieve is that I have forced that writer into a defensive position. There are times I have thought, I'd like to call up that guy and tell him what really happened, or how you really play the game, or where he was wrong, but I don't. The time for education is when the atmosphere is cool and clear, not when it is heated.

I saw this at work in the classroom when I was a principal, too. Whenever I had to arbitrate (read, referee) a dispute between teacher and student, the first step was to "send them to their corners." A cooling-down period was vital. The next task was to reopen their perspective so we could find a win-win solution. This requires healing the demoralization that occurs with the confrontation. The goal is always to find the win-win balance.

Easier said than done. The tendency is to assume immediately the role of judge and jury and choose one side or the other. It is the American way to prove the other guy wrong. That attitude falls short if you are seeking a win-win balance.

I forgot this wisdom one time and wrote an "educational" reply to a sportswriter who I felt was out of line in his comments. I felt uneasy about writing but let the "I'll show him" emotion blind me. It surprises me that I don't remember the particulars of the situation, but I do remember that after I presented the situation as clearly as I could, the writer's response in the paper the next day was "I still think he blew the call." I gained only more controversy by writing the letter.

This was my lesson that you don't get into an argument with people who buy their ink by the barrel and their paper by the ton.

The league is sensitive to these issues and takes the position of protecting officials. Commissioner Rozelle and Supervisor McNally take the brunt of the controversy when it comes.

Coaches call McNally on Monday morning, blistering an official for a call made in their game the day before. This happens as regularly as Monday comes in a week.

McNally listens. If it's a question on a call or something that the game film will show, he reviews the play situation. He then telephones the official(s) involved and says, "Tell me what happened on the play."

He wants an honest answer. No covering up. The worst thing the official can do is to say less than exactly what happened. If the official blew the call, he should admit it.

The Philadelphia Eagles and the Dallas Cowboys developed an intense rivalry after Eagles defensive end Mel Tom roughed up Dallas quarterback Roger Staubach in a game at Veterans Stadium in the mid-1970s. Staubach was not injured on the play, but the "player's code" was activated.

The next season, the Eagles were at Texas Stadium, and both sides were ready to resume where the previous year's game left off. The Cowboys were leading 19–0 in the third quarter. With third and 9 on the Dallas 35, Staubach was scrambling out of the pocket, looking for a receiver, when he slipped as he turned the corner and fumbled.

I was following on the play behind Staubach, saw him go down, but could not see the ball come out. The Eagles defenders closed on Staubach quickly. Thinking he still had the ball, I blew the whistle to protect the fallen runner. Trouble is, Staubach didn't have the ball, and I should have let the play continue.

While the sound of the whistle still hung in the air, I saw that Eagles defensive back Bill Bradley had recovered the ball and was running free and clear at the Cowboys' 20, easily on his way to a touchdown. No more than a few yards from the Eagles' sideline, Eagles head coach Ed Khayat put the bead on me. He began an angry protest of the mistake.

Taking a few steps toward the sideline, I said to him, "Ed, I blew the call. By rights you should have the touchdown, but I can't give it to you. Sorry."

It was amazing. Khayat responded, "Well, nothing you can do about it now. Forget about it."

I respect Khayat for handling his anger and disappointment so well. His emotions were justified. The best thing I could do was to admit my mistake. He understood there was no way to call it back and took the misfortune in stride.

I called McNally Monday morning to tell him what had happened. Khayat called later to tell McNally that he respected the fact that I had owned up to my mistake.

It's never easy to admit you made a mistake, but an official must live with the truth. If he doesn't have enough personal power to bear the responsibility of his error, he doesn't deserve the position power that comes with the uniform.

Whether there is merit to the criticism or not, McNally needs all the facts. He will protect the official from criticism to every extent possible. If the official made a technical error involving a rule, McNally will tell the coach and official alike, "We blew it."

McNally's use of the "editorial we" is deliberate. His standard of leadership dictates that he and the official are one in working the game. McNally always assumes responsibility for the technical competence of each and every NFL official.

If the criticism concerns a judgment call, as in pass interference or roughing the passer, McNally takes the position that the official used his knowledge and experience in making the call. His reply is something like "The official made the judgment based upon what he saw. This is the way we call it."

If the situation suggests that the official needs education on field mechanics, the rules, or the spirit of the rules, McNally becomes a teacher. He or one of the assistant supervisors works with the official to make the necessary improvement.

The league reserves the right to deal directly with the official. I always appreciate it when the league office involves me in the training process. Crew morale is better when I am there on the line with them, good or bad. There are no ivory towers on the gridiron.

Commissioner Rozelle supports McNally in dealing with the aftermath of an official being impugned. McNally handles the details of identifying the problem and defusing the anger. If there is negative publicity, Rozelle becomes involved, as he would anytime the league is being publicly discussed.

The commissioner's background as a public relations executive serves him well in dealing with public attention, good and bad. Even when the debate is heated, Rozelle consistently maintains his usual calm self-control. This may be why the league's policy requires that contact with the media during the season be handled only through the league office and not by individual officials.

Some refer to this policy as the "gag rule." While I don't agree with the policy, I respect that the league is taking the long view. The policy seems overprotective in minor situations, but the league wants it in place to handle major controversies when they arise.

I would prefer the league to leave the responsibility on my shoulders if there is controversy about something I did on the field. I am prepared to take both the credit and the blame as they are due.

The league understands the difficulty isn't simply an issue of officials being able to calmly and frankly explain their side of a controversial call. Unfortunately, experience has shown that the problem is the reverse. Sometimes you have a reporter who is unable (read, unwilling) to treat the story objectively. The league takes the position that it will act as a buffer in order to protect officials from those times when the fight isn't fair. Ink by the barrel. Paper by the ton.

23

For Love or Money

The impact of sports on our culture is greater now than it has ever been. Not since the days of Sparta have so many citizens been involved in sports, casually or professionally. We hear the influence in our metaphors ("kickoff meetings," "let's huddle on that," "it's half-time," "we're in the fourth quarter"). We see the widespread increase in awareness of fitness and health.

Sports is good for us—good for the nation, good for the fans. Sports provides good recreation and great vicarious release.

The size and prominence of the league are good. The better the delivery system, the more reliable the product.

The size of the "purse" may be another matter. This is the biggest "change" in the game in the last thirty years. The economics of being an owner, a coach, a player, or a fan is the same—"high price" for everyone.

Football uniforms don't have pockets, and I think there's good reason for that. The coin for the opening toss is the only money that should be out there, in pockets or minds.

"Red" Auerbach, former coach, general manager, and now president of the Boston Celtics, declares that "team pride is what wins championships." The Celtics' management strategy is to evaluate players and pay them according to what they contribute to the team, not according to individual statistics or performance.

This management strategy recognizes that a résumé is one thing and tonight's game is another. Winning in team sports is accomplished by individual players who willingly merge into one unit. Unity comes from giving priority to the good of the team over self-interest and individual glory. Winning in team sports requires team pride more than ego or going solo. It requires loyalty.

Loyalty rolls on a two-way street. If the Celtics' philosophy is to work, the players have to know that management respects them and will treat them fairly. They can't be "afraid of the boss" and see management as an adversary.

Loyalty stems from trust. This truth is evident in every human relationship that grows. From childhood through job changes, to the selection of a spouse and all the choices we make that involve forming a team, trust arises as the most important issue when we hope the relationship will endure. Without trust, there is no incentive to invest our emotions and become vulnerable to the goodwill and constancy of another.

The relationship between management and its athletes is no different than other natural relationships that have a su-perior-subordinate component—parent-child, teacher-student, employer-employee. In order for the inevitable issue of position power not to become divisive, both sides must bring to the association a feeling of trust. They must sense an atmosphere of fairness and respect. There can be no feeling of "bad," but that only "good" will come from a discussion of how to achieve our goals. The spirit of "win-win" must be in the air.

This requires self-confidence and flexibility. If either side en-ters the relationship with a feeling of arrogance—a sense of "I am more powerful than you" or "You need me more than I need you"—not only will the needed flexibility become arthritic, but the arrogance may cause the other person to take a defensive posture. Zap, there goes the chance for loyalty and trust to strengthen.

Trust is one of the strongest emotions in humans if both sides respect its value and strive to provide the emotional atmosphere that allows it to grow. Trust is also brittle. It is tough, but can be broken fast with a strong shock at the right angle. When trust breaks, it is difficult to mend. The repairs almost always show. All collaborative effort, whether it's team sports, marriage, parenting, schools, or making a movie, is premised on trust.

Halas's Bears, Lombardi's Packers, and Madden's Raiders, among others, are credible examples of teams built around the trust that endures even in a superior-subordinate relationship. In each, the coach trusted the players to pull the best from themselves. In like manner, the players trusted the coach to give his best to them.

Trust doesn't require pure democracy. With these teams there was a clear distinction: Halas was in charge of the Bears; Lombardi commanded the Packers; Madden was boss of the Raiders. Each coach held clear superiority, but there was always a sense of family. It was never far from anyone's mind that every "member of the family" had the same goal and that each one was willing to give his utmost to win.

This is the spirit you find in the huddle of winning teams— on the football field or in corporate staff rooms alike. The quarterback (chief operating officer) is the team leader. While the play (goal) may come from the bench (upstairs), the team leader is responsible for last-minute adjustments in implementing the game plan as he reads the defensive alignment (competition). Then everyone on the team breaks out to do his part.

Some argue this thinking is old-fashioned. They suggest that insisting on a sense of family as a necessity to winning teams is out of step with today's emphasis on individualism and self-interest. While developing a sense of family is more difficult today than it used to be, it is no less valuable than it was in Lombardi's era, Knute Rockne's, or "Pop" Warner's.

The last three Super Bowls provide three consecutive examples that getting the "family together" revitalizes performance. The Washington Redskins (Super Bowl XXII), the New

York Giants (Super Bowl XXI), and the Chicago Bears (Super Bowl XX) each prevailed because their teams had regained a sense of family. Team pride, with its twin strengths of trust and loyalty, created the extra individual incentive and team coordination that result in championship wins.

Lombardi was always direct on the question of a coach's responsibility. He knew his first task was to set a good example. Next, he protected the management climate so that trust and loyalty could develop in his players. Without team pride, he couldn't hope to pull from his players all the hard work and diligence he expected. He wanted every member to share his goal and to know they could rely as fully on each other as they could rely on him.

Whether Lombardi was aware of it or not, his thinking echoes the explanation given in *Chariots of Fire* for why Cambridge included sports in its curriculum. Sir John Gielgud, playing the Master of Trinity, explains it to Abrahams in one of their showdown meetings.

"Here in Cambridge," Gielgud intoned, "we have always been proud of our athletic prowess. We believe, we have *always* believed, that our games foster courage, honesty and leadership, but most of all an unassailable spirit of loyalty, comradeship and mutual responsibility." That's the bond that Lombardi was after.

Auerbach seeks no less. "Loyalty, comradeship and mutual responsibility," in the Cambridge vernacular, are the factors he's after in what he calls "team pride."

Auerbach has held with his management approach with the Celtics for more than three decades. He has had to endure the changing times, primarily the change in players' attitudes, but has held fast to his belief that loyalty develops team pride and team pride wins basketball games. The sixteen NBA championship banners hanging from the rafters of the Boston Garden are testimony.

Auerbach may not have attended my management seminars, but he nonetheless exemplifies that three conditions contribute to successful organizations: consistent ownership, consistent management, and consistent philosophy. When these three stabilizers are present, management can establish a direction for the team, and the team members can entrust their future to the organization. Loyalty becomes possible because there is reason to trust in the conditions. Implicit in trust is a sense of the future and that the relationship deserves to endure over time and travail.

It sounds like common sense to say that trust and loyalty depend on mutual respect. True, but the reason there is so much common sense in the world is because no one ever uses it.

Football is a microcosm of society. When you think about condemning players for demanding enormous amounts of money to "play" football, you have to also ask why we are willing to pay rock stars and other entertainers gigantic sums for short careers. In like manner, MBA graduates cavalierly demand starting salaries of above six figures. Twenty years ago, even ten years ago, there were only a small number of vocations that would provide six-figure incomes even after years of experience. The times they are a changin' . . . faster and faster.

The rapidity of change is a staggering challenge that everyone must face. Alvin Toffler told us seventeen years ago in *Future Shock* that the only permanent thing we can count on is change. Starting from man's first recorded history, knowledge doubled by the year 1900. By 1950, it had doubled again. By 1970, it had doubled again. It is doubling faster each decade. How do you keep up with such rapid change?

You don't. You do your best to form relationships that endure through change and adversity. You find situations that deserve trust. Trust depends on believing there is mutual goodwill no matter what change or uncertainty lies ahead. When you find a situation that inspires your trust (few enough these days), stick with it, and notice that it endures because it has a spirit that is both consistent and flexible.

* * *

If Lombardi was a master of the "old style" of management strategy that I admire so much, how would he do today? He would have trouble adjusting to the salary figures that are demanded, but more than that, he would be astonished by the demands for security being made by players and their agents.

In a similar way, I drew the conclusion while working in public school systems that tenure was wrong. Tenured teachers tend to become too secure, too complacent. There's something to be said for being on the cutting edge, to have to continue to perform to earn your salary.

I admire people who accept the responsibility that their best security is in using their best abilities, not in assuming any system can protect them. Tommy Lasorda worked for the Dodgers for over thirty years on a one-year contract. I like that. Self-assurance in action. We would improve all organizations if we systematically demanded routinely excellent performance.

As an example of routinely excellent performance and responsible decision making, I offer Jack Kemp, former All-Pro quarterback of the Buffalo Bills and now a congressman (New York-R). Politics aside, I was in favor of his campaign for the presidency because Kemp has demonstrated so often that he leads by example and is willing to deliver beyond the common norm. Football is a great teacher of what the extra effort yields.

Kemp ran an honest, straightforward campaign. An underdog from the beginning, he couldn't overcome the huge inertia of incumbency, but what makes him a victor in my book is that he kept to his game plan, didn't lapse into airing out somebody else's laundry to make his points, and he even had a few dollars in the campaign till when he withdrew. This speaks to his standard of leadership and to his conviction about pulling your own weight in fiscal planning and not pushing the unpleasant details off on someone else.

Kemp believes in self-reliance and teamwork. These two work together. They are not opposites. They are equally important if individual excellence is to merge into one coordinated, winning effort. This requires trusting in the system, but the system doesn't become worthy of that trust until individuals become self-reliant and start to contribute consistent excellence.

I felt that way as a coach. Next year's salary would be based on this year's results. That gave me a great incentive to do my best. It makes sense to have reward relative to performance and to have coaches set the example on the question of self-reliance and commitment.

The league uses this approach with officials. We work on a one-year contract. At the end of each season, our contracts expire. No one is automatically rehired. Each year means requalifying. At any time during the season you can be terminated on forty-eight-hour notice. For twenty-eight years, that's been fine with me. It ensures that I stay focused and keep my edge.

I feel there is a glitch in a person's self-esteem if he needs the protection of a long-term contract or for the system to protect him more than his own abilities. Players will argue, "But I can be injured and my career will be over." That can happen to an official, too.

Two officials, Dick Ferguson and Ralph Vandenberg, suffered serious knee injuries. They were sideline officials and unable to get out of the way of the play. Both took a collision that tore up a knee.

Being in the midst of heavy, forceful action makes pro football a hazardous job. Fine. Why should football players be paid more than policemen, firemen, bomb squads, toxic-spill clean-up teams, air-rescue teams, high-mountain rangers, or any other number of physically demanding occupations? There is no adequate way to compensate *in advance* for the risks people take to help others.

Life requires millions of people to face dangers every day for more important reasons than football. One can appropriately ask if football helps people or only entertains them.

Star performance deserves extra pay, but the idea of paying

big bucks for the prospect that injury may force a short career doesn't get my support. It's a hedge. For most players with high salary demands, it's a hedge against their skill level being surpassed by newcomers, not a true fear of injury.

I never go on the field thinking injury. Neither should a player. Personal concern of any kind is a distraction. It is antithetical to our purpose, which is concentration. Their talk of hazard clauses doesn't fit with what they say they're willing to do for their team.

Unfortunately, we see less love for the game today than we did in Lombardi's era. Lombardi would have played and coached for nothing but the love of the game. Players come to the league today saying, "Here's what I want."

If you ask players why they started playing football in high school, they will say it was because they enjoyed it. By the time they are drafted, they're thinking of million-dollar contracts.

In my opinion, that degrades the player. Worse, it erodes the conditions that allow trust and loyalty to survive. The "me-first" attitude destroyed the Roman Empire, gave us headaches in the 1960s that still persist, and destroys the trust on which teamwork depends.

The players' strike in the 1987 season accidentally provided an example of how much fun and simple love of the game can surface when all the contract protections are gone from the field. Every replacement player was on audition. As a result, the strike games were filled with surprising feats and joyfulness.

Players who had been cut from training camp, guys who the week before were dolefully back at the books, driving a truck, selling encyclopedias, or filling in as fitness instructors, were suddenly back in uniform, on the field, being yelled at by the coach and loving it. There was a new sense of freedom. The games had the earnestness and confusion of the best pickup games. The teams were less precise, awkward in formations and execution, running a little loose, but running with the ball, having fun, and getting the job done.

Play terminology and intricate sequences were abandoned. No more "Brown X Z right out Y hook on 2. Break."

The challenge was suddenly to pare it down and keep it simple. Huddle commands were plain talk, "Number twenty-three, you go down about there (nodding toward downfield) and turn toward the sideline. Number eighty-four, you take off and go as far as you can. I'll throw to the one who is open first. The rest of you guys, block like hell. Break."

It worked. These kids couldn't have been happier with a full book of "E" tickets and running into Doug Williams or Phil Simms at Disneyworld.

In the Houston-Denver strike game I worked, the Oilers left Houston without a punter. The special-teams coach had phoned a former college punter, a kid named Steve Superick, he knew was available but had never met. He told Superick to meet him at the team bus when they arrived at the Denver airport.

Superick showed up with his shoes and was getting on the team bus when Oilers Head Coach Jerry Glanville stopped him and demanded, "Where do you think you're going?"

Superick said, "I'm going to the game."

Glanville said, "You can't go on this bus. This is the team bus."

Superick smiled and said, "But I *am* on your team today. I'm your punter."

"Good. We need one," Glanville said. "Get on."

Houston won, 40–10. Superick punted twice.

The replacement players had fun, but they never lost sight of the purpose of competition—winning. They were industrious, willing to take risks, and became instantly loyal to the other guys who were joining in the effort that day.

When the regular players came back after a three-week absence, winning the division was on everyone's schedule. It was mainstream football again. The stars were back, replacements out. Some of the spirit of the game evaporates when any player becomes more important than the game.

* * *

Pro football (or any job you have in your twenties) should be thought of as a transition business. Players who think in terms of playing in the NFL for four or five years, during which they plan to earn enough money to retire on without having to do anything else, have got it wrong. Your first job out of college should be an entrée to other accomplishments, not a life deal by itself.

Plenty of ex-NFL players have distinguished themselves in their second careers. O.J. Simpson, Merlin Olsen, and Frank Gifford are visible ones, but there are many players who have made successful transitions. Gino Marchetti, for instance.

Marchetti was a defensive end for the Baltimore Colts during the 1960s. He had a great playing career, then went into the restaurant business and made himself a millionaire.

He certainly didn't make a million in football. There wasn't that kind of money floating around when Gino played. He carried the discipline he learned playing football to the business world. Then he worked. That's what it takes, on the field and off. Discipline and work.

Willie Davis, out of Grambling University, All-Pro defensive end of the championship Packers, has been the president and owner of a large beer distributorship in southern California and is now president of radio station KACE in Los Angeles. Davis candidly admits that the discipline Lombardi demanded from all his players taught him self-control and how to work in steps toward a goal. Coach would be proud.

Davis is right. If a player can be disciplined and dedicated on the field, he can be that way in business. It's a matter of attitude.

In an airport waiting room, I heard a line from a television drama. A kindly old gentleman was advising a granddaughter-type in-genue that her purpose should be "to retain the good from the past, sustain the good from the present, and obtain the good from the future."

That's pretty concise high talk for daytime drama. The meaning is dead center. If we all, as individuals in regular life or as owners, coaches, players, fans, and officials in pro sports, select our goals and make choices with the purpose of retaining, sustaining, and obtaining the good, excellence will naturally result. A high goal, full of options.

The game is people. People will shape its growth and determine its direction. It is dynamic because the intention of the participants is dynamic, fluxing, seeking a new balance continuously.

The changes in the game will always be related more to the business aspects, not coaching, because the principles of teamwork are perennial. No amount of money or technical sophistication will replace team pride, with its twin strengths of trust and loyalty, as the secret of winning teams. You can take that to the bank.

Index